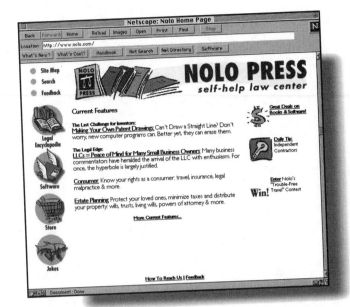

4TH EDITION

HOW TO FORM A

NONPROFIT CORPORATION

BY ATTORNEY ANTHONY MANCUSO

COMPANION COMPUTER DISK
FOR NONPROFIT INCORPORATORS

Included at the back of this book is a 3½" PC/MS DOS Nonprofit
Corporation Computer Disk containing files for the tear-out
incorporation forms included in this book. These files are provided
in standard file formats that can be read into, completed, and
printed with your PC wordprocessing program. For specific
instructions for using the forms on the disk, see the README.TXT
file included on the disk (insert the disk in your A: drive and use
the TYPE A:README.TXT or MORE <A:README.TXT command at
the DOS prompt to view this file on the screen).

N O L O   P R E S S   **B E R K E L E Y**

Your Responsibility When Using a Self-help Law Book

We've done our best to give you useful and accurate information in this book. But this book does not take the place of a lawyer licensed to practice law in your state. If you want legal advice, see a lawyer. If you use any information contained in this book, it's your personal responsibility to make sure that the facts and general information contained in it are applicable to your situation.

Keeping Up-to-Date

To keep its books up-to-date, Nolo Press issues new printings and new editions periodically. New printings reflect minor legal changes and technical corrections. New editions contain major legal changes, major text additions or major reorganizations. To find out if a later printing or edition of any Nolo book is available, call Nolo Press at (510) 549-1976 or check the catalog in the *Nolo News*, our quarterly newsletter. You can also contact Nolo Press at www.nolo.com.

To stay current, follow the "Update" service in the *Nolo News*. You can get a free one-year subscription by sending us the registration card in the back of the book. In another effort to help you use Nolo's latest materials, we offer a 25% discount off the purchase of the new edition of your Nolo book when you turn in the cover of an earlier edition. (See the "Recycle Offer" in the back of the book.) This book was last printed in October 1997.

FOURTH EDITION	October 1997
ILLUSTRATIONS	Mari Stein
BOOK DESIGN	Jackie Clark
COVER DESIGN	Toni Ihara
INDEX	Ken Cober
PRINTING	Bertelsmann Industry Services, Inc.

Mancuso, Anthony.
    How to form a nonprofit corporation / by Anthony Mancuso. --4th ed.

      p.   cm.
    Includes index.
    ISBN 0-87337-451-7
    1. Nonprofit organizations--Law and legislation--United States--Popular works. 2. Incorporation--United States--Popular works.
    I. Title
    KF1388.Z9M36 1997
    346.73'064--dc21

                                97-34980
                                CIP

Contents

Introduction

1 Overview of Nonprofit Corporations

2 Nonprofit Corporation Law

3 The Federal 501(c)(3) Nonprofit Income Tax Exemption

4 501(c)(3) Public Charities and Private Foundations

5 Other Nonprofit Tax Issues and Reporting Requirements

6 Steps to Organize a Nonprofit Corporation

7 Prepare Your Bylaws

8 Apply for Your Federal 501(c)(3) Tax Exemption

9 Final Steps in Organizing Your Nonprofit Corporation

10 After Your Corporation Is Organized

11 Lawyers and Accountants

Appendix

Incorporation Checklist

Incorporation Contact Letter

Name Availability Letter

Application for Reservation of Corporate Name

Articles Filing Letter

Bylaws

Minutes

State Sheets

Introduction

Qualifying as a 501(c)(3 Nonprofit

Since many commercial and non-commercial groups furnish services and products that provide an educational benefit to the public, a surprising number of groups can qualify for the IRC §501(c)(3) federal tax exemption covered in this book (such as booksellers, self-help centers, training courses, instructional seminars, etc.). Deciding to organize as a tax-exempt nonprofit does involve a few significant trade-offs however. For example, 501(c)(3) nonprofits are subject to the following operational rules and restrictions:

- Payment of profits or other private benefits to directors, officers, members or staff are prohibited. Reasonable salaries and standard employment benefits are allowed.

- Income from sources unrelated to the tax exempt purposes of the group must not be substantial.

- The assets of the organization must be dedicated to tax-exempt purposes. This means that if and when the group dissolves, any remaining assets must be distributed to another tax-exempt 501(c)(3) organization.

So, although many types of organizations can qualify for tax-exempt status under IRC §501(c)(3), a much smaller number actually decide to forego the incentives, prerogatives and perks of the commercial sector and incorporate as nonprofit organizations.

Interest in forming nonprofit corporations is on the rise. All sorts of groups—artists, musicians and dancers; people active in conservation, education, and health issues; organizations devoted to ethnic and community services, women's rights, help for the homeless; and countless other concerns—wish to organize their efforts as nonprofit corporations. All show an enormous dedication to doing good work amid challenging fiscal and social conditions, helping others to improve their lives and communities. It is understandable that there is often little time, money or enthusiasm left for attending to legal and tax formalities. This book is our effort to provide these organizations with the information and tools necessary to deal with these technicalities and obtain the substantial legal and tax benefits available to nonprofits.

Why Form a Nonprofit Corporation? Often the reason for forming a nonprofit corporation is simple—being organized as a tax-exempt nonprofit corporation is a common requirement for obtaining grant funds from government agencies and private foundations. There are also important federal, state, and local income, property, sales, excise and other tax exemptions available to nonprofit corporations. In addition, only tax-exempt nonprofit organizations provide donors with the incentive of an individual tax deduction for contributions made to the organization. There are additional benefits available to tax-exempt nonprofit corporations such as low cost nonprofit mailing, advertising and purchasing rates as well as other private and governmental discounts and preferences.

Of course, nonprofits, like all other product or service providers, need to prepare for and protect against possible lawsuits and potential liability for their activities and operations. Incorporating provides a valuable form of legal protection from personal liability. Under state corporation laws and court decisions, the nonprofit corporation protects its directors, officers and members from personal liability for claims brought against the corporation. Lawsuits against the nonprofit can only reach the corporate assets, not the bank accounts, houses or other property owned by the individuals who manage, work for, or participate as members of the corporation.

Many incorporators of nonprofit corporations also feel that the act of setting up the corporation is itself beneficial. Why? Because the act of preparing the standard paperwork necessary to organize a nonprofit corporation serves as a convenient means of dealing with important organizational issues that might otherwise be ignored in a more informal setting. For example, when preparing corporate Articles, Bylaws and tax exemption applications, you must define the nonprofit purposes of your group, describe your fundraising program, project expected sources of support, determine whether you will adopt a formal membership structure, specify the qualifications and procedures for selecting your board of directors, officers and members, and attend to a number of other details. This preliminary focus is essential in any collective undertaking. It is particularly valuable in the nonprofit arena where clarity of purpose and procedure is essential to meet the countless fiscal and program challenges that lie ahead.

Organizations Covered in this Book   This book deals with nonprofit corporations eligible for a federal corporate income tax exemption under Section 501(c)(3) of the Internal Revenue Code. IRC § 501(c)(3) nonprofits must be organized for religious, charitable, educational, scientific or literary purposes. These tax-exempt categories encompass a wide range of purposes and activities as discussed in the accompanying sidebar.

We do not deal with special nonprofit corporations organized to engage in special types of nonprofit activity, such as civic, patriotic, political, recreational, or social groups. While these groups may qualify for federal tax exemptions under other provisions of the Internal Revenue Code, they do not share all the benefits of 501(c)(3) tax exempt status and are not among the specific types of nonprofit corporations treated in this book.

How to Use this Book   We provide background information and specific line-by-line instructions and sample language necessary to prepare the federal tax exemption application required of all 501(c)(3) organizations. This book also contains a step-by-step guide to preparing the legal paperwork necessary to form a nonprofit corporation in each state. This paperwork includes Articles of Incorporation, Bylaws and the Minutes of your Board of Directors' Meeting. Since each state has separate legal requirements, we show you how to obtain and fill in your state's official form for your Articles. We included sample language you can use to complete most of the clauses found in your official form. To further help you complete your Articles according to state law requirements, and to help you fill in the tear-out corporate Bylaws and Minutes included in the Appendix to this book, we have supplemented this material with State Sheets containing each state's basic incorporation requirements. We refer you to this state specific information when filling in an official or tear-out incorporation form.

We have also included chapters to help you understand legal, tax and practical issues and areas of concern to initial and ongoing corporate operations. Steps to take after you have completed your incorporation papers, including ongoing legal and tax filing formalities, are covered in the final chapters of the book.

Because many incorporators will follow our suggestion and consult a legal and tax professional during the incorporation process, we include a chapter on finding a lawyer and accountant with nonprofit experience who will charge a reasonable fee to share their expertise with you. Since many incorporators will wish to look up some of the law themselves, this chapter includes basic information on how to perform your own self-help legal research.

Please scan this entire book at least once before you draw conclusions and fill out papers. It is not difficult to organize a nonprofit corporation, but many of the corporate and tax laws are picky or technical—often both—and you should get an overview of the whole subject before getting down to details. The Incorporation Checklist included in the Appendix provides an overview of the material in this book and a checklist for completing the steps involved in forming a nonprofit corporation.

We have enjoyed assembling and explaining this incorporation material. We hope it helps you with the legal and tax incorporation formalities necessary to incorporate your organization and brings you closer to attaining your nonprofit goals. Best of Luck!

Overview of Nonprofit Corporations

Nonprofit Corporations Can Make a Profit

"Nonprofit" does not mean literally that you cannot make a profit. Under the federal tax law and state corporate statutes, as long as your corporation is organized and operated for a recognized nonprofit purpose, it can take in more money than it expends in conducting its activities. For example, Friends of the Library, Inc., a 501(c)(3) nonprofit organized to encourage literary appreciation in the community and to raise money for the support and improvement of the public library, can make a profit from its sold-out lecture series featuring famous authors and from its annual sale of donated books. It may use its tax-free profits for its own operating expenses (including salaries for officers, directors and employees) or for the benefit of the library. What it cannot do [under IRC Section 501(c)(3)] is distribute any of the profits for the benefit of officers, directors or employees connected with Friends of the Library (as dividends, for example).

Nonprofits Can Collect Passive Income

Although it's not typical for the average group, a nonprofit corporation may make money from "passive" sources such as rents, royalties, interest, investments, etc. This income is, moreover, non-taxable in some cases.

This chapter provides a general overview of nonprofit corporations and their advantages and disadvantages, with a special emphasis on nonprofit corporations exempt from federal corporate income taxation under Section 501(c)(3) of the Internal Revenue Code. We also discuss basic corporate concepts and classifications to help you understand where nonprofits fit into the larger legal and corporate world.

If You Want to Know More Some important points are very briefly treated in this overview. Don't worry—important corporate concepts (such as limited liability, requirements for 501(c)(3) tax-exempt status, deductibility of charitable contributions, etc.) are explained in more detail in later chapters.

A. What Is a Corporation?

A corporation is a legal entity that enables a group of people to pool energy, time and money for profit or nonprofit activities. It acquires legal existence after complying with a particular state's incorporation procedures and formalities. A corporation is treated as a separate "person," distinct from the people who own, manage or operate it. It may enter into contracts, incur debts and pay taxes. The fact that the corporation exists as a separate entity gives directors, employees and members the benefits of limited liability. That is, business claims and lawsuits arising from corporate debts, transactions and activities may normally be advanced only against the corporation and corporate assets, not against any of the individuals associated with it or their own personal assets. We discuss the concept of limited liability and other unique advantages of the corporate form in later sections below.

B. Types of Corporations

State corporate statutes classify corporations in several ways. Let's look at two of the most basic divisions found in the corporation laws of the various states.

1. Profit and Nonprofit Corporations

State laws distinguish between profit (stock or business) corporations and nonprofit (nonstock) corporations. Profit corporations are authorized to issue shares of stock to shareholders in return for capital investments of money, property, or past services to the corporation. Shareholders receive a return on their investment only if dividends are declared and paid or if corporate assets remain to be divided among the shareholders (after payment of creditors) upon the dissolution of the corporation.[1]

Except for some hybrids such as consumer or producer co-ops,[2] nonprofit corporations generally can neither issue shares nor pay dividends under state law. Furthermore, under the federal tax code, 501(c)(3) tax-exempt nonprofit corporations cannot pay dividends or profits, as such, to members or other individuals and, on dissolution, must distribute their remaining assets to a similarly tax-exempt nonprofit group.

Nonprofit corporations do share some common attributes with profit corporations—for example, limited liability is available to founders, directors and profit corporations alike. More surprising, perhaps, is the fact that nonprofits may, like their for-profit counterparts, make a profit from nonprofit as well as commercial activities.

2. Domestic and Foreign Corporations

Corporations are also classified according to the state in which they are formed. For example, if a nonprofit corporation files Articles of Incorporation with the Oregon Secretary of State, it is considered a "domestic" nonprofit corporation in Oregon (or, more colloquially, an "Oregon corporation") and is subject to the corporate rules and procedures contained in Oregon's nonprofit corporation law. This Oregon corporation will be treated as a "foreign" (out-of-state) corporation under the laws of other states. Generally, each state requires foreign corporations which transact business in the state to file qualification papers as a "foreign" corporation and pay a qualification fee.

Should You Incorporate Out-Of-State? The distinction between domestic and foreign corporations leads to the following often-asked question: Why not incorporate in the state where incorporation fees or corporate taxes are lowest, state corporate taxes are minimal or non-existent, or nonprofit statutes are more flexible and then qualify to do business in your home state as a foreign corporation? Our answer is that although doing this is theoretically possible, in practice it's too much trouble and too expensive to incorporate out-of-state. Here are a few reasons why:

- The process of qualifying a foreign corporation to operate in most states is similar in terms of time and expense to incorporating a domestic corporation. Paperwork must be filed with the secretary of state and qualification fees must also be paid (which are at least as high as, and often higher than, regular incorporation fees). In short,

**Nonprofits Can Earn
Unrelated Income**

Nonprofits can also make money in ways
unrelated to their nonprofit purposes. This
type of income is usually subject to
taxation as unrelated business income
under state and federal corporate tax
rules, but such income is permissible and
often essential to the survival of the
nonprofit group. As you'll see, though, it's
best not to let unrelated business
activities reach the point where you start
to look more like a for-profit business than
a nonprofit one. This is the case if such
activities are absorbing a substantial
amount of staff time (or requiring additional paid staff or volunteers to run), or
are producing more income than your
exempt-purpose activities.

For example, many thousands of
books are donated to Friends of the
Library for its annual book sale, one of its
major fund raising events. Although the
sale is always highly successful, thousands of books are left over, and Friends
decides to sell the more valuable ones by
advertising in the rare and out-of-print
books classified sections in various
magazines. The response is overwhelming and soon there are six employees
cataloguing books. In addition, Friends
begins a business purchasing books they
don't have from other dealers and
reselling them to the public. Such a
situation could attract attention from the
IRS and prompt it to reconsider Friends'
501(c)(3) tax-exempt status.

you end up meeting the requirements and paying the fees in two
states, not one.

- Your corporation will still be subject to taxation in each state in
  which it earns or derives income or funds. If both states (the state of
  incorporation and the home state where the corporation will be
  active) impose a corporate income tax, the nonprofit corporation will
  need to file for and obtain two state corporate tax exemptions—one
  for each state. Similarly, double sales, property and other state tax
  exemptions may also often be necessary or appropriate.

- Your out-of-state corporation will still be subject to many, if not most,
  of the laws that affect corporations in your home state (in part
  because many of the corporate statutes which apply to domestic
  corporations also apply to foreign corporations with a specified
  percentage of payroll, property or sales within the state).

When Incorporating Out-of-State May Make Sense If you plan to
set up a multi-state nonprofit with corporate offices and activities in
more than one state (a tri-state environmental fund for example), then it
makes sense to consider incorporating in the state that offers the greatest
legal, tax and practical advantages. To help with this comparison, the
State Sheets in the Appendix list many basic nonprofit corporation law
provisions for each state. For further information on state-by-state
differences, you may be able to check a local nonprofit resource center
library. An experienced nonprofit lawyer or consultant may be able to
help you determine which state is the most convenient and least costly
to use as the legal home of your new nonprofit corporation.

C. What Are Valid Nonprofit Purposes?

While most for-profit corporations are formed for "any lawful purpose"
under state statutes, nonprofit corporations must usually be established to
accomplish specific purposes of benefit to the public at large, a segment
of the community, or a particular membership. Indeed, the essential
identity of each nonprofit, and its classification and treatment under the
tax statutes, is derived from the specific nonprofit purposes stated in the
corporation's Articles and Bylaws. For example, many different groups—
labor unions, chambers of commerce, social and recreational clubs,
fraternal societies, credit unions, farmers' co-ops, legal service organizations—may be eligible for a federal nonprofit organization tax exemption
under various sections of the Internal Revenue Code (see Table 3.1 for a
listing of special purpose IRC tax exemptions).

Note, however, that only those nonprofit corporations formed for religious, charitable, scientific, educational or literary purposes of benefit to the public may claim tax-exempt status under IRC § 501(c)(3). As explained in the introductory chapter, this is the all-important classification for, and the primary subject matter of, this book. We show you how to form a 501(c)(3) tax-exempt nonprofit—one which is not only exempt from corporate taxation under federal and state tax statutes, but also eligible to obtain tax deductible contributions from donors and other benefits not available to other tax-exempt nonprofit organizations.

D. Advantages of the 501(c)(3) Nonprofit Corporation

Now let's look at the specific advantages of forming a tax-exempt 501(c)(3) nonprofit corporation. Although the relative importance of each of the following factors will vary from group to group, if you are thinking about incorporating, at least one of the following points should have direct bearing on, and represent a significant benefit to, your organization.

1. Tax Exemptions

IRC 501(c)(3) nonprofit corporations are eligible for state and federal exemptions from payment of corporate income taxes, as well as other tax exemptions and benefits. At federal corporate tax rates of 15% on the first $50,000 of taxable income, 25% on the next $25,000 and 34% and higher on income over $75,000, it goes without saying—at least if you expect to earn a substantial profit, from services, exhibits or performances, for example—that you'll want to apply for an exemption. Furthermore, all but five states have corporate income taxes, and most also have sales and a panoply of other taxes. You'll surely want to put your nonprofit status to use to gain exemption from these.

We discuss the requirements and benefits associated with federal and state nonprofit tax exemptions in detail in later chapters. Chapter 8 is devoted exclusively to preparing the federal 501(c)(3) tax exemption application and takes you through this form, providing specific instructions and sample responses, one line at a time.

Out-of-State ("Foreign") Corporations

Each state sets a different threshold of activity for triggering its corporate qualification process for out-of-state corporations. Generally, mosts states say that any foreign corporation that plans to engage in a regular or repeated pattern of activity in the state must qualify to do so (by obtaining a Certificate of Authority from the secretary of state). Of course, many states have enacted specific statutory exceptions to their qualification rule. For example, in some states, out-of-state nonprofit corporations may engage in one or more of the following activities without having to obtain a Certificate of Authority from the secretary of state: maintaining, defending or settling any legal action or administrative proceeding, including securing or collecting debts and enforcing property rights; holding meetings of corporate directors or of the membership; maintaining bank accounts; making grants of funds; distributing information to members; making sales through independent contractors; engaging in interstate or foreign commerce; conducting a so-called "isolated transaction," which is completed within 30 days and is not one of a series of similar transactions; exercising powers as an executor, administrator or trustee, so long as none of the activities required of the position amounts to transacting business.

For specific information on the out-of-state corporation qualification rules in effect in a given state, check the state's nonprofit corporation law (look for a section labeled "Qualification of Foreign Corporations").

2. Receiving Public and Private Funds

One of the primary reasons for becoming a 501(c)(3) nonprofit corporation is so that your group will become eligible to receive both public and private grants. Generally, tax-exempt government foundations (the National Endowment for the Arts or Humanities, the Corporation for Public Broadcasting, the National Satellite Program Development Fund) as well as private foundations and charities (the Ford Foundation, the United Way, the American Cancer Society) are required by their own operating rules and IRS regulations to donate their funds to 501(c)(3) tax-exempt organizations, or else forfeit their own tax-exempt status. In addition, individual private donors can claim personal federal income tax deductions of up to 50% of adjusted gross income for donations made to 501(c)(3) tax-exempt groups. At death, a complete federal estate tax exemption is available for bequests made to 501(c)(3) groups. In short, if you plan to ask people to give you significant amounts of money in furtherance of your nonprofit purpose, you need to demonstrate to your donors that you have 501(c)(3) status.

3. Limited Liability

Limited liability can be a real incentive to forming a nonprofit corporation. It means that directors or trustees, officers, employees and members of the nonprofit corporation are not personally liable for corporate debts or liabilities, including unpaid business debts and unsatisfied lawsuit judgments, as they normally would be if they conducted their affairs without incorporating. Creditors can only go after corporate assets to satisfy liabilities incurred by the corporation—not the personal assets (car, home, bank accounts) of the people in the nonprofit corporation.

Example A nonprofit symphony is sued because someone falls due to a poorly maintained railing, and a judgment is entered against the corporation for an amount greater than insurance coverage. The amount of the judgment in excess of insurance is a debt of the corporation, but not of its directors, members, managers, etc. By contrast, if the premises were owned by an unincorporated association of musicians, the principals of the unincorporated group could be held personally liable for the excess judgment amount.

Exceptions to the Limited Liability Rule

Watch out. In a few situations, people involved with a nonprofit corporation may be personally liable for its debts. Here are some major areas of potential personal liability:

Loans If a nonprofit corporation takes a loan to cover its operating costs or buys properties subject to a mortgage, banks and commercial lending institutions may request the personal guarantee of its directors or officers that the money will be repaid. It is somewhat unusual for nonprofit directors to sign a personal guarantee, but obviously if they do they will be liable to repay the loan if the corporation is unable to do so.

Taxes State and federal governments can hold the corporate employee who is responsible for reporting and paying corporate taxes (usually the Treasurer) personally liable for any unpaid taxes, penalties and interest due for failure to pay taxes or file necessary returns. With proper planning, your nonprofit corporation should be tax exempt, but you may still have to file informational returns and annual reports with the secretary of state, as well as pay employee withholding taxes and taxes on income unrelated to your nonprofit purposes. IRS penalties for delinquent tax payments and returns are substantial, so keep this exception to limited liability in mind—particularly if you will be the Treasurer.

Dues Members of a nonprofit corporation are personally liable for any membership fees and dues they owe the corporation. In most cases, this is a minor obligation since dues are normally set at modest amounts.

Violations of Statutory Duties Corporate directors and officers have a "duty of care" to act responsibly (not negligently) when performing corporate duties, and may, on occasion, be held personally financially liable for breach of this duty. Personal liability of this sort is the exception, not the rule,[3] but in response to growing concern within the nonprofit community, many states have enacted special nonprofit immunity laws that protect volunteer directors, volunteer officers and other corporate personnel from liability for negligent corporate acts and omissions. However, exceptions to immunity protection under the statutes are typically made in cases of gross negligence, or malicious, intentional or criminal behavior.

The Impact of Federal Tax Law

Federal tax law, contained in the federal Internal Revenue Code (IRC), applies to all nonprofit corporations, regardless of where they are formed. Thus, a federally tax-exempt nonprofit corporation is exempt from federal corporate income taxes in all states, but generally must apply for separate state, county and local tax exemptions (from income, franchise, excise, sales, use, property and other taxes). Fortunately, many states follow the lead of the IRS and automatically grant state corporate income and other tax exemptions to nonprofit corporations exempt from federal corporate income taxation under IRC §501(c)(3). See your State Sheet for further information.

4. Separate and Perpetual Legal Existence

A corporation is a legal entity separate from the people who manage and work for it, or participate in its activities—a legal "person," capable of entering into contracts, incurring debts, receiving and maintaining funds, and, generally, doing anything a real person can do. This legal person is, in a sense, immortal, as the nonprofit corporation continues to exist as a legal entity despite changes in management or other corporate personnel caused by the resignation, removal or death of the people associated with it. It may, of course, be dissolved or drastically affected by the loss of key people, but its inherent perpetuality adds an element of certainty regarding the continuance of the group's activities, an attractive feature to the private and public donor who prefers funding activities that are organized to operate over the long term.

5. Employee Benefits

Another advantage of the nonprofit corporation is that its principals can also be employees and, therefore, be eligible for employee fringe benefits not available for the most part to self-employed business owners and operators. These include sick pay, group life insurance, accident and health insurance, payment of medical expenses and coverage by an approved corporate employee pension or retirement income plan. Note that the corporation's contribution to these employee plans is also deductible from its unrelated business income, should it have any.

6. Formality and Structure

There are inherent benefits in the formal documents—the Articles, Bylaws, Minutes of Meetings, Board Resolutions, etc.—of the nonprofit corporation. These form the outline of the group's organization and its operating rules and, aside from the benefits discussed above (obtaining tax exemptions, grants, etc.), they provide structure and procedures for decision making and dispute resolution. This is important for any collective activity, but for nonprofit groups it is a virtual necessity, especially where the board includes diverse members of the community with divergent interests and viewpoints. Without the clear-cut delegation of authority and specific operating rules in the Articles and Bylaws, running the organization can often be a divisive, if not futile, affair.

7. Other Advantages

Other varied advantages are associated with special areas of nonprofit activity or operations. These additional benefits can be helpful, and in some cases critical, to the success of a nonprofit organization. Here is a brief (and incomplete) listing of some supplemental nonprofit benefits:

- 501(c)(3)s receive lower postal rates on third class bulk mailings.

- 501(c)(3) performing arts groups are qualified to participate in the performance programs sponsored by federally supported colleges and universities; such programs are often a major venue for many performing arts groups.

- Many publications offer cheaper classified advertising rates to nonprofit organizations.

- Many Internet service providers offer discounted space to nonprofit organizations.

- Nonprofits are the exclusive beneficiaries of free radio and television public service announcements (PSAs) provided by local media outlets.

- Many stores (such as Price Club) offer lower membership rates to nonprofit employees.

- Nonprofit employees can be eligible to participate in job-training, student-intern, work-study, and other federal, state and local employment incentive programs (where salaries are substantially paid out of federal and state funds).

- 501(c)(3) educational organizations that offer formal instruction, have a regular faculty and curriculum and a regularly enrolled student body are eligible for a tax refund for gasoline expenses incurred (for example, in running school buses).

E. Disadvantages of a Nonprofit Corporation

There are, of course, disadvantages to forming a nonprofit corporation, especially for those groups which heretofore have operated informally without financial or employee record keeping and controls. First and foremost is the organizational paperwork. Next are the fees. Finally, the time and energy necessary to comply with the day-to-day operational rules (including periodic filings of forms with state and federal agencies) can represent a substantial drain on nonprofit personnel. We briefly discuss each of these areas below.

1. Paperwork

One disadvantage of forming any corporation is the red tape and paperwork. This begins with the preparation of initial incorporation documents (Articles of Incorporation, Bylaws, and Minutes of First Meeting of the Board of Directors). It continues with forms for amending Articles and Bylaws, Minutes of ongoing meetings, the annual report of your activities most states require you to file, and with the accounting and financial record-keeping you must do.

It's Not as Difficult as You Think In this book we show you how to prepare your own incorporation forms and Bylaws with a minimum of time and trouble. Of course, nonprofit corporations should schedule and hold board, officer and staff meetings frequently throughout the year to keep all participants apprised of, and involved in, ongoing activities and programs. Fortunately, keeping Minutes of these meetings is not all that difficult to do once someone volunteers for the task (typically the person you appoint as corporate secretary). Secretary of state annual report forms are standard forms (requesting the names and addresses of directors and officers) and can usually be completed and mailed in a few minutes.

Annual nonprofit informational tax returns do present a challenge to a new group unfamiliar with IRS forms and requirements. Other record-keeping and reporting chores, such as double-entry accounting procedures and payroll tax withholding and reporting, can be equally daunting. At least to start, most nonprofits rely on the experience of a tax

Federal Estate Tax Exemption

An advantage of forming a tax-exempt 501(c)(3) nonprofit corporation is that contributions made to such groups at death are exempt from federal estate taxation. For this reason, people with estates larger than $600,000 (the minimum threshold for federal estate tax for people who haven't given away large sums during life) often write substantial contributions into their estate plans for their favorite 501(c)(3) nonprofits. Not surprisingly, many nonprofits pursue an active estate plan contribution campaign (pointing out the estate tax benefits of leaving a large gift to the nonprofit in a will or trust document) as part of their overall campaign for public support.

advisor, bookkeeper, or other legal or tax specialist on the board or in the community to help them set up their books and establish a system for preparing tax forms on time.

See Chapter 11 for recommendations on finding legal and tax professionals for your nonprofit.

2. Incorporation Costs and Fees

Traditionally, the other main disadvantage of incorporating a nonprofit organization has been the cost of paying an attorney to prepare the incorporation forms and tax exemption applications. Putting a little time and effort into understanding the material in this book can help you eliminate this disadvantage, leaving you with only the actual cost of incorporation, which is considerably less for nonprofit than for for-profit corporations. Including the federal tax exemption application fee, total fees to incorporate in many states are less than $200.

3. Time and Energy

These are important factors to consider prior to incorporating. In most cases, the legal decision to incorporate is intimately bound to a broader decision to increase not just the structure, but the overall scope, scale and visibility of nonprofit operations. With a larger, more accountable organization comes a number of new tasks: setting up and balancing books and bank accounts, depositing and reporting payroll taxes, meeting with an accountant to extract and report year end figures for annual informational returns, etc. Although these financial, payroll and tax concerns are not, strictly speaking, exclusively corporate chores,[4] they do invariably follow from a decision to incorporate—most unincorporated nonprofits keep a low employment, tax and financial profile and get by with minimum attention to legal and tax formalities.

Example A women's health collective operates as an unincorporated nonprofit organization maintained by the part-time volunteer efforts of its two founders. It keeps an office open a few days per week where people can stop by to read and exchange information on community health services, share patient evaluations of local physicians, read medical literature on women's health issues and concerns, etc. The

Do You Need to Incorporate?

Many groups do fine and accomplish their nonprofit purposes as unincorporated nonprofit associations, without formal organizational paperwork and written operational rules. If you can continue to accomplish your nonprofit purposes and goals informally, you may be happier staying small.

If your group does not generate a surplus (does not make a taxable profit), does not need to attract tax deductible contributions, does not need to apply for public or private grant monies, and has no legal need to adopt the corporate form (such as providing nonprofit people with the protection of limited liability), it may decide it's best, at least for the present, not to form a tax exempt nonprofit corporation. For example, the botany club discussed in the next sidebar may decide to incorporate in a few years when it seeks funding and contributions to spearhead a drive to save open space in the community.

two founders donate their time so there is no payroll. The office space is donated by one of the founders and (non-tax-deductible) contributions made by people who stop by the office help defray some of the operating costs (phone, utilities, photocopying, etc.). The additional portion of the overhead is paid by the two organizers. Formal meetings are rarely held and the organization is run with an absolute minimum of paperwork and record keeping. The organization has never made a profit and tax returns have never been filed for the unincorporated organization.

The founders could decide to continue in this fashion into the indefinite future. However, a number of women have expressed interest in helping the founders expand the activities and revenues of the collective in order to provide additional services and serve a wider segment of the community. To be eligible for additional support brought by tax deductible contributions and grant funds made available by the city to tax-exempt nonprofits, and to qualify the group to employ student interns and work-study students, the founders decide to form a 501(c)(3) nonprofit corporation. Doing so will require the preparation and filing of Articles of Incorporation and a federal corporate income tax exemption application. An initial board of directors must be selected and organizational Bylaws prepared. Formal written Minutes of the first board of directors meeting documenting the beginning business of the corporation should be prepared and placed in the corporate records.

After incorporation, regular board meetings are held and documented with written Minutes, a double-entry bookkeeping system is set up and utilized, regular federal and state payroll and tax procedures and controls are implemented, exempt organization tax returns are filed each year, and the operations of the group are expanded. A full-time staff person is assigned to handle the increased paperwork and bookkeeping chores brought about by the change in structure and increased operations of the organization.

This example is intended to underline one essential consideration that should be placed high on your pre-incorporation checklist: You should make sure that you and your co-workers can meet the challenge of the extra time and effort that your incorporated nonprofit organization will require. If the extra incorporational and operational work would overwhelm or overtax your current resources, we suggest you hold off on your incorporation until you have obtained the added help necessary to smoothly (or at least more easily) accomplish this task.

An Unincorporated Botany Club

A senior citizens botany club is organized informally. Initially, six members take a monthly nature walk to study and photograph regional flora. Everyone chips in to buy gas for whoever drives to the hike's starting point. Recently, however, membership has increased to fifteen and the group has decided to collect dues from members to pay for increased expenses—gas money, guidebooks and maps, printing club T-shirts—associated with more frequent field trips. To avoid commingling club monies with personal funds, a treasurer is designated to open a bank account on behalf of the organization. Several people suggest that it is time to incorporate the club. Does this make sense? Probably not. There is no new pressing need to adopt the corporate form or to obtain formal recognition as a tax exempt nonprofit. (Most banks will allow an unincorporated group without a federal Employer Identification Number or IRS tax exemption to open up a non-interest bearing account.)

F. Summing Up

At this point you should appreciate the basic advantages of forming a nonprofit corporation. You should also have a rough idea, given the anticipated nature and scope of your activities and the energies of your group, whether forming a tax-exempt nonprofit corporation is a feasible undertaking for you and your co-founders. If you're still not sure, read on. The next chapter provides information on the legal rules and formalities associated with organizing and operating a nonprofit corporation. The succeeding chapters provide specific information on the requirements for qualifying as a tax-exempt 501(c)(3) organization with the IRS.

How to Avoid Tax Problems

We suggest you seek the help of a competent accountant from the moment you decide to organize your nonprofit. Make sure you choose someone experienced in the many special requirements of nonprofit bookkeeping. The accountant should help the nonprofit corporation (in particular its treasurer) set up a good record-keeping system. This should be periodically reviewed by the accountant to be sure that accepted bookkeeping standards are met and all tax forms are filed in a timely manner.

Notes

1 If you would like more information on small profit corporations, see *How to Form Your Own Corporation* (California, Florida, New York and Texas computer and book editions), by Mancuso (Nolo Press)—order information is at the back of this book.

2 Other nonprofit exceptions to this no-stock, no-dividend rule exist. For example, under Section 504 of the New York Not-For-Profit Corporation Law, a nonprofit corporation may issue subvention certificates to members in return for capital contributions to the corporation. Subvention rights attached to this certificate can include the payment of a return to members out of corporate assets.

3 Generally, as long as directors attend meetings and conscientiously carry out corporate responsibilities, they should have little to worry about.

4 Technically, any nonprofit organization (except certain specially excluded groups such as churches) with annual gross receipts of more than $25,000 must file an annual information return with the IRS. Likewise, any organization with employees must withhold, deposit and report payroll taxes under state and federal rules. Receipts and expenditures of any organization should be accurately reflected and accounted for on financial books. Of course, for a variety of reasons, these tasks are not taken care of until the group formalizes its operations by forming a nonprofit corporation.

Nonprofit Corporation Law

Special Nonprofit Purposes

In some states, nonprofits are specifically prohibited from incorporating for one or more special purposes and activities. For example, under the corporate statutes of Texas, nonprofit corporations cannot be formed for one of the following purposes or activities: group hospital service, rural credit unions, agricultural and livestock pools, mutual loan corporations, cooperative credit associations, farmers' cooperative societies, cooperative marketing corporations, rural electric cooperatives, telephone cooperatives, lodges, banks, insurance companies, and certain water supply companies.

As long as you plan to form a nonprofit whose purposes meet the 501(c)(3) federal tax exemption rules, you should have no problem. However, if you plan to incorporate some special activity which is subject to special licensing or other regulation in your state, check to see if doing so is allowed under your state's rules. To do this, call the office that handles corporate filings in your state (see your State Sheet in the Appendix).

In this chapter, we answer basic questions concerning organizing a nonprofit corporation and discuss the legal rules various states apply to nonprofits. This material is meant to give you further background in the law of nonprofits and to give you an overview of the legal provisions contained in the forms you will fill out in later chapters. It should also start you thinking about practical aspects of your group's organization and management.

A. For What Purposes May a Nonprofit Corporation Be Formed?

To qualify for your federal nonprofit tax exemption, you will want to organize and operate your nonprofit corporation for religious, charitable, educational, literary or scientific purposes permitted under Section 501(c)(3) of the Internal Revenue Code. These five federal tax-exempt purposes are included as allowable nonprofit purposes under the corporation laws of each of the states. As we've said, this federal tax exemption relieves your nonprofit from having to pay federal corporate income taxes, makes it eligible in most cases for a corresponding state income tax exemption, and allows your organization to apply for exemption from other state taxes (franchise, excise, sales and use, etc.). In addition, 501(c)(3) status enables your donors to deduct contributions made to your group on their individual or corporate income tax returns (or on an estate tax return if contributions are written into an individual's estate plan).

To make it clear that your corporation is being formed for a valid 501(c)(3) tax-exempt purpose, you will wish to include language to this effect in your Articles of Incorporation. In most states you will also want to insert additional language stating the specific purposes of the corporation (in some states, it is sufficient to state that the corporation is formed for "lawful purposes" under state law). In Chapter 6, we discuss each of the different types of purpose clauses used in nonprofit Articles of Incorporation.

B. What Activities May a Nonprofit Corporation Engage In Under State Law?

Generally, nonprofit corporations have the power to engage in any lawful activity related to their nonprofit purposes (as stated in their Articles of Incorporation and Bylaws), plus the right to engage in other activities specifically allowed by provisions of state nonprofit corporation laws. These other statutory provisions are so broad that, for practical purposes, they amount to carte blanche to engage in any lawful business activity.

Just so you'll know, here is a typical list of state statutory powers conferred on nonprofit corporations:

- perpetual duration (unless the duration of the corporation is expressly limited in the Articles or Bylaws);

- standing to participate in the legal process—to sue or defend in court, etc.;

- to own or hold both real and personal property and to dispose of it;

- to make contracts and incur liabilities;

- to elect or appoint officers and directors and to indemnify them against liability;

- to issue memberships;

- to receive money (contributions, bequests, dues, admission fees, charges for services) and make donations;

- to pay compensation and establish pension plans for employees;

- to operate a for-profit business (as discussed later, your organization will be taxed on any income unrelated to its tax-exempt purposes); and

- generally, to do anything lawful and necessary for the corporation to carry out its nonprofit purposes.

C. What Activities May a 501(c)(3) Nonprofit Corporation Engage in Under Federal Tax Law?

It is essential that you understand that even though your corporation may be permitted wide latitude in pursuing corporate purposes under state law, IRC Section 501(c)(3) establishes a number of overriding restrictions and limitations that apply to your nonprofit corporation. Meeting these rules is critical to qualifying for and maintaining your tax-exempt status. Specifically, to be eligible for your federal 501(c)(3) nonprofit tax exemption, your organization:

- must be organized and operated for charitable, educational, religious, literary or scientific purposes;

- can't distribute gains to directors, officers or members;

- must distribute any assets remaining on dissolution of the corporation to another tax-exempt group;

- can't participate in political campaigns for or against candidates for public office; and

- can't substantially engage in legislative or grass roots political activities except as permitted under federal tax regulations.

D. How Much Money Do You Need to Start a Nonprofit Corporation?

Nonprofit corporation law does not require a new nonprofit corporation to have a specified amount of money in the corporate bank account before commencing operations.[1] This is fortunate, of course, because many beginning nonprofits must, of necessity, start out on a "shoestring" of meager public and private support.

Nonprofit corporations do not issue shares, nor provide investment incentives, such as a return on capital through the payment of dividends, to investors, benefactors or participants in the corporation.[2] Nonprofits do, however, have their own means and methods of obtaining start-up funds. Obviously, the most common is obtaining revenue in the form of contributions, grants and dues from the people, organizations, and governmental agencies that support the nonprofit's purposes and goals. Also, if you are incorporating an existing organization, its assets are usually transferred to the new corporation—included in these assets may be the cash reserves of an unincorporated group which can help your corporation begin operations. It's also possible to borrow start-up funds from a bank, although for newly formed corporations, a bank loan may need to be secured by the personal assets of the incorporators—a pledge most nonprofit directors would be understandably reluctant to make.

Often, of course, nonprofits receive initial and ongoing revenues from services or activities provided in the pursuit of their exempt purposes (payments for art lessons or dance courses, school tuition, clinic charges, etc.).

Articles and Bylaws

The two basic incorporation documents used to form a nonprofit corporation are the Articles of Incorporation and the Bylaws. The Articles are considered the charter document of the corporation and are filed with the secretary of state's office to form the corporation. The Bylaws set forth the operating rules and procedures of the corporation. Both the Articles and Bylaws are submitted to the IRS when the corporation applies for its federal 501(c)(3) nonprofit corporate tax exemption. We discuss the requirements for these and other organizational forms in later chapters.

E. Can a Nonprofit Corporation Engage in For-Profit Pursuits?

Yes, regular commercial business activities can also be used to finance nonprofit operations. However, to avoid jeopardizing the nonprofit's federal 501(c)(3) tax exemption, these profit-making activities must be incidental sidelines, not substantial operations, of the nonprofit organization.

F. What are the Legal Rights and Duties of Nonprofit Organizers, Directors, Officers and Employees?

While a corporation is a legal person capable of making contracts, incurring liabilities, etc., it still needs real people to carry out its corporate purposes and activities. Corporate people are classified legally as incorporators, directors, officers, members and employees—each with separate legal rights and responsibilities. We look at the basic legal provisions affecting each type of corporate person in the sections below.

In the following sections, we occasionally refer to your State Sheet to find a particular legal rule in your state. These sheets are contained in the back of the book in the Appendix.

G. Incorporators

An incorporator is someone who signs and delivers the Articles of Incorporation to the proper state office (usually the secretary of state or corporations commission) for filing. In most states this can be done by one person (the State Sheets indicate if your state requires more than one incorporator). In practice, the incorporator is often selected from among the persons who serve as the initial directors of the corporation. Once the corporation is formed the incorporator's legal role is complete.

During the organizational phase, the incorporator's role may extend to being a "promoter" of the corporation—helping to obtain money, property, personnel, and whatever else it takes to get the nonprofit corporation started. If an incorporator acts as a promoter, she is considered by law to be its *fiduciary*. This is legal jargon that simply means she

Training Nonprofit Directors

The initial organizers of a nonprofit corporation should be prepared to develop the directors' skills and effectiveness. This will mean initial orientation and training programs concerning both the nonprofit's proposed operations and the specific skills necessary to achieve them. In addition, there should be continuing education later, so board members can improve their proficiency at handling operational issues that pertain to your nonprofit corporation.

For example, if your nonprofit corporation is organized to provide health care or education, board members will likely need considerable orientation as to city, state, and federal program requirements that impact your operations, as well as regular updates on changes made to these rules and regulations.

has a duty to act in the best interests of the corporation and make full disclosure of any personal interest and potential benefits she may derive from business transacted for the nonprofit.

Example   If the incorporator/promoter arranges for the sale of property she owns to the nonprofit corporation, she must disclose both her ownership interest and any gain she stands to make on the sale to the nonprofit's board of directors.

Generally a nonprofit corporation is not bound by an incorporator's pre-incorporation contract, unless it is later ratified by the board of directors or the corporation accepts the benefits of the contract (uses office space or equipment leased by the incorporator). The incorporator, however, may be personally liable unless the contracts are signed in the name of the corporation and he clearly informs the third party that the corporation does not yet exist, may never come into existence and, even if it does, may not ratify the contract.

In short, anyone making pre-incorporation contractual arrangements for office space, hiring employees, or borrowing money should take heed to make it clear that all agreements are subject to ratification by the corporation when, and if, it comes into existence. Knowing this, the other party may, of course, refuse to do business with you until the nonprofit corporation is legally organized.

H. Directors

Corporate directors, who meet collectively as the board of directors, are responsible—legally, financially and morally—for the management and operation of your nonprofit corporation. Most states require initial directors to be named in the Articles.

The State Sheets show the number of directors required in each state and list any additional director qualifications, such as age and residency. Because directors may need to sign contracts and other legal documents, they should be at least of the age of majority in your state (usually 18).

Before we discuss legalities and state law requirements, let's look at an overriding practical concern: how to select the best directors for your organization.

Selecting Directors

Choosing directors is among the most important decisions you will make when organizing your corporation. You should consider candidates from a number of perspectives, including:

Their practical qualifications This includes their managerial, technical and financial skills.

Their community relations value Your directors are a crucial link between your organization and its supporters and benefactors, so you want to make sure that the members of the community that you plan to serve will see your director as a credible and competent representative of your group and its nonprofit goals. Their status and integrity are crucial to encouraging and protecting public trust in your organization, and their connections are vital to attracting recognition, clients, donations and other support.

Their role in helping you qualify for 501(c)(3) tax-exempt status The IRS likes to see that you have a representative (and financially disinterested) governing body that reflects a range of public interests, not simply the personal interests of a small number of donors. Furthermore, IRS Form 1023 (the Application for Recognition of Exemption discussed in Chapter 8) specifically asks if any of your board members have been selected because they are either public officials or appointed by public officials. While it's by no means required, the presence of a sympathetic

Director Action by Written Consent or Conference Call

Many states authorize the taking of action by directors without a meeting by written consent or by a conference telephone hookup. In some states, the unanimous written consent of directors must be obtained; in others, only the consent of the number of directors needed to pass the resolution (normally a majority of a quorum) need be obtained. Check your state's nonprofit corporation law. Look for a section titled "Action by Written Consent" in the part dealing with "Directors" if you're interested in having your board take action without a meeting.

public official on your board can enhance its credibility with both the IRS and the community.

Directors' responsibilities include development and implementation of organizational policies and goals, budgeting, fund raising and disbursing a group's funds. The board of directors may hire an administrator or executive director to oversee staff and daily operations, or may supervise them directly. Either way, you will need directors with more than just a passing commitment to your nonprofit purposes. Your board of directors should be a practical-minded group, ready to put time and energy into the organization. Additional factors to take into account in putting together your board of directors include the following:

- Consider members of the community you wish to be identified with who have a proven commitment to the goals of your organization. The community you draw from may be local (city, county, state), regional or national. For example, if yours is an environmental group concerned with issues in the southern part of the state, you have both a geographic community (people in the area) and a community of interest (environmentalists generally). Your board should reflect a cross section of interested and competent people from both these communities.

- There should be enough directors to ensure a wide basis of support (particularly with regard to fund raising) but not so many as to impede the efficiency in the board's operation. Boards with between nine and fifteen members often work well.

- Look for people who have broad practical skills your group needs and who are willing to share them. Do you need the professional expertise of a doctor, lawyer or architect; or perhaps operational assistance in areas such as public relations, marketing or publishing?

- Look for people with contacts and real world savvy in the specific area of your nonprofit's interest. For example, if you are starting a new private school or health clinic someone familiar with your state's educational or public health bureaucracy will be a big help.

- Look for people with fundraising experience. While many large nonprofits have a staff fundraiser, smaller groups often can benefit from the advice of an experienced board member.

- Look for people with experience managing money, either a professional accountant or someone with expertise in record-keeping and budgeting. This is particularly important when you consider that many nonprofits get into difficulty because their recordkeeping and reporting techniques aren't adequate to produce information required by the federal and state governments; or because they are inattentive to financial responsibilities such as paying withholding taxes or accounting properly for public or private grant monies.

Before you contact prospective board members, we suggest that you prepare a job description that specifies at least the following:

- the scope of the nonprofit's proposed activities and programs;

- board member responsibilities and time commitments (expected frequency and length of board meetings, extra duties that may be assigned to directors);

- the rewards of serving on your board (the satisfaction of working on behalf of a cause you care about, the experience of community service, etc.).[3]

Doing this should go a long way in helping to avoid future misunderstandings on the part of board members as to what is expected of them.

Look for Conflicts of Interest   When selecting board members, you may need to inquire about or at least independently consider a prospective member's agenda or motives in joining the board. Obviously, people whose reasons for joining are more for personal benefit than they are for the benefit of the organization or the public should not be asked to serve. This doesn't mean that everyone with a remote or potential conflict of interest should be disqualified. It does mean that any slight or possible conflict of interest should be fully recognized and discussed. Consideration should be given to whether or not a conflict is sufficiently fundamental to disqualify a candidate. Sometimes the conflict is sufficiently limited and the director will be able to serve constructively if he refrains from voting on certain issues.

Director Compensation

Nonprofit directors normally serve without compensation. While state nonprofit statutes generally allow directors to be paid provided the payment is reasonable and related to the actual performance of services, most nonprofits limit themselves to reimbursing directors for any necessary expenses incurred in performing director duties (such as travel expenses—typically a gas or mileage allowance—to attend board meetings). We believe this is generally wise. Not paying nonprofit directors reinforces one of the important legal and ethical distinctions of the nonprofit corporation: its assets should not be used for the private enrichment of its incorporators, directors, agents, members or employees.

Director Term of Office

The term of office for directors is commonly set in the corporation's Bylaws. Some states set a maximum term for directors (typically one year) only if the term is not specified in the Articles or Bylaws; other states specify a maximum term in all cases.

The State Sheets show the state requirements for the director's term of office. If possible in your state, we suggest a three-year term in order to get the most of what a director has to contribute (and to return the satisfaction of long-term service—seeing goals fulfilled) and to ensure continuity in operations.

Also in the interest of continuity, staggered elections of board members may be a good idea. For example, rather than replacing the entire board at each annual election, you may wish to re-elect 1/3 of the board members each year to serve a three-year term. To start this staggered system out with a 15-member board, 5 of the initial directors would serve for 1 year, 5 others for 2 years, and the remaining 5 for the full 3-year term. At each annual re-election, 1/3 of the board would be elected to serve 3-year terms.

Director Quorum Rules

In order for the board of directors to take action at a meeting, a specified number of the total number of directors of the corporation—called a quorum—must be present.

Generally, state nonprofit statutes require a majority quorum—a majority of the full board must be present to hold a meeting—but some states allow the quorum requirement to be set lower. The State Sheets list the director quorum requirements in each state.

**Corporate Reports
Can Protect Directors**

To help directors accomplish their managerial duties, most state statutes allow directors to safely rely on information from reliable, competent sources within the corporation (officers, committees, supervisory staff, etc.), or on outside professional sources (lawyers, accountants). If the information on which the director relies is found to be faulty or incorrect and the decision turns out to be an inadvisable one leading to monetary damages or losses, the directors will not be held personally liable, unless there was an obvious need for the directors to distrust and look beyond the information presented to the board.

Director Voting Rules

Once a quorum is present at a meeting, the affirmative vote of a majority of those present at the meeting is usually necessary to pass a board resolution.

Example If the Bylaws of a corporation with ten board members specify that a quorum consists of a majority of the board, and, further, that action at a meeting may normally be taken by a majority of the directors present, then a quorum of at least six people (a majority of the ten-person board) must be present to hold a board meeting, and, at the very least, four votes (a majority of the six members present at a meeting) must pass the resolution. Note: If eight of the ten directors actually attend the meeting, action must be approved by at least five votes—again, a majority of those present at the meeting.

Director Executive Committee

State statutes permit the full board of directors to delegate some or even a significant part of the board's duties to an executive committee of two or more directors. This arrangement is often used when some directors are more committed to working many hours for the well-being of the nonprofit than others.

The State Sheets indicate the number of directors that must be appointed to an executive committee in each state.

Establishing an executive committee can work particularly well as long as the other directors keep an eye on what their more active colleagues are up to and actively participate in regular meetings of the full board. To reinforce this rule of passive director responsibility, many state statutes authorizing executive committees expressly state that the full board remains responsible for the actions of the executive committee.

Fortunately, keeping the full board abreast of executive committee actions isn't very difficult. The full board should receive regular, timely Minutes of executive committee meetings and should review and, if necessary, reconsider, important executive committee decisions at each regularly scheduled meeting of the full board. It should always be clear that the full board has the power to override decisions of the executive committee with which it disagrees.

How to Avoid Liability Problems

Although, as we've said, personal liability for directors occurs infrequently, it can happen in extreme cases of mismanagement. So, a few words of advice: all directors on the board, whether active participants or casual community observers, need to attend board meetings and stay informed of, and participate in, all major board decisions. If a woefully wrong-headed or ill-advised decision is taken by the board which leads to monetary damages, the best defense for any board member is a "no" vote recorded in the corporate Minutes.

Legalities aside, what is most likely to put nonprofit directors at risk of personal liability is bad financial management, such as failing to pay taxes, not keeping proper records of what money is collected and how it is disbursed, or commingling funds—either directors' personal funds with corporate funds or restricted with nonrestricted funds. This is why it makes sense to have an experienced financial manager on the board, or to use the services of a prudent accountant who demands regular audited financial statements of the group's books.

Other Committees Established By the Board Don't confuse this special executive committee of directors with other corporate committees. The board typically appoints several specialized committees to keep track of and report on corporate operations and programs. These may include finance, personnel, buildings and grounds, new projects, fundraising or other committees. These committees, often consisting of a mix of directors, officers and paid staff, do not normally have the power to take legal action on behalf of the corporation; their purpose is to report and make recommendations to the full board or the Executive Committee.

Example A finance committee might be appointed by the board of directors and be charged with overseeing the organization's fund raising, budgeting and expenditures, and bookkeeping. Periodically, this committee would make financial recommendations to the full board. The corporation's treasurer would be a logical person to chair such a committee. A personnel committee would typically establish hiring and employment policies, as well as interview candidates for important positions for ultimate consideration by the board. A plans and programs committee might have charge of putting together the group's action plan for accomplishing the overall purposes of the organization.

Again, all of these specialized committees are subordinate to the full board of directors, and their actions and their decisions should be subject to its specific approval. They are simply more manageable and focused working groups that can report and recommend to the full board on a periodic basis in order to help make better use of the board's time and its members' talents.

Director Duty of Care

Under state nonprofit corporation law statutes, corporate directors and officers have a legal duty to act responsibly and in the best interests of the corporation—this is called their statutory "duty of care."[4] If the directors meet this duty, they have no personal financial liability to the corporation for their actions or omissions while serving on the board. On the other hand, if, because of a flagrant breach of this duty, they cause financial harm to the corporation, to the members or to third parties, a court may hold them personally liable for the losses. For example, if the board is formally advised by the head of a committee that a flagrantly unsafe condition or practice exists within the corporation and the board fails to implement any of the remedial measures recommended by the committee or otherwise take steps to deal with the problem over a long period of time, a court might hold the directors personally liable for any ensuing damage.

However, don't be overly concerned about the prospect of personal liability. Broadly speaking, courts are reluctant to hold nonprofit directors personally liable except in the clearest cases of dereliction of duty or misuse of corporate funds or property. In the rare cases where liability is found, the usual penalties are not onerous or punitive—typically, restitution of the loss is ordered by the court. Further, the general trend in state statutes is now to hold directors liable only for fraudulent or grossly negligent behavior, not for ordinary negligence or poor judgment.[5] To this end, many states have enacted special volunteer immunity laws to protect volunteer directors (along with other volunteer personnel, and in some states paid personnel as well) from personal liability for violating their duty of care except in case of malicious, intentional, grossly negligent or criminal behavior.[6]

Director Self-Dealing

Directors must guard against self-dealing; that is, involving the corporation in any transaction (such as the purchase or sale of property, investment of funds, payment of fees or compensation) in which the director has a material financial interest. The nonprofit corporation acts of most states include special rules for validating self-interested director decisions of this sort. In most cases, the interest of the director must be disclosed prior to voting and only disinterested members of the board may vote on the proposal.

Example A vote by the board authorizing the corporation to lease or buy property owned by a director, or to purchase services or goods from another corporation in which a director owns a substantial amount of stock, might be considered a prohibited self-dealing transaction if not properly disclosed and approved, since a director has a material financial interest in each transaction.

Director Loans and Guarantees

Loans or guarantees of a loan to a director are expressly prohibited by most state laws, or if permitted, require approval by special disclosure or voting rules. In view of the stricture that a nonprofit's activities may not benefit individuals involved in its operations, it's easy to see why a loan to a director from tax-exempt funds over which he or she exercises control might appear questionable. As with self-dealing discussed above, we suggest you carefully review your state's nonprofit statutes before considering approval of loans or guarantees to directors.

Director Indemnification and Insurance

In addition to enacting director and officer immunity statutes, all but nine states have director indemnification statutes that require a corporation to indemnify a director for legal expenses incurred as a result of acts done on behalf of the corporation if the director is successful in the legal proceeding.

Directors' (and officers') liability coverage (also called acts and omissions coverage) is, of course, one way to insulate directors from possible personal liability for their actions on behalf of the corporation. Realistically, however, this type of insurance is normally priced far beyond the reach of the average small nonprofit organization. Rather than worry about needing this kind of coverage and not being able to afford it, it often makes more sense to do everything possible to minimize potential risks that might arise in the pursuit of your nonprofit purposes.

For example, make sure that employees perform their work in a safe manner and that staff required to perform skilled tasks are properly trained and licensed. In addition, the corporation should obtain specific coverage for any likely risks: motor vehicle insurance to cover drivers of corporate vehicles, general commercial liability insurance to cover the group's premises, etc.

I. Officers

Most states require a nonprofit corporation to have a president, a secretary and a treasurer. A vice president may be required or optional under state statutes. Typically, officers are selected from the board of directors. In a majority of the states, one person can hold two or more offices but this is usually a poor idea. Note however, that many states specifically prohibit one person from serving simultaneously as both the president and secretary of the corporation.

The State Sheets list the required officer positions and the rules for filling these positions in each state.

Officers may receive reasonable compensation for services they perform for a nonprofit corporation. Generally, compensation is appropriate if they really have day-to-day operational authority, but usually not if, as is typical, paid staff handles operations and the officers limit themselves to presiding over the board of directors and participating in making overall nonprofit policy decisions. However, in smaller nonprofit contexts, officers may also assume staff positions and be paid for performing these daily tasks.

Example In a larger nonprofit organization, a paid executive director or medical director (these are staff, not board of director, positions) will oversee routine operations of a medical clinic, and the paid principal or administrator (also staff positions) will do the same for a private school. However, in a smaller nonprofit, the corporate president or other officer may assume these salaried tasks.

If you do decide to pay a a salary to an officer who is also a member of the board of directors to avoid a conflict of interest or the appearance of possible unfairness, we suggest that your board approve the salary without counting the vote of the interested director. We think this is a wise precaution even though the nonprofit statutes in many states specifically allow board members to vote for their own compensation. Also note that public and private grant programs may impose overriding conflict of interest regulations on your nonprofit, forbidding the corporation from paying a salary to any member of the board or any officer of the corporation.

The powers, duties and responsibilities of corporate officers are usually set in the Bylaws. Most states do not regulate the job functions or duties of officers of a nonprofit corporation—you are free to define the powers and duties of these positions as you see fit in your Bylaws.

Generally, the actions and transactions of an officer are legally binding on the corporation—a third party is entitled to rely on the apparent authority of an officer (whether or not the officer was actually empowered by the board to enter into the transaction). To avoid confusion, if you delegate a special task to an officer outside the realm of the officer's normal duties, it's best to have your board pass a resolution granting the officer special authority to enter into the transaction on behalf of the corporation.

Formal Membership Rights in a Nonprofit Corporation

A formal (legally recognized) member of a nonprofit corporation is usually entitled under the state's nonprofit corporation law to vote on the following matters:

- election and removal of directors;
- amendment of Articles and Bylaws;
- approval of merger or consolidation with another corporation;
- election to wind up or dissolve the corporation;
- sale of corporate assets; and
- approval of a transaction involving an interested director or officer.

Officers have a duty to act honestly and in the best interests of the corporation. Loans and guarantees to officers (assuming the nonprofit is in a position to make them), are either prohibited or very strictly regulated, as they are with directors. Officers can be insured or indemnified against personal liabilities, and they can benefit from the same immunity statutes that relieve volunteer, and in some states paid, directors from personal liability for monetary damages.

J. Members

If a nonprofit corporation establishes a formal membership structure in its Articles of Incorporation or Bylaws, then members of the corporation will be granted fundamental rights to participate in the affairs and future of the nonprofit corporation. We refer to members who are given these special legal rights as "formal members."

It is optional for a nonprofit corporation to have formal members with legal voting rights. To avoid the problems, including the paperwork and expense, of having to put elections of directors and other major corporate decisions to a vote of the members, most nonprofits choose not to have formal membership structures.

This approach of not having formal members is organizationally simpler than adopting a formal membership structure because only the directors are legally entitled to participate in the operation of the corporation. People interested in a non-membership nonprofit, although they may play fundamental advisory roles, need not be notified nor allowed to vote for directors or approve changes to the corporation's Articles or Bylaws. Normally this works well since most people become involved in nonprofit organizations out of interest in the group's activities and purposes, or in some cases because they receive attendance privileges or discounts to nonprofit events or programs, not because they wish to participate in the legal affairs of the corporation.

Interested people who work with a nonprofit corporation to help it achieve its goals (and who may pay annual dues or fees) but who are not formal members are often called "supporters," "patrons" "contributors" or "advisors." For example, a patron may be issued an "informal" museum membership that entitles the person to free admissions, participation in educational programs and events, use of a special facility or attendance at exhibition previews, but it does not give the person any say as a formal (legal) member in the museum's operation and management. We discuss the decision to set up (or do without) a formal membership structure and show you how to adopt membership or non-membership Bylaws in Chapter 7.

Classes of Membership

Nonprofit corporations that do decide to set up a formal membership structure may decide to establish different classes of membership, such as voting and non-voting membership classes. If so, the rights, privileges, restrictions and obligations associated with each class of membership must normally be stated in the Articles of Incorporation. Again, most smaller corporations are better off without a formal membership structure and will opt instead to establish different levels of sponsorship or participation in the corporation without giving sponsors or patrons legal membership rights in corporate affairs.

Membership Quorum and Voting Rules

Most states allow nonprofits to set their own quorum requirement for members' meetings in the Articles or Bylaws. If the corporation does not adopt a membership quorum provision, state statutes typically set a quorum for members' meetings at a low percentage of the full membership. Other states specify a limit (such as one-third of the membership) below which the quorum cannot be set in any case. Some states simply say that a quorum is the actual number of voting members that attend the meeting (under this circularly phrased rule, a meeting of members can always be held if one or more members show up for the meeting).

The State Sheets indicate the membership quorum rules for each state.

Despite this flexibility under state statutes, to ensure representational meetings attended by a sufficient cross-section of the voting membership, many membership nonprofits will wish to set the members' quorum requirement at a majority (or some higher percentage) of the voting membership.

Reality Note Larger membership nonprofits rarely call and hold meetings of membership with the expectation that members will attend and vote at the meeting in person. Rather, membership proxies (written votes) are usually solicited by mail well in advance of the meeting. The corporate secretary tallies and reports these votes at the membership meeting. The main business of the membership, the re-election of the board, is usually accomplished by using this proxy-by-mail procedure (or by relying on a specific nomination and balloting by mail procedure authorized by the state's nonprofit corporation statutes). Our membership provisions provide a simple membership balloting procedure which allows members to elect directors and transact other business by mail without a meeting.

Unless the Articles or Bylaws state otherwise, each member is entitled to cast one vote on any matter submitted for approval to the members. Again, it's possible to have several classes of membership with different voting rights attached to each membership.

K. Employees

Employees of nonprofit corporations are no different from employees of for-profit corporations. They work for and under the supervision of the corporation and are paid a salary in return for their services. Nonprofit employers, for the most part, pay the same employment taxes and employee benefits as for-profit employers [although 501(c)(3) tax-exempt nonprofits are exempt from paying federal unemployment taxes for employees]. Paid directors and officers are considered employees for purposes of withholding, Social Security, state unemployment and other payroll taxes the employer must pay. Employees likewise have the usual duty to report and pay their taxes, and the usual personal liability for failing to do so.

Employee Immunity

Employees are generally not personally liable for any financial loss their acts or omissions may cause to the corporation or to outsiders as long as they are working within the course and scope of their employment. If the harm is done to outsiders, it is the corporation, not the employees, which must assume the burden of paying for the loss.

An important exception to the rule of employee non-liability concerns the employee whose duty is to report or pay federal or state corporate or employment taxes. The responsible employee (or officer or director) can be held personally liable for failure to report or pay such taxes. The IRS may take a broad view as to who is "responsible" for such duties—see Chapter 10C.

Employee Compensation

Salaries, whether paid to officers or regular employees, should be reasonable and given in return for services actually performed. A reasonable salary is one roughly equal to that received by employees rendering the same services elsewhere (in other nonprofits or commercial businesses). If salaries are unreasonably high, they are apt to be treated as a simple distribution of net corporate earnings and could jeopardize the nonprofit's tax-exempt status. Of course, nonprofit personnel are usually paid comparatively (if not unreasonably) low salaries, so this caution is mostly a technical one.

Employee Benefits

Among the major advantages associated with being an employee of a corporation are the employment benefits it can provide. These are often more favorable than those allowed non-corporate employees. Benefits (which are deductible by a nonprofit corporation if taxes are owed by the corporation in connection with an activity that uses the services of these employees) include corporate pension plans, corporate medical expense reimbursement plans and corporate group accident, health, life and disability insurance. Generally, amounts paid by the corporation to provide for these benefits (such as the payment of insurance premiums by the corporation) are not included in the employee's individual gross income and, therefore, not taxed to the employee. Also, the benefits themselves (insurance proceeds, etc.) are often not taxed when the employee receives them. These corporate employee benefits can sometimes be an important collateral reason for forming a nonprofit corporation.[7]

L. How Is a Nonprofit Corporation Dissolved?

Dissolution of a corporation may be either voluntary or involuntary. Voluntary dissolution occurs when a corporation decides to wind up its affairs by a vote of the board of directors, or the board in conjunction with the formal membership. The decision to dissolve may come as the result of running out of program or administrative funds, an internal dispute within the nonprofit, or simply because the nonprofit program has accomplished its purposes or done as much as is reasonably possible in its area of endeavor.

A corporation dissolves voluntarily by filing Articles of Dissolution (or a similar document) with the secretary of state and, in some cases, obtaining a tax clearance from the state Department of Taxation or Revenue. (Your secretary of state materials should contain information on obtaining the forms and instructions necessary to dissolve a nonprofit corporation in your state).

Involuntary dissolution may occur if the corporation has failed to file its required annual financial report or pay state taxes for which it is liable for a given number of years. In such instances, the dissolution of the corporation will be initiated by the secretary of state or the attorney general, depending on which department has jurisdiction over the misfeasance. The nonprofit corporation itself may petition the court to involuntarily dissolve it if its board is deadlocked, if it has been inactive for a number of years, or for other specific reasons specified under state statutes.

After a board decision to dissolve, the corporation must cease transacting business except to the extent necessary to wind up its affairs. All corporate debts and liabilities, to the extent of the corporation's remaining assets, must be paid or provided for. If any corporate assets are left after paying corporate debts, a 501(c)(3) tax-exempt nonprofit corporation must, as we'll see, distribute them to another 501(c)(3) group.

M. Summing Up—More Questions?

Hopefully, this chapter on the basic legal provisions affecting nonprofit corporations has answered more questions than it has raised. It's not possible (and at this stage you probably wouldn't want us) to include a complete corporate law course here. If you do get stuck, or face a particularly complex or unusual legal question or problem, it makes sense to do your own legal research or to consult a lawyer with experience in nonprofit corporation law (or often to do both). In Chapter 11 we discuss how to choose a lawyer and approach doing your own legal research.

Notes

1 By contrast, the for-profit corporation statutes of some states specify a minimum capitalization requirement—often $1,000—which must be paid into the corporation at the time it is organized.

2 A few special types of nonprofit corporations are allowed under state law to issue shares or membership participation rights in return for capital contributions. We do not cover nonprofits of this type in this book.

3 The corporate kits advertised at the back of the book include director certificates which express appreciation to the recipient for serving on the board and contributing toward the realization of the nonprofit goals of the corporation.

4 State statutes defining this duty are usually phrased using general, imprecise legal terminology, requiring judges to interpret these terms subjectively on a case-by-case basis. Here's one example: "A director shall perform the duties of a director … in good faith, in a manner such director believes to be in the best interest of the corporation and with such care, including reasonable inquiry, as an ordinarily prudent person in a like position would use under similar circumstances."

5 For an analysis of past and likely future directions in standards of care for nonprofit directors, see *Standards of Conduct for Directors of Nonprofit Corporations*, James S. Fishman, Vol. 7, Pace Law Review, p. 389 (1987). This volume should be available at law school libraries (or call the Pace University School of Law, Law Library, White Plains, NY). For an excellent legal treatment of this entire area together with hypothetical scenarios and cites to legal decisions, see *Board Liability, Guide for Nonprofit Directors* by Kurtz, published by Moyer Bell Limited, Mt. Kisco, NY, and available from Nolo Press.

6 Currently all states but Alaska, Hawaii, Iowa, Kentucky, Louisiana, Maine, Michigan, Mississippi, Missouri, Montana, Nebraska, North Dakota, New Hampshire, New Jersey, Nevada, Washington and the District of Columbia have some kind of nonprofit director immunity statute.

7 Nonprofits may also establish profit-sharing plans and similar arrangements—see IRC § 401(a)(27). Tax-exempt nonprofits may not, however, set up 401(k) plans (qualified cash or deferred arrangements—§ IRC 401(k)(4)(B). For information on setting up qualified employee plans and other benefits, consult your tax advisor.

The Federal 501(c)(3) Nonprofit Income Tax Exemption

**Humane Societies
and Sports Organizations**

Groups organized for the prevention of cruelty to children or animals or fostering national or international amateur sports competitions can also claim a 501(c)(3) tax exemption. However, these groups must meet narrowly defined 501(c)(3) requirements, and, for humane societies, special state requirements. See IRS Publication 557 for specifics on each of these special 501(c)(3) groups and contact your state attorney general's office for special incorporation requirements for humane societies.

Corporations, like individuals, are normally subject to federal and state income taxation. One reason for establishing a nonprofit corporation is to be exempt from paying corporate income taxes. Exemption is not automatic—a corporation must apply and show that it is in compliance with nonprofit exemption requirements to receive it. This chapter focuses on the basic federal tax exemption available to nonprofits under Section 501(c)(3) of the Internal Revenue Code.

A. Special-Purpose Nonprofit Tax Exemptions

Before looking at the IRC §501(c)(3) tax exemption provisions, let's glance at some special tax exemption categories contained in other sections of the Internal Revenue Code. Table 3.1 contains a listing of these special tax exemption categories, with a brief description of each type of organization, the IRS exemption application used to apply for the exemption, the annual information return applicable to each group, and whether or not contributions to each organization are tax deductible.

As you can see, these nonprofits are very narrowly defined and chances are that these categories do not apply to you. If, after scanning over this table, you think that you may wish to form one of these special nonprofit groups rather than a 501(c)(3) corporation, you should consult a nonprofit professional or do your own research. IRS Publication 557 and IRS Form 1024 contain additional information and instructions on forming some of these special-purpose nonprofits.

B. 501(c)(3) Nonprofit Tax Exemption

IRC §501(c)(3) exempts from payment of federal income taxes groups organized and operated exclusively for charitable, religious, scientific, literary, and educational purposes. The Articles of Incorporation of a 501(c)(3) group must limit corporate purposes to one or more allowable 501(c)(3) purposes and must not empower the corporation to engage, other than as an insubstantial part of its activities, in activities not in furtherance of one or more of these tax-exempt purposes. This formal requirement is known as the 501(c)(3) *organizational test.*

Multiple 501(c)(3) Purposes Are Permitted It is common and permissible for a group to engage in more than one 501(c)(3) tax-exempt activity. For example, its activities may be characterized as charitable or educational, or both, such as a school for blind or physically handicapped children.

Cross Purposes Are Not Allowed It is not permissible to engage simultaneously in 501(c)(3) exempt purpose activities and in activities exempt under other 501(c) subsections. So while you may perform charitable and educational functions together [both are valid 501(c)(3) purposes), you cannot, for example, form a 501(c)(3) for both educational and social or recreational purposes [the latter two purposes are exempt under IRC §501(c)(7)]. This problem rarely occurs, as the non-Section 501(c)(3) subsections are custom-tailored to very specific types of organizations (such as war veterans organizations and cemetery companies).

C. 501(c)(3) Tax-Exempt Purposes

Now let's take a closer look at the most common 501(c)(3) purposes and the requirements associated with each.[1]

1. Charitable Purposes

Benefit to the Public The word "charitable" as used in Section 501(c)(3) is broadly defined to mean "providing services beneficial to the public interest." Note that this definition is considerably broader than the traditional meaning of the term, "the relief of poverty or distress." In fact, other 501(c)(3) purpose groups—501(c)(3) educational, religious and scientific groups—are often also considered charitable in nature since their activities usually benefit the public.

Groups which seek to promote the welfare of specific groups of people within the community (e.g., services for handicapped or elderly persons or members of a particular ethnic group) or which seek to advance other exempt activities (e.g., environmental education) will generally be considered to be organized for charitable purposes since these activities can be viewed as benefiting the public at large and are charitable in nature.

Charitable Class A charitable organization must be set up to benefit an indefinite class of individuals, not particular persons. However, the number of beneficiaries may be relatively small as long as the benefited class is open and the identities of the beneficiaries are not specifically listed.

Table 3.1 Special Nonprofit Tax Exempt Organizations

IRC §	Organization and Description	Application Form	Annual Return	Deductibility of Contributions[1]
501(c)(1)	FEDERAL CORPORATIONS corporations organized under an Act of Congress as federal corporations specifically declared to be exempt from payment of federal income taxes.	No Form	None	Yes, if made for public purposes
501(c)(2)	CORPORATIONS HOLDING TITLE TO PROPERTY FOR EXEMPT ORGANIZATIONS corporations organized for the exclusive purpose of holding title to property, collecting income from property, and turning over this income, less expenses, to an organization which, itself, is exempt from payment of federal income taxes.	1024	990	No
501(c)(4)	CIVIL LEAGUES, SOCIAL WELFARE ORGANIZATIONS OR LOCAL EMPLOYEE ASSOCIATIONS civic leagues or organizations operated exclusively for the promotion of social welfare, or local associations of employees, the membership of which is limited to the employees of a particular employer within a particular municipality, and whose net earnings are devoted exclusively to charitable, educational or recreational purposes. Typical examples of groups which fall under this category are volunteer fire companies, home owners or real estate development associations, or employee associations formed to further charitable community service.	1024	990	Generally, No[2]
501(c)(5)	LABOR, AGRICULTURAL OR HORTICULTURAL ORGANIZATIONS organizations of workers organized to protect their interests in connection with their employment (e.g., labor unions) or groups organized to promote more efficient techniques in production or the betterment of conditions for workers engaged in agricultural or horticultural employment.	1024	990	No
501(c)(6)	BUSINESS LEAGUES, CHAMBERS OF COMMERCE, ETC. business leagues, chambers of commerce, real estate boards or boards-of-trade organized for the purpose of improving business conditions in one or more lines of business.	1024	990	No
501(c)(7)	SOCIAL AND RECREATIONAL CLUBS clubs organized for pleasure, recreation, and other nonprofit purposes, no part of the net earnings of which inure to the benefit of any member. Examples of such organizations are hobby clubs and other special interest social or recreational membership groups.	1024	990	No
501(c)(8)	FRATERNAL BENEFICIARY SOCIETIES groups which operate under the lodge system for the exclusive benefit of their members, which provide benefits such as the payment of life, sick or accident insurance to members.	1024	990	Yes, if for certain 501(c)(3) purposes
501(c)(9)	VOLUNTEER EMPLOYEE BENEFICIARY ASSOCIATIONS associations of employees which provide benefits to their members, enrollment in which is strictly voluntary and none of the earnings of which inure to the benefit of any individual members except in accordance with the association's group benefit plan.	1024	990	No
501(c)(10)	DOMESTIC FRATERNAL SOCIETIES domestic fraternal organizations operating under the lodge system which devote their net earnings to religious, charitable, scientific, literary, educational or fraternal purposes and which do not provide for the payment of insurance or other benefits to members.	1024	990	Yes, if for certain 501(c)(3) purposes
501(c)(11)	LOCAL TEACHER RETIREMENT FUND ASSOCIATIONS associations organized to receive amounts received from public taxation, from assessments on the teaching salaries of members, or income from investments, to devote solely to providing retirement benefits to its members.	No Form[3]	990	No

IRC §	Organization and Description	Application Form	Annual Return	Deductibility of Contributions[1]
501(c)(12)	BENEVOLENT LIFE INSURANCE ASSOCIATIONS, MUTUAL WATER AND TELEPHONE COMPANIES, ETC. organizations organized on a mutual or cooperative basis to provide the above and similar services to members, 85% of whose income is collected from members, and whose income is used solely to cover the expenses and losses of the organization.	1024	990	No
501(c)(13)	CEMETERY COMPANIES companies owned and operated exclusively for the benefit of members solely to provide cemetery services to their members.	1024	990	Generally, Yes
501(c)(14)	CREDIT UNIONS credit unions and other mutual financial organizations organized without capital stock for nonprofit purposes.	No Form[3]	990	No
501(c)(15)	MUTUAL INSURANCE COMPANIES certain mutual insurance companies whose gross receipts are from specific sources and are within certain statutory limits.	1024	990	No
501(c)(16)	FARMERS' COOPERATIVES associations organized and operated on a cooperative basis for the purpose of marketing the products of members or other products.	No Form[3]	990	No
501(c)(19)	WAR VETERAN ORGANIZATIONS posts or organizations whose members are war veterans, formed to provide benefits to their members.	1024	990	Generally, No[4]
501(c)(20)	GROUP LEGAL SERVICE ORGANIZATIONS organizations created for the exclusive function of forming a qualified group legal service plan.	1024	990	No
501(c)(25)	TITLE HOLDING COMPANY a corporation or trust organized to acquire, hold title to and collect income from real property and remit it to tax-exempt organizations that are shareholders or beneficiaries. Participation in the trust is limited to certain qualified plans, government entities and 501(c)(3) organizations.	1024	990	No
501(d)	RELIGIOUS AND APOSTOLIC ORGANIZATIONS religious associations or corporations with a common treasury which engage in business for the common benefit of members. Each member's share of the net income of the corporation is reported on his individual tax return. This is a rarely used section of the Code used by religious groups which are ineligible for 501(c)(3) status because they engage in a communal trade or business.	No Form	1065	No
521(a)	FARMERS' COOPERATIVE ASSOCIATIONS farmers', fruit growers' and like associations organized and operated on a cooperative basis for the purpose of marketing the products of members or other producers, or for the purchase of supplies and equipment for members at cost.	1028	990-C	No

For specific information on the requirements of several of these special-purpose tax exemption categories, see IRS Publication 557, *Tax-Exempt Status for Your Organization*.

1 An organization exempt under a subsection of IRC Section 501 other than (c)(3)—the types listed in this table—may establish a fund exclusively for 501(c)(3) purposes, contributions to which are deductible. Section 501(c)(3) tax-exempt status should be obtained for this separate fund of a non-501(c)(3) group. See IRS Publication 557 for further details.

2 Contributions to volunteer fire companies and similar organizations are deductible, but only if made for exclusively public purposes.

3 Application is made by letter to the key District Director.

4 Contributions are deductible if 90% or more of the members are war veterans.

**Nonprofit Purposes—Sometimes
Simply a Matter of Definition**

You'll notice in going through the material
in this section that many IRS tax-
exemption criteria are generally stated
and seemingly applicable to a wide
range of activities, commercial and non-
commercial alike. In fact, this is often the
case. For instance, many nonprofit
scientific organizations perform research
that would qualify as 501(c)(3) scientific
research in the public interest. Similarly,
many commercial publishing houses
publish educational materials that could
qualify for a 501(c)(3) tax exemption. The
dividing line between commercial and
tax-exempt activities becomes further
blurred by the fact that tax-exempt
organizations may charge a reasonable
fee for their services and products (and,
indeed, may make a profit from pursuing
their tax-exempt purposes).

So how does the IRS decide whether
a particular organization is tax exempt?
The answer lies in the very act of
applying for a tax exemption. By defining
and organizing your activities as
nonprofit, tax-exempt activities, you
agree to give up any proprietary interest
in the enterprise and irrevocably
dedicate organizational assets to tax-
exempt purposes. This, in itself, evidences your nonprofit intent and purpose
and distinguishes your activities from
similar commercial endeavors.

Examples A nonprofit corporation established to benefit an
impoverished individual, Jeffrey Smith, is not charitable under
501(c)(3). But one whose general charitable purpose is to benefit needy
individuals in a particular community is a charitable organization and
may select Jeffrey Smith as a beneficiary. A foundation that awards
scholarships solely to undergraduate members of a designated fraternity
has been held to be a charitable organization even though the number of
members in the benefited group or class is small.

Services Need Not Be Free 501(c)(3) charitable organizations are
not required to offer services or products free or at cost. However, doing
so, or at least providing services at a substantial discount from the going
commercial rate, helps convince the IRS of the group's bona fide
charitable intentions. Charging full retail prices for services or products
usually demonstrates little benefit to the public.

Examples of Valid Charitable Purposes Here are examples from
IRS regulations of valid 501(c)(3) charitable activities and purposes:

- relief of the poor, distressed or underprivileged;

- advancement of religion;

- advancement of education or science;

- erection or maintenance of public buildings, monuments or works;

- lessening the burdens of government;

- lessening neighborhood tensions;

- elimination of prejudice and discrimination;

- promotion and development of the arts;

- defense of human and civil rights secured by law;

- providing facilities and services to senior citizens;

- maintaining a charitable hospital;

- providing a community fund to support family relief and service
  agencies in the community;

- providing loans for charitable or educational purposes;

- maintaining a public interest law firm.

The following are specific examples of activities that have been held
to be tax-exempt 501(c)(3) charitable activities:

Assistance to Low Income Families An organization formed to build
new housing and to renovate existing housing for sale to low income
families on long-term, low payment plans; also, a day care center for
children of needy working parents.

Self-Help Programs A group created to market the cooking and needlework of needy women; a self-help housing program for low income families.

Assistance to the Aged Homes for the aged where the organization satisfies the special needs of an aged person for housing, health care and financial security. The requirements for housing and health care will be satisfied if the organization is committed to maintaining residents who become unable to pay and if services are provided at the lowest possible cost.

Ministering to the Sick An organization that takes care of patients' non-medical needs (reading, writing letters, etc.) in a privately-owned hospital.

Rescue and Emergency Services An organization that provides emergency and rescue services for stranded, injured or lost persons; a drug crisis center and a telephone hotline for persons with drug problems.

Legal Assistance to Low Income Families A legal aid society offering free legal services to indigent persons.

2. Religious Purposes

Groups falling within this category include general types of religious organizations and more formal institutionalized churches. Let's look at general religious-purpose (non-church) organizations first.

Qualifying as a 501(c)(3) Religious Organization

Traditionally, the IRS and the courts have been reluctant to question the validity or sincerity of religious beliefs or practices. As long as the organization's belief appears to be "truly and sincerely held" and the practice and rituals associated with it are not illegal or against public policy, the IRS generally does not challenge the validity of the religious tenets or practices. However, the IRS will question the nature and extent of religious activities (as opposed to religious beliefs) if they do not appear to foster religious worship or advance a religious purpose, or if they appear commercial in nature.

Examples A group which holds weekly meetings and publishes material celebrating the divine presence in all natural phenomena should qualify as a religious purpose group. An organization which sells a large volume of literature to the general public, some of which has little or no connection to the religious beliefs held by the organization, may be regarded by the IRS strictly as a regular trade or business, not as a tax-exempt religious organization.

Belief in a Supreme Being Is Not Necessary A religious group need not profess belief in a Supreme Being to qualify as a religious organization under 501(c)(3). The Supreme Court has stated that serious Constitutional difficulties would result if 501(c)(3) were interpreted to exclude those beliefs that do not encompass a Supreme Being in the conventional sense, such as Taoism, Buddhism and Secular Humanism.[2]

Advancement of Religion Activities that advance religion are exempt under 501(c)(3)—the IRS is likely to classify these activities as charitable and religious (the advancement of religion is also classified as a charitable purpose). Here are specific examples of activities that have been held to advance religion under 501(c)(3):

Monthly Newspaper The publication and distribution of a monthly newspaper carrying church news of interdenominational interest accomplishes a charitable purpose by contributing to the advancement of religion.

Coffee House A nonprofit organization formed by local churches to operate a supervised facility known as a coffee house, in which persons of college age are brought together with church leaders, educators, and leaders from the business community for discussions and counseling on religion, current events, social and vocational problems was held to be advancing religion and thus exempt under 501(c)(3).

Genealogical Research An organization formed to compile genealogical research data on its family members in order to perform religious observances in accordance with the precepts of their faith was held to be advancing religion.

Missionary Housing A group established to provide temporary low-cost housing and related services for missionary families on furlough in the U.S. from their assignments abroad was held to be operated exclusively for charitable purposes.

Qualifying as a 501(c)(3) Church

You can also qualify under the 501(c)(3) religious-purpose category as a church, but doing so is more difficult to accomplish than qualifying simply as a 501(c)(3) religious organization. One of the advantages of qualifying as a church is that these organizations automatically qualify for 501(c)(3) *public charity status*—a status which all 501(c)(3) groups will want to obtain, as we explain in Chapter 4.

How the IRS Defines a Church Under IRS rulings, a religious organization should have the following characteristics to qualify as a church (not all are necessary but the more the better):

- a recognized creed or form of worship;
- a definite and distinct ecclesiastical government;
- a formal code of doctrine and discipline;
- a distinct religious history;
- a membership not associated with any other church or denomination;
- a complete organization of ordained ministers;
- a literature of its own;
- established places of worship;
- regular congregations;
- regular religious services.

Courts have used similar criteria to determine whether or not a religious organization qualifies as a church. For example, the U.S. Tax Court[3] has looked for the presence of the following "church" factors:

- services held on a regular basis;
- ordained ministers or other representatives;
- a record of the performance of marriage, other ceremonies, and sacraments;
- a place of worship;
- some support required from members;
- formal operations;
- satisfies all other requirements of federal tax law for religious organizations.

All religious-purpose groups claiming church status must complete a special IRS schedule containing specific questions on some of the church characteristics listed above when preparing their federal tax exemption application.

We discuss this application and the special church schedule in Chapter 8.

Traditional churches, synagogues, associations or conventions of churches (and religious orders or organizations that are an integral part of a church and engaged in carrying out its functions) may qualify as a

501(c)(3) church without difficulty. Less traditional and less formal religious organizations may have a harder time. Such groups may have to answer additional questions to convince the IRS that they qualify as a tax-exempt church.

Church Audits Some churches stand a greater chance of being audited by the IRS than others. Not surprisingly, the IRS is more likely to examine and question groups that promise members substantial tax benefits for organizing their households as tax-deductible church organizations.

IRS Church Guide The Internal Revenue Service is developing a guide designed to assist churches and clergy in complying with the requirements of the Internal Revenue Code. The publication is intended to be a "user-friendly" compilation, set forth in question-and-answer format. A draft copy of the guide, tentatively titled *Tax Guide for Churches and Other Religious Organizations*, is available at no charge from the Internal Revenue Service by asking for it by name and sending your request in writing to: Freedom of Information Reading Room, P.O. Box 795, Ben Franklin Station, Washington, DC 20044 . Most church and religious-purpose groups will find the information in this material extremely helpful when preparing their federal exemption application.

3. Scientific Purposes

Tax-exempt status is allowed to groups that engage in scientific research carried on in the public interest. Under IRS regulations, research incidental to commercial or industrial operations (such as the normal inspection or testing of materials or products or the design or construction of equipment and buildings) does not qualify under IRC §501(c)(3).

Public Interest Research Generally, research is considered in the public interest if the results (including any patents, copyrights, processes or formulas) are made available to the public (i.e., if the scientific research is published for others to study and use); if the research is performed for the United States or a state, county or city government; or if the research is conducted to accomplish one of the following purposes:

- aiding in the scientific education of college or university students;

- discovering a cure for a disease;

- aiding a community or region by attracting new industry, or by encouraging the development or retention of an existing industry.

Example A research organization, operated by a group of physicians specializing in heart defects and investigating the causes and treatment of cardiac and cardiovascular conditions and diseases, was recognized as an exempt 501(c)(3) scientific organization. The physicians practiced medicine apart from the organization's research program; although some of their private patients were accepted for study, they were selected on the same criteria as other patients; the organization's facilities were maintained separately from private practice facilities and were used exclusively for research.

Another Example Clinical testing of drugs for pharmaceutical companies was held not to be "scientific" under § 501(c)(3) since the clinical testing in question was incidental to a pharmaceutical company's commercial operations.

If you are applying for a scientific exemption under IRC 501(c)(3), your responses to the narrative portions of the federal exemption application (covered in Chapter 8) should show that your organization is conducting public interest research and should provide the following information:

- an explanation of the nature of the research;

- description of past and present research projects;

- how and by whom research projects are determined and selected;

- who will retain ownership of control of any patents, copyrights, processes, or formulas resulting from the research.

This and other specific information required to be submitted to the IRS by scientific groups is listed on page 14 of IRS Publication 557.

501(c)(3) Private School Non-Discrimination Requirements

If you do set up a 501(c)(3) private school, you must include a non-discrimination statement in your Bylaws and must publicize this statement to the community served by the school. [In an 8 to 1 ruling, the U.S. Supreme Court upheld the validity of these private school non-discrimination rules. *Bob Jones v. U.S.*, 433 CCH S.Ct. Bull. B2702 (1983)].

Essentially, this statement must make it clear that the school does not discriminate against students or applicants on the basis of race, color or national or ethnic origin.

For further information on these IRS private school anti-discrimination rules and procedures, see IRS Publication 557.

4. Literary Purposes

This is a seldom-used 501(c)(3) category, since most literary-purpose nonprofits are classified as educational by the IRS. Nevertheless, valid 501(c)(3) literary purposes include traditional literary efforts such as publishing, distribution, book sales, etc., which are directed toward promoting the public interest rather than engaging in a commercial literary enterprise or specifically serving the interests of particular individuals (such as the proprietors of a publishing house). Generally, this means that literary material must be available to the general public and must pertain to the betterment of the community. Beyond paying reasonable salaries, profits must be put to use for nonprofit purposes.

What distinguishes public interest publishing from a private publishing house? A combination of factors. If you publish materials that are clearly educational and make them available to the public at cost (or at least below standard commercial rates), then you stand a chance of qualifying as a 501(c)(3) organization. However, if your material seems aimed primarily at a commercial market and is sold at standard rates through regular commercial channels, chances are that your literary organization will be viewed by the IRS as a regular business enterprise ineligible for a 501(c)(3) tax exemption.

Example Publishing of material promoting highway safety or the education of handicapped children qualify as bona fide 501(c)(3) literary purposes. Publishing efforts more private than public in nature—publishing textbooks at standard rates for example—will have difficulty qualifying as tax-exempt literary activities under Section 501(c)(3).

An IRS Literary Organization Ruling A nonprofit publishing house applied for its 501(c)(3) exemption. It published only books (tracts actually) related to esoteric Eastern philosophical thought. The books were to be sold commercially but at modest prices. The IRS granted the tax exemption after requesting and reviewing the manuscript for the nonprofit's first publication. Apparently, the IRS agreed that the material was sufficiently specialized to render it non-commercial in nature.

5. Educational Purposes

501(c)(3) tax-exempt educational purposes are broad, encompassing instruction for both self-development and for the benefit of the community. The IRS allows advocacy of a particular intellectual position or viewpoint if there "is a sufficiently full and fair exposition of pertinent facts to permit an individual or the public to form an independent opinion or conclusion. However, mere presentation of unsupported opinion is not (considered) educational." If the group takes political positions, it may not qualify.

Example   If an educational group publishes a newsletter with a balanced analysis of an issue (or at least with some room devoted to debate or presentation of opposing opinions), this should qualify as a 501(c)(3) tax-exempt activity. If its newsletter is simply devoted to espousing one side of a issue, platform or agenda, tax exemption may be denied or revoked.

Educational exempt-purpose activities include:

- publishing public interest educational materials;
- conducting public discussion groups, forums, panels, lectures, workshops, etc.;
- offering a correspondence course or one that uses other media such as television or radio;
- a museum, zoo, planetarium, symphony orchestra, performance groups, etc.;
- serving an educational institution, such as a college bookstore, alumni association or athletic organization;
- publishing educational newsletters, pamphlets, books or other material.

Formal School Not Necessary   To qualify as a 501(c)(3) educational organization a group need not provide instruction in traditional school subjects, nor, for that matter, organize itself as a formal school facility with a regular faculty, established curriculum and a regularly enrolled student body .

Additional Federal and State School Requirements People setting up non-traditional schools should remember that although they do not need a regular faculty, full-time students nor even a fixed curriculum to qualify for a 501(c)(3) educational purpose tax exemption, as a practical matter they may need all of these things to qualify for state or federal support, to participate in federal student loan programs and to obtain accreditation.

Child Care Centers   Providing child care outside the home qualifies as a 501(c)(3) educational purpose under special provisions contained in IRC §501(k) if:

- the care enables parent(s) to be employed; and
- the child care services are available to the general public.

However, a child care facility that gives enrollment preference to children of employees of a specific employer will not be considered a 501(c)(3) educational-purpose organization.

Political Expenditures Test

Under the political expenditures test in IRC § 501(h), limitations are imposed on two types of political activities: lobbying expenditures and grassroots expenditures.

Lobbying expenditures are those made for the purpose of influencing legislation, while grassroots expenditures are those made to influence public opinion.

For examples of activities within these categories, read the section on *Lobbying Expenditures* in IRS Publication 557. The monetary limits are different for each category, and the formulas for computing them are somewhat complicated.

D. Other Tax Exemption Requirements

In addition to being organized for one or more allowable tax-exempt purposes, a 501(c)(3) must meet other requirements.

1. Insubstantial Unrelated Activities Requirement

A 501(c)(3) nonprofit may not substantially engage in activities unrelated to the group's tax-exempt purposes. Or, put affirmatively, this means that your nonprofit corporation may conduct activities not directly related to its exempt purposes as long as they don't represent a substantial portion of total organizational activities. This leeway is granted in recognition of the fact that most nonprofits may need to do unrelated business in order to survive. For example, a nonprofit dance group might rent unused portions of its studio space to an outside group to use for storage. Another nonprofit may invest surplus funds to augment the income of the organization.

Most groups need not be overly concerned with this limitation unless activities unrelated to exempt purposes come to involve a significant amount of the group's energy or time, or if they produce "substantial" income. If these activities are themselves nonprofit, they should be included in the organization's exempt purposes and be classified as related activities. The IRS keeps an eye out for tax-exempt groups that regularly engage in profit-making businesses with little or no connection to their exempt purposes (i.e., a church running a truck company). Business activities necessary to implement the group's exempt purposes, such as hiring and paying employees, and paying rent for space used for the group's exempt purpose or activities, are considered related activities.

Most new nonprofits work full-time simply tending to their exempt purposes and do not explore unrelated money making activities until later, if at all. However, if you plan to engage in unrelated business from the start, be careful. It's hard to pin down exactly when such activities become substantial enough to jeopardize the corporation's tax-exempt status. Also, income derived from unrelated business activities is subject to federal and state corporate income tax, even if it is not substantial enough to affect the group's 501(c)(3) tax-exempt status.

2. Limitation on Private Inurement (Profits and Benefits)

No 501(c)(3) nonprofit corporation may be organized or operated to benefit individuals associated with the corporation (directors, officers, or members) or other persons or entities related to, or controlled by, these individuals (such as another corporation controlled by a director). In tax language, this limitation is known as the "prohibition on private inurement" and means that 501(c)(3) groups can't pay profits to, or otherwise benefit, private as opposed to public interests.

Two specific 501(c)(3) requirements implement this prohibition on self-inurement:

- no part of the net earnings of the corporation may be distributed to individuals associated with the corporation; and

- the assets of a 501(c)(3) group must be irrevocably dedicated to another exempt group.

Payment of reasonable salaries to directors, officers, employees or agents for services rendered the corporation in furtherance of its exempt purposes is allowed.

3. Limitation on Political Activities

501(c)(3) tax-exempt nonprofit corporations are absolutely prohibited from participating in political campaigns for or against any candidate for public office.[4] Participation in or contributions to political campaigns can result in the revocation of 501(c)(3) tax-exempt status and the assessment of special excise taxes against the organization and its managers.[5]

Influencing Legislation Tax-exempt 501(c)(3) nonprofit organizations are also prohibited, "except to an insubstantial degree," from acting to influence legislation.[6] Generally, if a nonprofit corporation contacts, or urges the public to contact, members of a legislative body, or if it advocates the adoption or rejection of legislation, the IRS considers it to be acting to influence legislation.

Also, under IRS regulations, lobbying to influence legislation includes:

- any attempt to affect the opinions of the general public or a segment of it; and

- communication with any member or employee of a legislative body, or with any government official or employee who may participate in the formulation of legislation.

However, lobbying to influence legislation does not mean:

Making the Political Expenditures Election

If your 501(c)(3) nonprofit elects the political expenditures test, you must file IRS form 5768, *Election by an Eligible Section 501(c)(3) Organization to Make Expenditures to Influence Legislation,* within the tax yearin which you wish the election to be effective.

- making available the results of nonpartisan analysis, study, or research;

- providing technical advice or assistance to a government body, or to its committee or other subdivision, in response to a written request from it, where such advice would otherwise constitute the influencing of legislation;

- appearing before, or communicating with, any legislative body with respect to a possible decision that might affect the organization's existence, powers, tax-exempt status, or the deduction of contributions to it;

- communicating with a government official or employee, other than for the purpose of influencing legislation.

Also excluded from the definition of lobbying efforts are communications between an organization and its members with respect to legislation (or proposed legislation) of direct interest to the organization and the members, unless these communications directly encourage members to influence legislation.

Example A Housing Information Exchange keeps its members informed of proposed legislation affecting low income renters. This should not be considered legislative lobbying activity unless members are urged to contact their political representatives in support of, or in opposition to, the proposed legislation.

In determining whether a group's legislative activities are substantial in scope, the IRS looks at the amount of time, money or effort expended on legislative lobbying. If they are substantial in relation to other activities, 501(c)(3) tax status may be revoked and, again, special excise taxes can be levied against the organization and its managers.[7]

The Alternative Political Expenditures Test Since it is impossible to know ahead of time how the IRS will assess the "substantiality" of a group's legislative activity, the IRC allows 501(c)(3) public charities (as you'll see in Chapter 4, we assume you will qualify for public charity classification), to elect an alternative "expenditures test" to measure permissible legislative activity.[8]

Example If your nonprofit corporation plans to do considerable lobbying activity, carried on primarily by unpaid volunteers, then electing the expenditures test might be a good idea. Why? Because the minimal outlay of money to engage in these activities will probably keep you under the applicable expenditure limits. If you didn't make this election, your 501(c)(3) tax exemption might be placed in jeopardy if the IRS considered your political activities to be a substantial part of your overall purposes and program.

If you plan to engage in more than a minimum amount of political lobbying or legislative efforts, you need to decide whether it is to your advantage to elect the expenditures test based on the facts of your situation. If you find that these alternative political expenditures rules are still too restrictive,[9] you might consider forming a social welfare organization or civic league under IRC Section 501(c)(4)—this exemption requires a different federal exemption application, IRS Form 1024, and does not carry with it all the attractive benefits of 501(c)(3) status (access to grant funds, tax deductible contributions, etc.). See Table 3.1 above and IRS Publication 557 for further information on 501(c)(4) organizations.

Political Action Organizations Another way the IRS can challenge a 501(c)(3) group's political activities is to determine that it is an action organization, one so involved in political activities that *it is not organized exclusively for a 501(c)(3) tax-exempt purpose*, and then revoke its tax-exempt status.[10] Intervention in political campaigns or substantial attempts to influence legislation, as discussed above, are grounds for applying this sanction. In addition, if a group has the following two characteristics, it will be classified as an action organization and lose its 501(c)(3) status:

1. its main or primary objective or objectives—not incidental or secondary objectives—may be attained only by legislation or defeat of proposed legislation; and

2. it advocates or campaigns for the attainment of such objectives rather than engaging in nonpartisan analysis, study, or research and making the results available to the public.

In determining whether a group has these characteristics, the IRS looks at the surrounding facts and circumstances, including the group's Articles and activities, and its organizational and operational structure.

The point here is to be careful not to state your exempt purposes in such a way that they seem only attainable by political action. Even if you indicate that your activities will not be substantially involved with legislative or lobbying efforts, the IRS may decide otherwise and invoke this special classification to deny or rescind 501(c)(3) status.

Example A group that has a primary purpose of "reforming the judicial system in the United States" will likely sound like a political action organization to the IRS since this sounds like a political goal which must be accomplished mostly by political means. However, if the group rephrases its primary purpose as "educating the public on the efficacy of mediation, arbitration and other alternative non-judicial dispute resolution mechanisms," it stands a better chance of having the IRS approve its application, even if it lists some political activity as incidental to its primary educational purpose.

Notes

1 For an in-depth discussion and analysis of the requirements that apply to each type of 501(c)(3) nonprofit, supplemented annually with the latest IRS and court rulings in each area, see *The Law of Tax-Exempt Organizations* by Bruce R. Hopkins, published by John Wiley & Sons, New York, N.Y. (check a nonprofit resource center library).

2 Saint Germain Foundation, 26 T.C. 648 (1956).

3 *Pusch v. Commissioner*, 39 T.C.M. 838 (1980), affirmed 628 F. 2d 1353 (5th Cir. 1980).

4 Certain voter education activities conducted in a non-partisan manner may be undertaken by 501(c)(3) groups—see IRS Revenue Ruling 78-248 at your local county law library and consult an attorney for recent developments on this issue if you want to engage in this type of political activity. Your organization may request an IRS letter ruling on its voter education activities by writing to the address listed in IRS Publication 557, Chapter 3, section on "Political Activity."

5 See IRC §§ 4955, 6852 and 7409.

6 In the past, courts have said that the expenditure of more than 5% of the corporation's budget, time or effort for political activity was "substantial"—more recently, the courts have tended to look at the individual facts of each case.

7 See IRC § 4912.

8 This expenditures test and its provisions for lobbying and grassroots expenditures are not available to churches, an integrated auxiliary of a church, a member of an affiliated group of organizations which includes a church, or to private foundations.

9 Federally funded groups may be subject to even more stringent political expenditure tests than those discussed here (for example, political activity and expenditure restrictions imposed by the federal Office of Management and Budget).

10 Unlike the penalties mentioned earlier for excess political expenditures, a group classified as an action organization may apply for and qualify as a 501(c)(4) social welfare group.

501(c)(3) Public Charities and Private Foundations

n this chapter we discuss one of the most difficult areas of nonprofit tax law: qualifying for 501(c)(3) public charity status. You'll see that it is essential to do this to avoid falling into the less favorable tax status of a 501(c)(3) private foundation. Private foundations are subject to special operating rules and restrictions which most nonprofits find unworkable; public charities avoid these limitations.

This chapter covers the most technical and cumbersome part of the nonprofit incorporation process. We wish we could skip this technical area of 501(c)(3) tax law. However, since you will encounter the distinction between public charity and private foundation tax status when you fill out your federal tax exemption application, it's important to come to terms with this material. For now it is enough to read this material through to get a general understanding. Then later, as part of Chapter 8 when you focus on the details of how to prepare your federal tax exemption application, we will ask you to return to this chapter to re-read the sections you'll need.

A. The Importance of Public Charity Status

All 501(c)(3) tax-exempt nonprofit corporations are classified by the IRS as either private foundations or public charities. Initially, and this is the important point, *they are presumed to be private foundations*. This is not in your best interests. Most 501(c)(3) groups would find it impossible to operate under the restrictions imposed on 501(c)(3) private foundations. In short, you must overcome this presumption and show how you qualify as a public charity on your federal 501(c)(3) tax exemption application.[1]

Before looking at how to qualify as a public charity, let's look at the basic characteristics and treatment of private foundations and public charities under Section 501(c)(3).

B. Private Foundations—Background

Broadly speaking, the reason that private foundations are subject to strict operating limitations and special taxes, while public charities are not, is to counter tax abuse schemes by wealthy individuals and families. Before the existence of private foundation restrictions, a person with lots of money could set up his own 501(c)(3) tax-exempt organization (e.g., The William Smith Foundation) with a high-sounding purpose (i.e., to wipe out the potato bug in Northern Louisiana). The potato bugs, though, were never in any danger, because the real purpose of the foundation was to hire all of William Smith's relatives and friends down to the third generation. Instead of leaving the money in a will and paying heavy estate taxes, William Smith neatly transferred money to the next generation tax-free by use of a tax-exempt foundation which just happened to hire all of his relatives.

To prevent schemes such as this, Congress enacted the private foundation operating restrictions, special excise taxes and other private foundation disincentives discussed in the next section.

C. Private Foundation Rules

Let's briefly look at why private foundation restrictions are so burdensome.

1. Operating Restrictions

Here is a summary of the limitations and restrictions that apply to 501(c)(3) private foundations:

- restrictions on self-dealing between private foundations and their substantial contributors and other disqualified persons;
- requirements that the foundation annually distribute its net income for charitable purposes;
- limitations on holdings in private businesses;
- provisions that investments must not jeopardize the carrying out of the group's 501(c)(3) tax-exempt purposes; and
- provisions to assure that expenditures further the group's exempt purposes.

Violations of these provisions result in substantial excise taxes and penalties against the private foundation and, in some cases, against its managers, major contributors and certain related persons. Keeping track of and meeting these restrictions is unworkable for the average 501(c)(3) group, which is the main reason why you'll want to avoid being classified by the IRS as a private foundation.

To learn more about private foundation excise taxes, see IRS Publication 578, *Tax Information for Private Foundations and Foundation Managers*.

2. Limitation on Deductibility of Contributions

Generally, personal income tax deductions for individual contributions to private foundations are limited to 30% of the donor's adjusted gross income, whereas those to public charities are generally deductible to the extent of 50% of adjusted gross income.[2]

Note Of course, since the overwhelming number of individual contributors do not contribute an amount even close to the 30% limit, this limitation of private foundation status is not very important. The real question of importance to contributors is whether your organization is a qualified 501(c)(3) to which tax deductible charitable contributions may be made at all.

IRS Publication 526, *Charitable Contributions*, discusses in more depth the rules limiting deductions to private foundations (called *30% limit organizations*) and public charities (*50% limit organizations*). 501(c)(3)s (both public charities and private foundations) and other qualified groups eligible to receive tax deductible charitable contributions are listed in IRS Publication 78, *Cumulative List of Organizations*.

D. Special Types of Private Foundations

The IRS recognizes two special types of private foundations that have some of the advantages of public charities: private operating and private non-operating foundations. We mention them briefly below since they are included in IRS nonprofit tax publications and forms. Few readers will be interested in forming either of these special organizations.

Why Bother with Internal Revenue Code Sections?

On the federal 501(c)(3) tax exemption application, the different public charity classifications are identified by reference to specific Internal Revenue Code (IRC) sections. We include these IRC sections to help you understand and fill out the federal form. Don't let the numbers distract you—they're included for reference, not intimidation.

In Chapter 8 we show you how to cross-reference each IRS public charity classification and IRC section to the simple three-part public charity classification used in this chapter.

1. Private Operating Foundations

To qualify as a private operating foundation, the organization generally must distribute most of its income to tax-exempt activities and must meet one of three special tests (an assets, support or endowment test). This special type of 501(c)(3) private foundation is allowed a few benefits not granted to regular private foundations, including the following:

- As with public charities, individual donors can deduct up to 50% of adjusted gross income on contributions to the organization.

- The organization may receive grants from a private foundation without having to distribute the funds received within one year (these funds, moreover, can be treated as "qualifying distributions" by the donating private foundation).

- The private foundation excise tax on net investment income does not apply.

All other private foundation restrictions and excise taxes apply to private operating foundations.

2. Private Non-Operating Foundations

This special type of private foundation is one that either:

- distributes all the contributions it receives to public charities and private operating foundations (discussed just above) each year; or

- pools its contributions into a common trust fund and distributes the income and corpus to public charities.

Individual contributors to private non-operating foundations may deduct 50% of their donations. However, the organization is subject to all excise taxes and operating restrictions applicable to regular private foundations.

E. How to Qualify for 501(c)(3) Public Charity Status

We have no doubt convinced you that, in the nonprofit world, being classified as a private foundation is a fate worse than death. So the burning question becomes how to be sure to qualify for public charity status. There are three basic ways to do this:

1. organize a particular type of nonprofit organization such as a church, school or hospital which automatically qualifies for public charity status (see Section F1 below);

2. receive support primarily from individual contributions, government or other public sources to qualify for public charity status as a publicly supported organization (see Section F2 below);

3. receive most of your revenue from activities related to your tax-exempt purposes to qualify under a special public charity support test that applies to many smaller nonprofits (see Section F3 below).

Here are examples of three different groups using these three different methods to qualify for public charity status.

Automatic Public Charity Status   A church that maintains a facility for religious worship would most easily obtain *automatic* public charity status (Section F1 below). A church qualifies for recognition as a public charity because of the nature of its activities rather than its sources of support.

Publicly Supported Organization   An organization to operate a center for rehabilitation, counseling, or similar services and which plans to carry on a broad-based solicitation program and depend primarily on government grants, corporate contributions and individual donations would most likely seek public charity status as a *publicly supported organization* (Section F2 below).

Support Test   An arts group deriving most of its income from exempt-purpose activities (lessons, performances, renting studio facilities to other arts groups) would probably choose the *support test* discussed in Section F3 below. This public charity test, unlike those that apply to publicly supported organizations, allows groups to count income derived from the performance of their exempt purposes as qualified support.

F. 501(c)(3) Public Charities and Their Requirements

Let's now look at each of the three primary public charity tests together with the IRC sections that apply to each. When reading this material for the first time, simply try and get a sense of which test will most likely apply to your nonprofit organization. You can always return to this material later to refresh yourself on some of the technical details and requirements of each category.

1. Automatic Public Charity Status

The IRS automatically recognizes certain 501(c)(3) groups as public charities because they perform particular services or engage in certain activities. Those that can automatically qualify are:

Churches [IRC Sections 509(a)(1) and 170(b)(1)(A)(i)]: In determining which groups qualify as churches, the IRS uses the criteria discussed in Chapter 3C2 above.

Schools [IRC Sections 509(a)(1) and 170(b)(1)(A)(ii)]: Certain educational institutions whose main function is formal instruction and that have a regularly enrolled student body qualify as public charities.

School requirements are stricter than those for obtaining an educational purpose tax exemption under Section 501(c)(3) (see Chapter 3C5) and are geared toward primary, secondary preparatory or high schools and colleges and universities. This doesn't mean that less structured educational institutions can't automatically qualify for public charity status as a school, but rather that it's more difficult. However, the farther an educational group is from the "institutional" criteria

You Can Let the IRS Decide Your Public Charity Classification

For many groups, the most difficult part of applying for a federal 501(c)(3) tax exemption is deciding whether their organization will be a publicly supported public charity as discussed in Section F2 or one which meets the support test discussed in Section F3. To decide this an organization must second-guess future sources of support and tackle quite a few tax technicalities. Fortunately, if you have doubts, the IRS will help. Simply check a box on the federal form and the IRS will decide this question for you based upon the financial and program information submitted with your application.

For the specifics on making this election, see the Chapter 8 instructions to Part III, Line 9(j) of the federal tax exemption application.

mentioned, the harder it is to qualify as a public charity under the above IRC sections. Non-traditional groups have a better chance of obtaining public charity status if they have some conventional institutional attributes, such as regional accreditation and a state-approved curriculum.

Hospitals and Medical Research Organizations [IRC Sections 509(a)(1) and 170(b)(1)(A)(iii)]: Corporations whose main function is providing hospital or medical care, medical education or medical research automatically qualify as public charities under these IRC sections.

Health organizations such as rehabilitation groups, outpatient clinics, community mental health or drug treatment centers should qualify as hospitals if their principal purpose is to provide hospital or medical care.[3] Using consultation services of certified medical personnel such as doctors and nurses helps to establish a group's medical care purpose.

Medical education and research organizations do not qualify under these IRC sections unless they actively provide on-site medical or hospital care to patients as an integral part of their functions. Medical research groups must also be directly and continuously active in medical research with a hospital and this research must be the organization's principal purpose.

Public Safety Organizations [IRC Section 509(a)(4)]: Groups organized and operated exclusively for public safety testing automatically qualify for public charity status. Generally, these organizations test consumer products to determine their fitness for use by the general public.

Government Organizations Certain government organizations operated for the benefit of a college or university are automatically classified as public charities [under IRC Sections 509(a)(1) and 170(b)(1)(A)(iv)]. Also, government units described in IRC Section 170(c)(1) that receive gifts or contributions for public purposes qualify as public charities [under IRC Sections 509(a)(1) and 170(b)(1)(A)(v)]. You won't be forming a government corporation, but we mention these organizations because they are included in the list of public charities on the federal tax exemption application form.

Supporting Organizations [IRC Section 509(a)(3)]: Organizations operated solely for the benefit of, or in connection with, one or more of the above organizations, or those described in sections F2 or F3 below, are also automatically classified as public charities (except those that benefit a public safety organization).

For further information on organizations listed above, see IRS Publication 557, page 16, "Section 509(a)(1) Organizations." For supporting organizations, see page 24 of Publication 557, "Section 509(a)(3) Organizations."

2. Publicly Supported Organizations

Certain publicly supported organizations qualify for 501(c)(3) public charity status [under IRC Sections 509(a)(1) and 170(b)(1)(A)(vi)]— again, don't worry about these code sections for now; they are included as references to help you when you prepare your federal exemption application.

To be classified as a publicly supported public charity, a group must regularly solicit funds from the general community. It must normally[4] receive money from government agencies, and a number of different private contributors or agencies.

Examples Museums, libraries and community centers to promote the arts that rely on broad based support received from individual members of the community or from various public and private sources should qualify under this public charity test.

Your organization will probably be denied this status if you expect to rely primarily on a few private sources or occasional large grants to fund your operations. Further, this support test is difficult for smaller, grassroots groups to meet because it does not include as qualifying public support income from the performance of tax-exempt purposes—a source of support commonly relied upon by these groups.

Below we look at the various tests and factors the IRS uses to determine if a 501(c)(3) nonprofit meets the requirements of this public charity category. Because these laws are complex and because many new groups are uncertain about sources of future income, it might be wise to consult a tax advisor or nonprofit lawyer before deciding to pursue this public charity classification. (You can let the IRS decide if this is the best public charity category for you—see the sidebar text.)

For more detailed information on this public charity category, see IRS Publication 557, page 16, "Publicly Supported Organizations."

How Much Public Support Do You Need Under This Test?

Generally, an organization is publicly supported if it:

1. normally receives at least 1/3 of its total support from governmental units, from contributions made directly or indirectly by the general public, or from a combination of the two;[5] or

2. receives at least 1/10 of its support from these sources and meets an "attraction of public support" requirement.

Qualified support (support included in the numerator of the fraction) includes funds from private and public agencies as well as contributions from corporate and individual donors. However, limitations are placed on the amount of qualified support received from one individual or corporation. Also, some membership fees may be included as qualified support. We discuss these areas further below.

Short-Cut for Those with Sufficient Support If 1/3 of your organization's total support is qualified support, you are the type of group listed under #1 just above and you can skip the following subsection. The attraction of public support requirement discussed below need only be met by the types of groups listed in #2 above where 1/10 or more, but less than 1/3, of the organization's total support is qualified support.

Attraction of Public Support

The IRS considers a number of factors, listed below, in determining whether a tax-exempt nonprofit group meets the attraction of public support requirement. Only Factor 1 absolutely must be met; the rest are not specifically required. Of course, the more you meet, the better your chances are of meeting the attraction of public support requirement.

Factor 1. Continuous Solicitation of Funds Program

Your group must continually attract new public or governmental support. It will meet this requirement if it maintains a continuous program for soliciting money from the general public, community, or membership—or if it solicits support from governmental agencies or churches, schools or hospitals that also qualify as public charities (see section F1 above). Although this mandates broad-based support, the IRS allows new groups to limit initial campaigns to seeking "seed" money from a select number of the most promising agencies or people.

Factor 2. Percentage of Financial Support

At least 10% of your group's total support must come from the public. For this purpose, the greater the percentage of public support, the better; remember that if your public support amounts to 1/3 or more, you do not have to meet the attraction of public support factors listed in this subsection.

Factor 3. Support from a Representative Number of People

If your group gets most of its money from government agencies or from a representative number of people as opposed to getting it from a particular individual or a group with a special interest in its activities, it will more likely meet the attraction of public support requirement.

Factor 4. Representative Governing Body

A nonprofit corporation whose governing body represents broad public interests, rather than the personal interest of a limited number of donors, is considered favorably by the IRS. An organization's governing body is more likely to be treated as representative if it includes:

- public officials;
- people selected by public officials;
- people recognized as experts in the organization's area of operations;
- community leaders or others representing a cross-section of community views and interests (such as members of the clergy, teachers, civic leaders); or
- for membership organizations, people elected under the corporate Articles or Bylaws by a broad-based membership.

Factor 5. Availability of Public Facilities or Services

If an organization continuously provides facilities or services for the general public, this will be considered favorably by the IRS. This would include a museum open to the public; an orchestra that gives public performances; a group that distributes educational literature to the

Advance and Definitive Rulings

There are two ways to request public charity status as a publicly supported organization.

If your organization has been operating for one tax year consisting of at least eight months at the time of completion of your federal exemption application, you can ask for a definitive ruling on your public charity status. The IRS will use the past support received by the group to determine if it qualifies as a publicly supported organization.

Existing groups may, and new groups must, request an advance ruling on their public charity status. If your expected sources of support seem likely to qualify you as a publicly supported organization, the IRS will grant you a tentative ruling. Later, at the end of an advance ruling period consisting of the corporation's first five tax years, the IRS will give a definitive ruling. If the group's public support during the advance ruling period satisfies the requirements of this public charity test, the organization will qualify as a publicly supported organization.

In granting advance rulings, the IRS always looks to see if your organization will meet the attraction of public support factors discussed earlier in this section, whether you plan to meet the 1/3 or 1/10 public support test.

For further information on definitive and advance public charity ruling requests, see Chapter 8.

public; or an old age home that provides nursing or other services to low-income members of the community.

Factor 6. Additional Factors

Corporations are also more likely to meet the requirement if:

- members of the public having special knowledge or expertise (such as public officials, or civic or community leaders) participate in or sponsor programs;

- the organization maintains a program to do charitable work in the community (such as job development or slum rehabilitation); or

- the organization gets a significant portion of its funds from another public charity or a governmental agency to which it is, in some way, held accountable as a condition of the grant, contract or contribution.

Factor 7. Additional Factors for Membership Groups Only

A membership organization is more likely to meet the attraction of public support requirement if:

- the solicitation for dues-paying members attempts to enroll a substantial number of people in the community or area, or in a particular profession or field of special interest;

- membership dues are affordable to a broad cross-section of the interested public; or

- the organization's activities are likely to appeal to people with some broad common interest or purpose—such as musical activities in the case of an orchestra, or different forms of dance in the case of a dance studio.

Technical Terms and Requirements for Publicly Supported Organizations

Now we reach a tricky part. We've explained that an organization must normally receive at least 1/3 (or 1/10 if it also meets the attraction of public support requirement discussed above) of its total support from government units, from contributions by the general public, or from a combination of these sources. We call this 1/3 or 1/10 figure "public support." To keep your percentage high enough, you'll want the IRS to:

- classify as much of your income as possible as public support; and

- keep your total support figure as low as possible.

By doing this, your final percentage of public support will be higher. Of course, the IRS has more than a fair number of rules, and exceptions to the rules, to define "public support" and "total support." We provide a guide to the basic technical terms used under this public charity category below. Start by skimming through this material, then go back and read areas that may apply to your organization.

What Does "Normally" Mean?

An organization must "normally" receive either 1/3 or 1/10 of its total support from public support sources. This means that one tax year is not critical. The IRS bases its decision on four year's cumulative receipts. Your organization will meet either the 1/3 or 1/10 support test for both its current and the following tax year if, during the four tax years before its current tax year, its cumulative public support equals 1/3 or 1/10 of its cumulative total support.

Example Open Range, Inc. is a nonprofit organization for medical research on the healthful effects of organic cattle ranching. ORI's cumulative total support was $60,000 for 1986 through 1990, and its cumulative public support was $25,000. The organization will, therefore, be considered a publicly supported public charity for 1990 and the following tax year. This remains true even if, for one or more of the previous four years, public support did not equal 1/3 of the total support—it's the cumulative total that counts.

What Is a "Government Unit"?

Money received from a "government unit" is considered public support. Government units include federal or state governmental agencies, county and city agencies, etc. The most common example of governmental support is a federal or state grant.

Limits on Contributions from the General Public

Direct or indirect contributions by the general public are considered public support. Indirect contributions include grants from private trusts or agencies also funded by contributions from the general public, such as grants from Community Chest or the United Fund. However, there is a major restriction. The total contributions of one individual, trust, or corporation made during the preceding four tax years may be counted *only* to the extent that they do not exceed 2% of the corporation's total support for these four years. Money from government units, publicly supported organizations and unusual grants is not subject to this 2% limit. These exceptions are discussed below.

Example If your total support over the previous four-year period was $60,000, then only $1,200 (2% of $60,000) contributed by any one person, private agency or other source counts as public support.

Why Less Is More, More or Less Note that the total amount of any one contribution, even if it exceeds this 2%, four-year limitation, is included in the corporation's total support. Paradoxically, therefore, large contributions from an individual or private agency can have a disastrous effect on your status as a publicly supported charity. This is because you only get to include such contributions as public support to the extent of 2% of the previous four years' total income, while at the same time the total income figure is increased by the full amount of the contribution. This makes it more difficult for you to meet the 1/3 or 1/10 public support requirement.

Example On Your Toes, a ballet troupe, received the following contributions from 1987 through 1990:

1987	$10,000	from individual X
1988	20,000	from individual Y
1989	60,000	from Z Community Chest
1990	10,000	as an additional contribution from individual X

Total Support: $100,000

All support for the four-year period is from contributions, direct or indirect, from the general public. However, in view of the 2% limit, On Your Toes will have trouble maintaining its publicly supported public charity status because while all contributions count toward *total support*, only $2,000 (2% x $100,000) from any one contributor counts as *public support*. Therefore, the troupe's public support for this period is only $6,000 ($2,000 from each contributor, X, Y and Z), which falls $4,000 short of the minimum 1/10 public support requirement.

Now suppose On Your Toes received $2,000 each from 50 contributors over the four-year period. It still has $100,000 total support, but because no one contributor gave more than 2% of the four years' total support, it can count the entire $100,000 as public support.

A Suggestion To qualify as a publicly supported public charity, solicit smaller contributions through a broad-based fund-raising program and don't rely constantly on the same major sources. This way, you'll beat the 2% limit and have a better chance of qualifying contributions as public support.

Exceptions to the 2% Limit Rule

In a few circumstances, contributions are not subject to the 2% limit:

Money from Government Units or Publicly Supported Organizations Contributions received from a government unit or other publicly supported organization are not subject to the 2% limit, except those specifically "earmarked" for your organization by the original donor.

Example Ebeneezer Sax gives one million dollars to National Public Music, a national government foundation that promotes musical arts. NPM then gives your organization the million as a grant. If Sax made the contribution to NPM on the condition that the foundation turn it over to your organization, it's earmarked for you and the 2% limit applies.

Except for earmarked contributions or grants, you can rely on large contributions or grants from specific government agencies or other publicly supported organizations every year, since all such contributions will be counted as public support.

Money from "Unusual Grants" Another major exception to the 2% limit is for "unusual grants" from the private or public sector. A grant is unusual if it:

- is attracted by the publicly supported nature of your organization;
- is unusual—this means you don't regularly rely on the particular grant and it is an unexpectedly large amount; and

- would, because of its large size, adversely affect the publicly supported status of your organization (as we've seen, because of the 2% limit, large grants can cause trouble).

If a grant qualifies as an unusual grant, you can exclude the grant funds from both your public support and total support figures for the year in which they are given.

Example   The National Museum of Computer Memorabilia, Inc. is a nonprofit corporation that operates a museum of computers and artificial intelligence memorabilia. The years 1987 through 1989 are difficult ones and the museum raises very little money. But in 1990 the organization receives an unexpected windfall grant. A look at the receipts for 1987 to 1990 helps illustrate the importance of the unusual grant exception. All amounts are individual contributions from the general public unless indicated otherwise:

1987	$1,000	from A
	1,000	from B
1988	1,000	from C
1989	1,000	from D
	1,000	from E
1990	100,000	from Z, a private grant agency
Total Receipts:	$105,000	

Assume that the 1990 grant qualifies as an unusual grant. The total support computation for the four year period would be:

1987	$1,000	from A
	1,000	from B
1988	1,000	from C
1989	1,000	from D
	1,000	from E
1990	0	the $100,000 grant drops out from total support
Total Support:	$5,000	

Since the total support is $5,000, the museum can only count a maximum of 2% times $5,000, or $100, received from any one individual during this period as public support. Therefore, the public support computation for this period looks like this:

1987	$100	from A
	100	from B
1988	100	from C
1989	100	from D
	100	from E
1990	0	the $100,000 contribution also drops out from the public support computation

Total Public Support: $500

The museum meets the 10% support test since total public support of $500 equals 10% of the total support of $5,000 received over the four year period. If the organization also meets the attraction of public support requirement (which must be met by groups whose public support is less than 1/3 of total support), it will qualify as a publicly supported public charity for 1990 and 1991.

If the $100,000 contribution did not qualify as an unusual grant, the nonprofit would not meet the 10% public support test. Total support would equal total receipts of $105,000; a maximum of 2% times $105,000, or $2,100, from each individual and the grant agency would be classified as public support. Public support received over the four year period would consist of $1,000 from individuals A, B, C, D and E and the maximum allowable sum of $2,100 from the grant agency, for a total public support figure of $7,100. The percentage of public support for the four-year period would equal $7,100 divided by $105,000, or less than 7%, and the group would not qualify as a publicly supported public charity in 1990. Again, you can see how a large grant can hurt you if it does not qualify as an unusual grant.

Some Membership Fees as Public Support

Membership fees are considered public support as long as the member does not receive something valuable in return, such as admissions, merchandise, or the use of facilities or services. If a member does receive direct benefits in exchange for fees, the fees are not considered public support. These fees are, however, always included in the total support computation.

What's Not Public Support?

Unrelated Activities and Investments Net income from activities unrelated to exempt purposes as well as "gross investment income," which include rents, dividends, royalties and returns on investments, are not considered public support *and are added to the total support figure.*

Sales Assets or Performing Tax-Exempt Activity The following types of receipts are not considered either public support or part of total support (as with unusual grants, they drop out of both computations altogether):

- Gains from selling a capital asset. Generally, capital assets are property owned by the corporation for use in its activities. Capital assets do not include any business inventory or resale merchandise, business accounts or notes receivable, or real property used in a trade or business—gains from selling these assets would be characterized as "gross investment income" and *are not* considered public support, but *are added to the total support figure.*

- Receipts from performing tax-exempt purposes. Examples include money received from: admissions to performances of a symphony; fees for classes given by a dance studio; tuition or other charges for attending seminars, lectures or classes given by an exempt educational organization.

An Exception for Some Exempt-Purpose Receipts Since we're dealing with tax laws, you'd probably expect at least one complicating exception. Here it is. If your organization relies primarily on gross receipts from activities related to its exempt purposes, like an educational nonprofit that receives most of its support from class tuitions, this exempt-purpose income will not be considered public support, *but will be computed in total support.* If your group falls in this category, it will probably not be able to qualify as a publicly supported public charity and should attempt to qualify under the public charity support test discussed in Section F3 below.

3. The Support Test

Don't worry if your Section 501(c)(3) group does not qualify as a public charity either automatically or through the public support test. There is another way to qualify as a public charity. The support test discussed below [under IRC Section 509(a)(2)] is likely to meet your needs if your 501(c)(3) group intends to derive income from performing exempt-purpose activities and services.[6]

How Much Public Support Do You Need Under This Test?

To qualify under this public charity support test, a 501(c)(3) nonprofit organization must meet two requirements:

1. The organization must normally receive more than 1/3 of its total support in each tax year as qualified public support. Qualified public support is support from any of the following sources:

- gifts, grants, contributions or membership fees; and
- gross receipts from admissions, selling merchandise, performing services, or providing facilities in an activity related to the exempt purposes of the nonprofit organization; and

2. The organization must normally not receive more than 1/3 of its annual support from unrelated trades or businesses or gross investment income.[7] Gross investment income includes rent from unrelated sources, interest, dividends and royalties—sources of support far removed from the activities of most smaller nonprofit organizations.

Again, the most important aspect of this test, and the one that makes it appropriate for many 501(c)(3) groups, is that it allows the 1/3 qualified public support amount to include the group's receipts from performing its exempt purposes. Hence, this public charity classification is appropriate for many self-sustaining nonprofits that raise income from their tax-exempt activities, such as performing arts groups, schools and other educational purpose organizations, and nonprofit service organizations.

Example School tuition, admissions to concerts or plays, or payments for classes at a pottery studio count as qualified public support under this public charity test.

Technical Terms and Requirements of the Support Test

In this subsection we look at specific technical terms, concepts and requirements of this public charity category. Skim through this material and then re-read portions of specific interest or application to your organization.

For more detailed information on this public charity category, see IRS Publication 557, page 21, "509(a)(2) Organizations." Again, if you are unsure whether your organization qualifies for the public charity support test covered below, you can let the IRS decide by checking a box on your federal tax exemption application (see Chapter 8 for further information).

Support Must Be from Permitted Sources

Qualified public support under this test must be from permitted sources including:

- government agencies;
- other 501(c)(3) public charities—generally, those that qualify as public charities under one of the tests described in sections F1 and F2 above.

Permitted sources do not include:

- disqualified persons—people who would be considered disqualified if the organization were classified as a private foundation. These include substantial contributor, the organization's founders, and certain related persons (for a discussion of disqualified persons, see "Who Are Disqualified Persons?" in Chapter 8); or
- groups that qualify for public charity status as Related Organizations or Public Safety Organizations (see these categories in Section F1 above).

Membership Fees and Dues Get Special Treatment

Dues paid to provide support for or to participate in the nonprofit organization, or in return for services or facilities provided only to members, are considered valid membership dues and can be counted as qualified public support. On the other hand, fees or dues paid in return for a discount on products or services provided to the public or in return for some other monetary benefit will not be included as valid membership fees. However, these payments may still be counted as qualified public support if the fee entitles the member to special rates for exempt purpose activities—in this case the payments qualify as receipts related to the group's exempt purposes.

Example People pay $50 to become members of All Thumbs, a nonprofit group dedicated to rebuilding interest in the unitar, a near-extinct one-stringed guitar-like musical instrument. All Thumbs' members are allowed $50 worth of reduced rate passes to all unitar concerts nationwide. Although these fees can't be counted as valid membership fees since they are paid in return for an equivalent monetary benefit (a $50 discount), they still count as receipts related to the performance of the group's exempt purposes (paid in return for attendance at unitar concerts—putting on these concerts is an exempt purpose and activity of the group). Therefore the fees may be counted by the organization as qualified public support.

Limitation on Large Exempt-Purpose Receipts

There is one major limitation on the amount of income received in return for exempt-purpose activities that can be included in the 1/3

If Your Nonprofit Sells Services or Information

Under IRC §6711, if a tax-exempt nonprofit (including any 501(c)(3) organization, whether classified as a public charity or private foundation) offers to sell to individuals information or routine services that could be readily obtained free, or for a nominal fee, from the federal government, the nonprofit must include a statement that the information or service can be so obtained. Failure to comply with this disclosure requirement can result in a substantial fine.

If your nonprofit plans to sell services or information, check to see if the same service or information is available from the federal government. If so, you may need to make the required disclosure to clients and customers. For further information on these disclosure requirements, see IRS Publication 557, page 8.

qualified public support figure. Specifically, in any tax year, receipts from the performance of exempt purpose services from individuals or government units which exceed $5,000 or 1% of the organization's total support for the year, whichever is greater, must be excluded from the organization's qualified public support figure. This limitation applies only to exempt-purpose receipts and not to gifts, grants, contributions or membership fees received by the organization.

Example Van-Go is a visual arts group that makes art available to people around the nation by toting it around in specially marked vans. In 1990, Van-Go derives $30,000 total support from the sale of paintings. The funds are receipts related to the performance of the group's exempt purposes. Any amount over $5,000 paid by any one individual cannot be included in computing its qualified public support for the year, although the full amount is included in total support. Of course, if Van-Go's total support for any year is more than $500,000, then the limitation on individual contributions will be 1% of the year's total support, since this figure exceeds $5,000.

Some Gifts are Gross Receipts

Generally, when someone pays money or gives property without getting anything of value in return, it is considered a gift or contribution. But gifts made in return for admissions paid, merchandise sold, services performed, or facilities furnished to the contributor are considered gross receipts from exempt-purpose activities and are subject to the $5,000 or 1% limitation.

Example At its annual fund raising drive, the California Cormorant Preservation League rewards $100 contributors with a book containing color prints of cormorants. The book normally retails for $25. Only $75 of each contribution is considered a gift; the remaining $25 payments are classified as gross receipts from the performance of the group's exempt purposes and are subject to the $5,000 or 1% limitation.

Some Grants are Gross Receipts

The $5,000 or 1% limitation also applies to grants. However, it is sometimes hard to distinguish money received as grants from exempt-purpose gross receipts. The rule used by the IRS is that money paid so that the granting agency gets some economic or physical benefit, such as a service, facility or product, are classified as gross receipts related to the exempt activities of the nonprofit organization. Money contributed to benefit the public will be treated as bona fide grants by the IRS, not as exempt-purpose receipts.

Example A pharmaceutical company, Amalgamated Mortar & Pestle, provides a research grant to a nonprofit scientific and medical research organization, Safer Sciences, Inc. The company specifies that the nonprofit must use the grant to develop a more reliable child-proof cap for prescription drug containers (the results of the nonprofit research will be shared with the commercial company). The money is treated as receipts received by Safer Sciences in carrying out its exempt purposes and is subject to the $5,000 or 1% limitation.

Another Example Safer Sciences gets a grant from the federal Center for Disease Control to build a better petri dish for epidemiological research. Since the money is used to benefit the public, the full amount will be included in the nonprofit organization's qualified public support figure.

Unusual Grants Can Be Excluded from the Support Computations

As with the publicly supported public charities discussed in Section F2 above, IRS rules allow groups seeking public charity status under the public support test discussed in this section to exclude "unusual grants" from their support computations. These are grants and contributions, not regularly relied on and attracted by the publicly supported nature of the organization, which, because of their substantial size, might adversely affect the organization's ability to meet the 1/3 qualified support requirement of this public charity test.

Rents Related to Exempt Purposes Are Not Gross Investment Income

Rents received from people or groups related to the group's exempt purpose are generally not considered gross investment income. Remember: Under this public charity test, the organization must normally not receive more than 1/3 of its annual support from unrelated trades or businesses or from gross investment income.

Example Good Crafts, Inc., a studio that provides facilities for public education in historic crafts, rents a portion of its premises to an instructor who teaches stained glass classes. Such rent would probably not fall into the negative gross investment income category.

It may be important, therefore, that your group rent to another person or group whose activities are directly related to your exempt purposes.

We suggest you consult a nonprofit lawyer or tax advisor if you'll rely on rental income even from related groups. It's a tricky subject.

A Technicality If, as more and more nonprofits must, you plan to supplement your support with income from activities unrelated to your exempt purposes, check with your tax advisor to make sure this additional income will not exceed 1/3 of your annual support and jeopardize your ability to qualify under this public charity category.

There's That Word "Normally" Again

We've mentioned that the public charities discussed here must normally meet the support requirements of this test. This means that the IRS looks at the total amount of support over the previous four-year period to decide if the organization qualifies as a public charity for the current and the following tax year.

Advance vs. Definitive Public Charity Rulings

Like the publicly supported public charities discussed earlier, the groups discussed here may qualify for public charity status under a definitive or advance ruling.

For further information on advance and definitive rulings, see the sidebar in Section F2 above and Chapter 8.

G. Summing Up

Now that we've looked at the three ways to achieve 501(c)(3) public charity status, we suggest you go back and re-read the three examples given in Section E of this chapter. These summarize the three public charity tests explained in the previous sections and provide typical examples of how these tests are used by 501(c)(3) nonprofit organizations. Again, don't worry if you don't have a thorough command of this material. When you prepare your federal tax exemption application, you can come back to this chapter and re-read the sections that apply to you. And remember: If you are unsure whether the Section F2 or F3 public charity public support test applies to your organization, you can ask the IRS to make this determination for you.

Notes

1 A few special groups are not required to apply for public charity status—the same groups that are not required to file a 501(c)(3) tax exemption application. We think it's foolhardy in most cases not to apply for, and obtain, official notification from the IRS that you are a public charity. For a discussion of this issue, see the section entitled "Should You Apply for Tax-Exempt Status?" in Chapter 8A.

2 Special percentages apply to contributions of securities, real estate and certain types of tangible personal property. See IRS Publication 526.

3 Convalescent homes, homes for children or the aged, or institutions that provide vocational training for the handicapped are not recognized by the IRS as fitting within this public charity category.

4 The word "normally" has a special meaning which we discuss below.

5 Note that support received from other publicly supported organizations is also counted as qualifying public support.

6 To make matters even more confusing, IRS publications sometimes refer to groups that meet this IRC 509(a)(2) support test as "publicly supported organizations." We do not follow this practice—for us, publicly supported organizations are only those that qualify under the support test described in section F2 of this chapter.

7 If you pay tax on income from unrelated businesses or activities, the amount of the tax paid will be deducted from this income before it is counted in this 33-1/3% figure.

Other Nonprofit Tax Issues and Reporting Requirements

I n this chapter we discuss additional federal and state tax issues affecting nonprofits. We also discuss solicitation of funds rules and other state reporting requirements that apply to nonprofit corporations.

A. Federal Tax Deductions for Contributions

A donor may claim a personal federal income tax deduction for contributions made to a 501(c)(3) tax-exempt organization. These contributions are termed "charitable contributions."

- Corporations may make deductible charitable contributions of up to 10% of their annual taxable income.

- Individuals may deduct up to 50% of adjusted gross income in any year for contributions made to 501(c)(3) public charities and to some types of 501(c)(3) private foundations, as explained in Chapter 4.

What May Be Deducted The following types of contributions are deductible on the donor's tax return:

- cash;

- property—generally donors may deduct the fair market (resale) value of donated property; special rules apply to gifts of appreciated property (property which has increased in value);

- unreimbursed car expenses, including the cost of gas and oil, paid while performing services for the nonprofit organization; and

- unreimbursed travel expenses incurred while away from home performing services for the nonprofit organization, including the cost of transportation, meals and lodging.

What May Not Be Deducted Certain types of gifts cannot be deducted as charitable contributions. Nondeductible gifts include:

- the value of volunteer services;

- the right to use property;

- contributions to political parties—these, however, may be taken as a tax credit, subject to dollar and percentage limitations;

- direct contributions to needy individuals;

- tuition—even amounts designated as "donations" that must be paid in addition to tuition as a condition of enrollment are not deductible;

- dues paid to labor unions;

- the cost of raffle, bingo, lottery tickets or other games of chance; and

- child care costs paid while performing services for the nonprofit organization.

What May Be Partially Deducted Contributions received in return for a service, product or other benefit—such as membership fees paid in return for special membership incentives or promotional products or "donations" charged for attending a performance—are only partially deductible. In these instances, a deduction is allowed only for the portion of the gift that exceeds the fair market value of the service, product or benefit received by the donor.

Example If a member of a 501(c)(3) organization pays a $30 membership fee and receives a record album that retails for $30, nothing is deductible. But if a $20 product is given in return for the payment, $10 of the fee paid is a bona-fide donation and may be deducted by the member as a charitable contribution.

501(c)(3) nonprofit groups should clearly state the dollar amount that is deductible when receiving contributions, donations, or membership fees in return for providing a service, product, discount or other benefit to the donor.

Reporting Requirements Deductions for charitable contributions made by individuals are claimed by itemizing the gifts on IRS Schedule A and filing this form with the individual's annual 1040 income tax return. IRS rules require donors to obtain receipts for all charitable contributions claimed on their tax returns. Receipts must describe the contribution and show the value of any goods or services received from the nonprofit by the donor as part of the transaction.

The IRS requirements for deducting and reporting charitable contributions change from year to year, and may vary depending on the amount and type—cash or property—of contribution. For current information see IRS Publication 526, *Charitable Contributions*. For information on valuing gifts, see IRS Publication 561, *Determining the Value of Donated Property*. For additional information, see IRS Publication 1391, *Deductibility of Payments Made to Charities Conducting Fund-Raising Events*.

B. Federal Estate and Gift Tax Exemptions

An important source of contributions for 501(c)(3) nonprofits is gifts made as part of an individual's estate plan (as part of a will or trust document). When the individual dies, these amounts are distributed to the 510(c)(3) organization and are excluded from the taxable estate on the individual's unified estate and gift tax return. The tax savings can be enormous: taxable estates over $600,000[1] are taxed at a rate starting at 37% (and can be taxed as high as 55%).

Even though property which passes to a surviving spouse is not included in an individual's taxable estate, more and more people are realizing that their taxable estate will total more than $600,000. Thus many people are motivated to engage in estate planning, including making charitable gifts to nonprofit organizations.

Traditionally, colleges and universities and larger environmental and health organizations have actively solicited this type of charitable giving by providing information about estate planning and the benefits of charitable bequests to members and donors. Increasingly, smaller nonprofits too are starting to get, and get out, the message and are pursuing similar strategies in their fundraising efforts. You should be familiar with the tax benefits of charitable bequests as an effective way of persuading potential donors to give to your cause.

Gifts   Gifts made during an individual's life are not subject to taxation. However, if made to an individual or non-qualified organization, they reduce the donor's $600,000 unified estate and gift tax credit to the extent they exceed $10,000 in one calendar year. If made to a 501(c)(3) nonprofit they do not reduce this federal and estate gift tax credit.

For further information on federal and state estate and gift taxes and individual estate planning techniques, see *Plan Your Estate* by Clifford (Nolo Press).

C. Federal Unrelated Business Income Tax

All tax-exempt nonprofit corporations, whether private foundations or public charities, may have to pay tax on income derived from activities unrelated to their exempt purposes. The first $1,000 of unrelated business

Some States Require an Advance Tax Payment

In a small number of states, incorporators must make a franchise tax, trust fund or other advance payment when filing nonprofit Articles of Incorporation with the secretary of state.

Connecticut charges a $30 franchise fee.

Michigan collects a $20 combined filing and franchise fee.

Texas imposes a $150 (annual) franchise tax that is waived for a domestic nonprofit corporation's first 15 months of operation. If the state exemption is ultimately denied the corporation pays only this amount with no added penalties. A foreign nonprofit corporation seeking authorization in Texas must make a $500 cash trust deposit while its tax-exemption application is pending.

Virginia assesses a $50 initial charter fee and a $25 (annual) registration fee.

income is not taxed, but after that, the normal federal corporate tax rate applies: 15% on the first $50,000 of taxable corporate income; 25% on the next $25,000; and 34% on taxable income over $75,000 (with a 5% surtax on taxable income between $100,000 and $335,000).

As explained in Chapter 3, Section D1, if unrelated income is substantial, it may jeopardize the organization's 501(c)(3) tax exemption.

1. Activities That Are Taxed

Unrelated business income derives from activities not directly related to a group's exempt purposes. An unrelated trade or business is one that is regularly carried on and not substantially related to a nonprofit group's exempt purposes. It is irrelevant that the organization uses the profits to conduct its exempt-purpose activities.

Example Enviro-Home Institute is a 501(c)(3) nonprofit organized to educate the public about environmentally sound home design and home construction techniques. Enviro-Home develops a model home kit that applies its ideas of appropriate environmental construction and is very successful in selling the kit. The IRS considers this unrelated business income because it is not directly related to the educational purposes of the organization.

Another Example A halfway house that offers room, board, therapy and counseling to recently released prison inmates also operates a furniture shop to provide full-time employment for its residents. This has been ruled not to be an unrelated trade or business, since the shop directly benefits the residents (even though it also produces income).

2. Activities That Are Not Taxed

A number of activities are specifically excluded from the definition of "unrelated trades or businesses."[2] These include the following types of activities:

- those in which nearly all work is done by volunteers;
- those carried on by 501(c)(3) tax-exempt organizations primarily for the benefit of members, students, patients, officers, or employees (such as a hospital gift shop for patients or employees);

- those that sell mostly donated merchandise, such as thrift shops;

- exchanging or renting lists of donors or members;

- distribution of low-cost items, such as stamps or mailing labels worth less than $5, in the course of soliciting funds;

- sponsoring of trade shows by 501(c)(3) groups—this exclusion extends to the exempt organization's suppliers, who may educate trade show attendees on new developments or products related to the organization's exempt activities.

Also excluded from this tax is income not derived from services (termed "gross investment income" in the IRC). Remember: this tax applies to unrelated activities, not necessarily to unrelated income. Examples of nontaxable income include:[3]

- dividends, interest, and royalties;

- rent from land, buildings, furniture and equipment. Some forms of rent are taxed if the rental property was purchased or improved subject to a mortgage or if the rental income is based on the profits earned by the tenant;

- gains or losses from the sale or exchange of property.

It is often difficult to predict whether the IRS will tax an activity or income as unrelated business. Furthermore, IRS regulations and rulings and U.S. Tax Court decisions contain a number of specific rules classifying specific activities as unrelated businesses that are subject to tax. In short, you should consult a tax specialist if you plan to engage in activities or derive income from sources not directly related to your exempt purposes. Please note, this isn't the same thing as saying you shouldn't engage in an unrelated activity—many nonprofits must engage in commercial businesses unrelated to their exempt purposes to survive. You simply need good tax advice in this situation, so you don't risk jeopardizing your 501(c)(3) tax-exempt status.

D. State Corporate Income Tax Exemptions

Most states have a corporate income tax, but nonprofit groups are eligible to apply for an exemption in all cases. Fortunately, in the overwhelming majority of states there is little or nothing to do, as state authorities will rely on your federal 501(c)(3) exemption determination to conclude that you are also entitled to a state corporate income tax exemption.

In about half the states, a nonprofit corporation that has received its federal exemption is automatically exempt from state corporate income taxes. A few states exempt nonprofits on the basis of their having filed nonprofit Articles with the secretary of state (obtaining a federal tax exemption is not necessary to obtain the state tax exemption).

Notification to the department of revenue or a separate exemption application is required in approximately one-third of the states, but their decision is based on the federal determination. Finally, only in a handful of states is an independent evaluation of nonprofit purposes, activities and financial statements made to determine exemption.

The State Sheets show the method your state uses to grant a corporate income tax exemption to nonprofit organizations.

Generally, a corporation that has filed for its federal tax exemption need not pay state corporate income taxes prior to receiving a federal determination, which can take a few months or more in special cases. If the federal application is denied—and the state exemption determination is based upon obtaining the federal exemption—the corporation may be liable for state income taxes it would have paid as a for-profit corporation while the application was pending.

Even if your organization receives a state tax exemption, it may still be required to file an informational tax return yearly. For forms and information about exemption requirements, contact the tax agency listed on your State Sheet. It may take considerable patience and persistence to get all the tax information you need, since some states' exempt organization tax units are small and under-staffed.

Also keep in mind that just as at the federal level, there are state taxes on unrelated business income generated by a regular activity that has nothing to do with your exempt purposes. If you will have unrelated business income, you might wish to see a tax accountant in your state to be certain about your state corporate tax liabilities and necessary state filings.

**Exceptions to State
Solicitation Regulations**

Typically, grants, unrestricted gifts, bona fide membership fees and payments for goods and services not received in connection with a solicitation are exempted from state solicitation rules and regulation.

E. Other State Taxes

Each state imposes additional taxes that may apply to your nonprofit activities and operations. In many cases, your tax-exempt 501(c)(3) can apply for an exemption from one or more of these additional taxes.

Most states have enacted a sales tax. Some states exempt nonprofits from payment when purchasing goods. Only a few exempt nonprofits from collecting sales tax when selling goods, and then only under restricted circumstances, such as fund-raising events—bake sales, crafts fairs, benefit dinners, performances, etc.—that take place occasionally during the year.

In addition, there are state and local use, excise and property taxes, hotel and meal taxes, and business license fees from which a nonprofit corporation may be eligible to apply for exemption.

The materials you receive from the secretary of state should include a listing of state tax agencies. Contact these agencies to learn more about your tax responsibilities—and exemption possibilities.

F. State Solicitation Regulations

Fundraising is a way of life for most nonprofit organizations, which must depend either on public or private grants, or on contributions solicited from the general public, for all operating funds. This activity—solicitation of contributions from the general public by a 501(c)(3) public charity—is regulated by most states.[4]

Generally, state regulation of charitable solicitations is meant to serve two purposes:

- to curb fundraising abuses by monitoring the people involved and their activities;
- to give the public access to information on how much an organization spends to raise whatever ultimately goes into funding its charitable, educational, religious, etc., purposes.

At present a majority of the states require groups that solicit within the state to register, usually with the attorney general. Most of these states also require the registration of paid fundraisers and solicitors, both the people who administer the programs and those who go door-to-door or use the telephone or other media to solicit money. A registration fee, a bond or both may also be required for solicitors, ranging from as little as $15 to $800 or more.

Several cases affecting how much information solicitors must disclose—about methods and what happens to the money they collect—have come before the U. S. Supreme Court. The issue has been raised as a First Amendment question. At present, states may require professional solicitors to tell prospective donors where to check for financial information on their campaigns, including what percentage of the money collected actually goes to charity, but fundraisers needn't submit scripts of their pitches to the state for review.

In addition to solicitor regulation, many states have detailed contribution reporting requirements, and demand information on the amount spent (on paid solicitors, advertising and promotion, mailings, etc.) to raise the total amount solicited. This information may have to be supplied either annually or for each individual fundraising campaign.

While it is the large scale fundraising operations—those that use telemarketing and massive direct mail solicitation—that are the targets of these regulations, all organizations soliciting the general public in states where they apply must comply with them. Small groups must still meet local and state requirements, so find out what your obligations are by checking with your city government. At the state level, the attorney general's office is usually the one in charge of solicitation registration; if not, find out from your secretary of state what registration and reporting requirements, if any, you must comply with.

G. State Nonprofit Corporate Report Requirements

Nonprofit corporations in most states must periodically file reports with the secretary of state, in effect re-registering their existence. Generally this is an annual report, but in a few states a report is required less frequently.

The State Sheet lists the corporate report requirements for each state.

The contents of the state corporate report—generally submitted on a form supplied by the secretary of state—vary. Most states want only a simple recital of minimal information to confirm that a corporation is still operating, under the same name, at the same address and for the purposes stated in its Articles of Incorporation. Sometimes the names and addresses of directors and/or officers must be included, and the report must be signed by one of these people. Many states also collect a filing fee with the annual report.

A few states, however, require detailed financial and other information as well, which may include some of the following:

- a disclosure of salaries, loans, guarantees and other payments or benefits made to or conferred on directors and officers;

- the amount of money invested in real or personal property in the state;

- a complete financial statement listing all assets and liabilities, revenues and receipts, expenses and disbursements (except for the smallest nonprofits, your accountant or treasurer should prepare a balance sheet and income statement at least annually);

Each state has its own filing date or period; this information is obtainable from your secretary of state. Although completing the corporate report is a mere formality in most states, requiring the submission of very little information, compliance is important, since a failure to file may, in some cases, result in the imposition of a fine and the suspension of corporate powers by the secretary of state.

Notes

1 As noted later in the text, this federal estate and gift tax credit amount is lessened by the amount of large taxable gifts made during an individual's life. Specifically, taxable gifts to a non-spouse which exceed $10,000 in a given year are subtracted from the individual's unified estate and gift tax credit of $600,000. Gifts made to 501(c)(3) nonprofits which exceed $10,000 in a year are not taxable (they do not reduce the $600,000 credit).

2 Some of these exceptions have been hotly contested by commercial business interests at several congressional hearings. The primary objection to these loopholes to the unrelated business income tax is that nonprofits receive an unfair advantage by being allowed to engage in these competing activities tax-free. Expect more hearings and future developments in this volatile area of nonprofit tax law.

3 See Section 512(b) of the Internal Revenue Code for the complete list of these untaxed sources of income and the exceptions that exist for certain items.

4 Regulation of charitable solicitation is currently an active area of both legislation and litigation. At the federal level, Congress has proposed putting multi-state nonprofit fundraising activities under Federal Trade Commission (FTC) regulation, and thereby under federal court jurisdiction; single-state efforts would remain under state and local jurisdiction. In 1989 alone, nine state legislatures enacted new laws or tightened existing ones regulating charitable solicitation.

Steps to Organize a Nonprofit Corporation

COMPANION COMPUTER DISK
FOR NONPROFIT INCORPORATORS

Included at the back of this book is a 3½" PC/MS DOS Nonprofit Corporation Computer Disk containing files for the tear-out incorporation forms included in this book. These files are provided in standard file formats that can be read into, completed, and printed with your PC wordprocessing program. For specific instructions for using the forms on the disk, see the README.TXT file included on the disk (insert the disk in your A: drive and use the TYPE A:README.TXT or MORE <A:README.TXT command at the DOS prompt to view this file on the screen).

Nonprofit Nomenclature

Different states use different words in their nonprofit statutes, regulations and bureaucracies. We have tried to use the most common terms to describe nonprofit forms, procedures and officials. For example, we refer to the charter document used to form the nonprofit corporation as the Articles of Incorporation. In some states, this document is given another name such as the Certificate of Incorporation. Similarly, we refer to the office that handles corporate filings as the secretary of state's office since this is the official designation used in most states for this function. Just keep in mind that your state may occasionally use different corporate terminology than we use in the text.

This chapter and those that follow show you how to form your nonprofit corporation in a sequence of small, manageable steps. Fortunately, most incorporation steps, particularly those involving legal formalities (such as reserving a corporate name, preparing and filing Articles and preparing Bylaws) are straightforward. For the most part you will fill in blanks on standard incorporation forms, based upon information you already have at your fingertips. In short, although the entire incorporation process may seem complex at first, we're sure you'll do fine if you relax, work at your own pace and follow our instructions one step at a time.

Because the content and format of certain corporate documents differ from state to state, it's essential that you contact your secretary of state or other corporate official to obtain official incorporation forms and information. We show you how to do this. To help you complete your incorporation forms as required by your state's nonprofit corporation law, we have included tear-out State Incorporation Sheets in the Appendix (referred to as State Sheets throughout this book), which list the incorporation form requirements for each state. In addition, we provide sample clauses, forms and information designed to show you how to use this state specific information to prepare your nonprofit incorporation forms.

How to Use the Incorporation Checklist In the Appendix you will find a tear-out Incorporation Checklist which shows each incorporation step referenced to the chapter and step where it is covered. You may wish to chart your progress by checking off the Done column as you complete each incorporation step in this book.

Step 1. Order Materials from Your Secretary of State

To get started, contact your secretary of state to obtain nonprofit incorporation information and materials.

Materials that many states supply include the following:

- a nonprofit Articles of Incorporation form with instructions for filling it in;

- nonprofit corporation statutes which contain the technical requirements for organizing and operating a nonprofit corporation in your state. You may need to refer to these statutes when completing your Articles of Incorporation and corporate Bylaws. Some states don't supply the statutes free, but tell you how to obtain them for a fee. The fee, if charged, is usually modest and worth paying to have this valuable reference material on hand;

Note In most states, the nonprofit laws are contained in a separate nonprofit law or act. In a few states, the nonprofit laws are interspersed with, and are obtained as part of, the state's regular business corporation act or law.

- a fee schedule showing current charges for filing, copying and certifying various corporate forms;

- forms and instructions to check corporate name availability and reserve a corporate name; and

- forms and instructions for post-incorporation procedures. These may include materials to amend Articles, change the corporation's registered office or registered agent, or register an assumed corporate name (one which is different from the corporate name shown in the incorporation papers).

To Order Your Nonprofit Material

√ In the Appendix we provide a tear-out incorporation contact letter requesting specific information on forming a nonprofit corporation in

Keeping or Changing Your Name

If you are incorporating an existing organization, you'll probably wish to use your current name as your corporate name if it has become associated with your group, its activities, fund-raising efforts, products, services, etc. Many new corporations do this by simply adding "Inc." to their old name (e.g., The World Betterment Fund decides to incorporate as The World Betterment Fund, Inc.). Using your old name is not required, however, and if you have been thinking about a new name for your organization, this is your chance to change it.

your state. The secretary of state information on your State Sheet lists the name and address of the corporate filings office in your state. Complete the letter by typing the name of your corporate filings office in the salutation of the letter. Then type your name, address and telephone number in the box at the bottom. Enclose a stamped, self-addressed envelope and mail the letter to your corporate filing office.

√ You may prefer to call your secretary of state instead. If so, the phone number of the corporations division or similar office in your state is listed on your State Sheet.

√ Check your state's web site (using the URL (address) in the State Sheets). The site may have information about what your state provides, or may even have everything you need online.

When You Receive Your Nonprofit Information Packet

√ If any information is missing (check your State Sheet) or there is a charge for forms and information you wish to order, make sure to send a follow-up letter or make a follow-up phone call to the secretary of state.

√ Get a large file folder (an accordion file, cardboard box, etc.) and place all forms, statutes and other legal material you receive from the secretary of state in it. You will need to refer to this information throughout your incorporation steps and don't want to misplace this material. We show you how to set up a more formal corporate records book in Chapter 9, Step 8.

To save time later, you may wish to call the IRS now and order the tax forms and publications listed at the beginning of Chapter 8, Step 6.

Step 2. Choose a Corporate Name

Your next step is choosing a name for your nonprofit corporation. Before looking at the legal requirements, let's briefly discuss the importance of choosing the right name for your new corporation.

A. The Importance of Your Corporate Name

As a practical matter your corporate name is one of your most important assets and represents the "goodwill" of your nonprofit organization. We don't mean this in any strictly legal, accounting or tax sense, but rather that people in the community, grant agencies, other nonprofits, and those you do business with will identify your nonprofit primarily by its name. For this reason, as well as a number of practical reasons such as not wanting to print new stationery or checks, change promotional literature, create new logos, etc., you will want to thoughtfully pick a name you'll be happy with for a long time.

B. Corporate Name Legal Requirements

Let's look at the basic legal name requirements for nonprofit corporations applicable in most states:

Requirement #1

Your proposed corporate name (the name stated in your Articles of Incorporation) must not be the same as, or confusingly similar to, a name already on file with the secretary of state.

The list of names maintained by the secretaries of state includes the following types of names:

- existing corporations formed in your state;
- out-of-state corporations qualified to do business in your state;
- names reserved for use by individuals planning to incorporate in your state (name reservation periods vary from 30 to 120 days and often can be renewed at least once);
- names registered in your state by out-of-state corporations;
- in some states, names registered as trademarks or service marks and those registered as assumed corporate names (we discuss these special types of business names below).

In resolving this issue of name similarity, the secretary's office will usually only look at similarities between the names themselves, not at similarities in the types and locations of the businesses using the names. If you attempt to form a corporation with a name that is similar in sound or wording to the name of another corporation on the corporate name list, your name may be rejected and your Articles of Incorporation returned to you.

Example Your proposed corporate name is Open Spaces Society, Inc. If another corporation is on file with the secretary of state with the name Open Spaces International, Inc., your name will probably be rejected as too similar.

Requirement #2

In many states, your corporate name must include a corporate designator, such as Incorporated, Corporation, Company or Limited or one of their abbreviations.

Although corporate designators are typically included at the end of a corporate name (The Foundation For Health, Incorporated), the designator may normally be placed anywhere in your corporate name (The Incorporated Heath Care Foundation).

See the corporate name section of your State Sheet to determine if your state requires a corporate designator in your name.

Requirement #3

The statutes of various states forbid the use of specific words in the name of a nonprofit corporation. Mostly, prohibited names are those associated with specialized business, nonprofit, professional or governmental entities or corporations. So try to avoid names from each of these categories—here are several examples of specialized corporate names controlled by separate state statutes:

Accounting	Insurance
Attorney	Physician
Banking	Reserve
Cooperative	Trust
Engineering	United States
Federal	

Of course if you are forming a specialized nonprofit corporation, such as a consumers' or producers' cooperative, or a nonprofit organization named "Solar Engineering Data Sciences" which collects research on solar engineering, you may be entitled to use one of these special words in your corporate name.

In Case of A Name Conflict

If the use of your proposed name is crucial to you and you are told by the secretary of state that it is unacceptable because it is too close to an existing name already on file, there are a few things you can do:

- Submit a written request for a review of your name's acceptability to the legal counsel in the secretary of state's office. The legal questions here are not always easy to resolve. For now, we simply note that if you do get into this sort of squabble, you will probably want to see a lawyer who is versed in the complexities of tradename or trademark law or do some additional reading and research on your own.
- Obtain the written consent of the other corporation. Sometimes, a profit corporation will let you use your proposed similar name if they are not worried about competition or public confusion between their commercial operations and your nonprofit activities. If your secretary of state will accept this written approval, obtain

the name and address of an officer of
the other corporation from the
secretary's office. Mail the officer a
written consent statement to sign,
together with an explanatory letter
(preceded, perhaps, by a preliminary
phone call), indicating why you'd like
them to agree to your use of your
similar name (because you will be
engaged in nonprofit activities clearly
different from their profit-making
business in a different locale, for
example). If the officer signs the
consent, re-file your Articles together
with a copy of the signed statement.

- Decide that it's simpler to pick
another name for your nonprofit
corporation. We normally recommend
this third approach.

Additional Legal Points

Here are a couple of additional legal points relevant to your choice of a corporate name:

- *Filing your corporate name with the secretary of state does not guarantee your right to use it*

Having your name approved by the secretary of state when you file your Articles of Incorporation is not a guarantee that you have the absolute legal right to use it—as explained further below, another organization may already be using it as a trademark or service mark. If they are, they may be able to prevent you from doing so, depending on their location, type of business and other circumstances. We show you how to so some checking on your own to be relatively sure that no one else has a prior claim to your proposed corporate name.

- *Using a name different from your formal corporate name is allowed*

If you want to adopt a formal corporate name in your Articles which is different from the one you have used, or plan to use, locally to identify your nonprofit organization, you can do this by filing an assumed or fictitious business name statement with your secretary of state (and/or your county clerk).

- *You can change your corporate name by amending your articles*

If you decide to change your formal corporate name after filing your Articles, you can do so by:

- making sure that your new corporate name is available for your use (as explained further below); then
- filing amended Articles of Incorporation with the secretary of state showing your new corporate name.

C. Practical Suggestions When Selecting a Name

Now that we've looked at the basic state legal requirements related to your choice of a corporate name, here are some practical suggestions to help you do it.

Use Common Nonprofit Terms In Your Name

There are a number of words that broadly suggest 501(c)(3) nonprofit purposes or activities. Choosing one of these names can simplify the task of finding the right name for your organization and can help alert others to the nonprofit nature of your corporate activities. Here are just a few:

Academy	House
Aid	Human
American	Humane
Appreciation	Institute
Assistance	International
Association	Learning
Benefit	Literary
Betterment	Mission
Care	Music
Center	Orchestra
Charitable	Organization
Coalition	Philanthropic
Community	Philharmonic[1]
Congress	Program
Conservation	Project
Consortium	Protection
Council	Public
Cultural	Refuge
Education	Relief
Educational	Religious
Environmental	Research
Exchange	Resource
Fellowship	Scholarship
Foundation	Scientific
Friends	Service
Fund	Shelter
Health	Social
Help	Society
Heritage	Study
Home	Troupe
Hope	Voluntary
Hospice	Welfare
Hospital	

Names to Avoid

When selecting a corporate name, we suggest you avoid, or use with caution, the types of words described and listed below. Of course there are exceptions and if one of them relates to your particular nonprofit purposes or activities, it may make sense to use the word in your name.

- *Avoid words that, taken together, signify a profit making business or venture*

  Booksellers Corporation   *Commercial Products Inc.*
  Jeff Baxter & Company   *Entrepreneurial Services Corp.*

- *Avoid words that describe or are related to special types of nonprofit organizations [those that are tax exempt under provisions of the IRC other than Section 501(c)(3)]*

  Business League
  Chamber of Commerce
  Civic League
  Hobby, Recreational or Social Club
  Labor, Agricultural or Horticultural Organization
  Political Action Organization
  Real Estate Board
  Trade Group

For a complete listing of these special tax-exempt nonprofit groups, see Table 3.1.

Example   The name Westbrook Social Club, Inc. would clearly identify a social club, tax exempt under IRC §501(c)(7)—you shouldn't use this type of name for your 501(c)(3) nonprofit. However, The Social Consciousness Society might be an appropriate name for a 501(c)(3) educational purpose organization. Also, although The Trade Betterment League of Pottersville would identify a 501(c)(6) business league and The Millbrae Civic Betterment League a 501(c)(4) civic league, The Philanthropic League of Castlemont may be suitable for a 501(c)(3) charitable giving group.

Do You Want to Bypass Name Checking Procedures?

It may take a few weeks or more for the secretary to respond to a written name availability request. Also, even if your proposed corporate name is available at the time of your name availability request, this is not, of course, a guarantee that your name will be available when you later file your Articles of Incorporation. For these reasons, you may wish to dispense with a written name availability check and attempt to reserve your corporate name, as explained below, or file your Articles and hope that your name is available for use.

Filing your Articles without preliminary name checking or reservation makes sense if your state offers an expedited (24 hour) filing procedure for a small additional fee—you'll know in a day or two if your proposed name is available and if your Articles were filed.

Note: Of course, if your state allows you to check a proposed corporate name over the phone, we suggest you take the time to do this in all cases.

- *Avoid words or abbreviations commonly associated with nationally known nonprofit causes, organizations, programs or trademarks*

You can bet that the well-known group has taken steps to protect its name as a trademark or service mark. Here is a small sampling of some well known nonprofit names and abbreviations:

AAA
American Red Cross
American Ballet Theatre or ABT
American Conservatory Theatre or ACT
Audubon
Blue Cross
Blue Shield
Environmental Defense Fund
National Geographic
National Public Radio or NPR
Sierra Club
Public Broadcasting System or PBS

- *Avoid words using special symbols or punctuation that may confuse the secretary of state's computer name-search software*

!@#$%^&*()+?><

Pick a Descriptive Name to Aid Identification

It's often a good idea to pick a name that clearly reflects your purposes or activities (Downtown Ballet Theater, Inc.; Good Health Society, Ltd.; Endangered Fish Protection League, Inc.). Doing this allows potential members, donors, beneficiaries and others to locate and identify you easily. More fanciful names (The Wave Project, Inc., Serendipity Unlimited Inc.) are usually less advisable because it normally takes a while for people to figure out what they stand for, although occasionally their uniqueness may provide better identification over the long term.

Example   Although the name Northern California Feline Shelter, Inc. will alert people at the start to the charitable purposes of the nonprofit group, Cats' Cradle, Inc. may stay with people longer once they are familiar with the activities of the organization.

- *Limit your name geographically or regionally, if necessary, to avoid name conflicts or confusion*

If you use general or descriptive terms in your name, you may need to further qualify it to avoid conflicts or public confusion.

Example Your proposed name is The Philharmonic Society, Inc. Your secretary of state rejects this name as too close to a number of philharmonic orchestras on file. You refile using the proposed name, The Philharmonic Society of Bar Harbor, and your name is accepted.

Another Example Suppose you are incorporating the AIDS Support Group, Inc. Even if this name does not conflict with the name of another corporation on file in your state, it is an excellent idea to limit or qualify the name to avoid confusion by the public with other groups in other parts of the country that share the same purposes or goals. This could be done by changing the name to the AIDS Support Group of Middleville.

- *Choose a new name rather than limiting your proposed name with a local (or other) identifier if there is still the likelihood of public confusion between your name and the name of another group*

Example Your proposed nonprofit name is The Park School, Inc. If another corporation (specializing in a nationwide network of apprentice training colleges) is already listed with the name Park Training Schools, your secretary of state may reject your name as too similar. You may be able to limit your name and make it acceptable (The Park Street School of Westmont, Inc.) but this may not be a good idea for two reasons:

1. members of the public who have heard of the Park Training Schools may believe that your school is simply a Westmont affiliate of the national training program; and

2. you may be infringing the trademark rights of the national group (they may have registered their name as a state or federal trademark).

- *Use a corporate designator in your name*

Even if not legally required in your state, you may wish to include a corporate designator in your name to let others know that your organization is a corporation.

Example Hopi Archaeological Society, Inc.; The Children's Museum Corporation; Mercy Hospital, Incorporated; The Hadley School Corp.

Take Your Time When Choosing a Corporate Name

Finding an appropriate and available name for your organization takes time and requires patience. It's usually best not to act on your first impulse—try a few names before making your final choice. Ask others both inside and outside the organization for feedback. And of course, remember: your proposed name may not be available for your use—have one or more alternate names in reserve in case your first choice isn't available.

D. Check to See If Your Proposed Name Is Available

Since your Articles of Incorporation will be rejected by the secretary of state if the name you've chosen is not available, it's often wise to check in advance before submitting your Articles.

Check Your Proposed Name By Phone

The materials you received from your secretary of state as part of Step 1 above should list the telephone number you can call to check the availability of one or more proposed corporate names. If not, call the main number of the corporate filings office listed on your State Sheet and ask to speak to someone in the corporate name availability section.

Check Your Proposed Name By Mail

A few states will not advise you of the availability of a proposed corporate name over the phone—your secretary of state materials should indicate if you live in one of these states. If you do, you can usually check by mail, although there may be a small charge for checking each name. To request a corporate name check by mail, complete the tear-out secretary of state Name Availability Letter in the Appendix, following the sample form. Special instructions follow the sample letter and are keyed to the circled numbers.

If You Use Another Company's Tradename or Trademark

Legal remedies for violation of tradename or trademark rights vary under federal and state laws and court decisions. Generally, the business with the prior claim to the name can sue to enjoin (stop) you from using your name or can force you to change it. Money damages may be awarded by the court for lost sales or loss of goodwill suffered by the name's rightful owner due to your use of the name. If you violate a trademark or service mark registered with the U.S. Patent and Trademark Office, treble damages (three times the actual money damages suffered as a result of the infringement), defendant's profits and court costs may be awarded and the goods with the offending labels or marks may be ordered to be confiscated and destroyed.

Note that distinctive names qualify for the principal federal register and are afforded significant legal presumptions and protections over descriptive marks registered on the supplemental federal register.

For further information see *Patent, Copyright & Trademark—The Intellectual Property Law Dictionary* by Elias (Nolo Press).

Sample Name Availability Letter

Your Address
Date

Name and Address
Corporations Division
Secretary of State

Corporate Name Availability:

Please advise if the following proposed corporate names, listed in order of preference, are available for corporate use:

      (first choice for corporate name)   ①
      (second choice)

Enclosed is a stamped, self-addressed envelope for your reply. My name, address and phone number are included below if you wish to contact me regarding this request.

Name:

Address:

Phone:

[I enclose a check for $_____ in payment of the fee for checking the availability of the above names.] ②

Thank you for your assistance.

(your signature)

Special Instructions

① Your secretary of state materials will indicate if you can check the availability of more than one name. If so, list your proposed names in order of preference here.

② If there is a fee for checking the availability of one or more names by mail, type and complete this bracketed sentence on the tear-out letter.

    Payment Note A few secretaries of state require payment by money order or certified check only. Check your materials to see if there are special payment requirements in your state.

A name check is just a preliminary indication of the availability of your proposed corporate name. So don't order your stationery, cards, etc., until your name has been formally accepted following a more complete name search by the secretary of state and after your Reservation of Corporate Name has been approved or your Articles of Incorporation have been filed.

Checking Your Name by Computer

Most of the business name listings mentioned below, including Yellow Page listings and business directory listings as well as the federal and state trademark registers, are available as part of several commercial computer databases. For example, the federal and state registers can be accessed through the Trademarkscan® service which is part of the Trademark Research Center forum (Go Traderc) on the CompuServe database (call 1-800-848-8990 for subscription information) or the Dialog database (call 1-800-462-3411).

If you own, or have access to, a computer and a modem and are already signed up on one of these databases, you can check your proposed name against the names in the federal and state registers in just a few minutes time (for an extra charge for your time while using the Trademarkscan® service).

Yellow Page listings can often be searched for free on the Internet. Also, you can use one of the Internet's search engines to search for corporate names.

E. Reserve Your Corporate Name

Most states allow you to reserve an available corporate name. During the reservation period, only you may file Articles with this name or a similar name. The reservation period and the fees vary. In many states, you can renew your reservation if you don't get around to filing your Articles during the first reservation period.

Once you have decided on a corporate name and established its availability, it makes sense to reserve it if you will not be filing your Articles immediately, because:

- available corporate names are becoming hard to find, particularly in states with a lot of corporate filing activity; and

- reserving a name allows you to hold on to it while you complete your initial paperwork.

To reserve a corporate name, follow any instructions included in your secretary of state materials. If you have no information, call the corporations filings office of your secretary of state listed on your State Sheet and ask for instructions. If the secretary does not provide a form, you can use the tear-out reservation of corporate name letter included in the Appendix. Here is a sample of the tear-out form.

Sample Application for Reservation of Corporate Name

Date

Name and Address
Corporate Filings Office
Secretary of State Address

Corporate Name Reservation:

Please reserve the following corporate name for my use for the allowable period specified under the state's corporation statutes:

(your proposed corporate name)

I enclose the required payment of $(fee) . My name, address and phone number are included below if you wish to contact me regarding this request.

Name:

Address:

Phone:

Thank you for your assistance,

(your signature)

Note   Make sure that the person signing this letter will be available to sign Articles of Incorporation on behalf of your organization—the corporate name is reserved for this person's use only.

F. How to Perform a Name Search

As we've said, approval by the secretary of state's office doesn't necessarily mean that you have the legal right to use a name; it simply means that your name does not conflict with that of another corporation already on file with the secretary of state and that you are presumed to have the legal right to use it within your state. Another organization (corporate or non-corporate, profit or nonprofit) may, in fact, already have the legal right to use this same name as a federal or state trademark or service

Nonprofits and Commercial Trademarks

Fortunately, disputes involving tradenames, trademarks and service marks tend to arise primarily in the private, commercial sector, and much less in the nonprofit world. This is primarily because customer confusion as to names of commercial products or services can result in much larger amounts of misdirected revenues. Also, most smaller local nonprofits do not "market" their products or services as aggressively as regular commercial concerns and therefore don't tend to run afoul of another business' trademark or service mark. Besides, engaging in a substantial amount of commercial activity of this sort may jeopardize the nonprofit organization's tax exempt status.

mark used to identify their goods or services. Most secretaries of state do not even check their own state trademark/service mark registration lists to see if your proposed corporate name is available; none check the federal trademark register. Also, another organization may already be presumed to have the legal right to the name in a particular county if they are using it as a tradename (as the name of their business or organization) and have filed an assumed (or fictitious) business name statement with their county clerk. The secretaries of state of many states do not register or check assumed names, even assumed corporate names—this is most often done at the county level.

Without discussing the intricacies of federal and state trademark, service mark and tradename law, the basic rule is that the ultimate right to use a particular name will usually be decided on the basis of who was first to actually use the name in connection with a particular trade, business, activity, service or product.[2] In deciding who has the right to a name in case of a conflict, the similarity of the types of businesses or organizations and their geographical proximity are usually taken into account. To avoid problems, we suggest using the name selection techniques discussed in Step 2, Section C above and performing the kind of common sense checking described further below.

Of course, disputes involving trade names, trademarks and service marks tend to arise in the private, commercial sector. Further, it is unlikely that your nonprofit will wish to "market" products and services as aggressively as a regular commercial concern and thereby run afoul of another business's trademark or service mark (besides, engaging in a substantial amount of commercial activity of this sort could jeopardize your tax exempt status). Nonetheless, as a matter of common sense, and to avoid legal disputes later on, you should do your best to avoid names already in use by other profit and nonprofit organizations, or in use as trademarks or service marks.

In many circumstances, you will know that your name is unique and unlikely to infringe on another organization's name. This would be the case, for example, if you called your group the Sumner County Crisis Hotline or the Southern Arizona Medieval Music Society. By qualifying your name this way, you know that you are the only nonprofit in your area using the name. However, in some circumstances you may be less sure of your right to use a name. For example, the names Legal Rights For All or The Society To Cure Lyme Disease may be in use by a group in any part of the country.

Below we list self-help name checking procedures you may wish to use to be more certain of the uniqueness of your proposed corporate name. These name search procedures should be performed prior to filing your Articles. Obviously, you can't be one-hundred percent certain since you can't possibly check all names in use by all other groups. However, you can check obvious sources likely to expose names similar to the one you wish to use. Here are our suggestions:

Check state trademarks and service marks   Call the trademark section of your secretary of state's office and ask if your proposed corporate name is the same or similar to trademarks and service marks registered with the state (some offices may ask for a written request and a small fee before performing this search).

Check state and county assumed business name files   Your secretary of state materials should indicate whether assumed (or fictitious) corporate names are registered with your secretary of state's office, at the county level, or both.[3] If they are registered at the state level, call the assumed name section at the secretary of state's office and ask if your proposed corporate name is the same or similar to a registered assumed (or fictitious) corporate name. Also call your local County Clerk's office to ask how you can check assumed business name filings—in most states, noncorporate assumed or fictitious business name statements, or "doing business as" (dba), statements are filed with the county clerk's office. In most cases, you will have to go in and check the assumed business name files in person—it takes just a few minutes to do this.

Check Directories   Check major metropolitan phone book listings, nonprofit directories, business and trade directories, etc., to see if another company or group is using a name similar to your proposed corporate name. Larger public libraries keep phone directories for many major cities throughout the country as well as trade and nonprofit directories. A local nonprofit resource center or business branch of a public library may have a special collection of nonprofit research materials—check these first for listings of local and national nonprofits.

A Likely Resource   One commonly consulted national directory of nonprofit names is the *Encyclopedia of Associations* published by Gale Research Company.

Check the Federal Trademark Register   If your name is the type that might be used to market a service or product or to identify a business activity of your nonprofit corporation, you will wish to check federal trademarks and service marks. Go to a large public library or special business and government library in your area that carries the federal Trademark Register. This consists of a listing of trademark and service mark names broken into categories of goods and services.

Of course, if you wish to go further in your name search, you can pay a private records search company to check various databases and name listings. Alternatively, or in conjunction with your own efforts or search procedures, you can pay a trademark lawyer to oversee or undertake these searches for you (or to render a legal opinion if your search turns up a similar name). Most smaller nonprofit organizers, particularly those who believe that a specialized or locally-based name is not likely to conflict with anyone else's name, will not feel the need to do this and will be content to undertake the more modest self-help search procedures mentioned above.

G. Protect Your Name

Once you have filed your Articles of Incorporation, you may wish to take additional steps to protect your name against later users. For example, if your name is also used to identify your products or services, you may wish to register it with your secretary of state and with the United States Patent and Trademark Office as a trademark or service mark. Registration in other states may also be appropriate if you plan to conduct operations there.

Federal registration costs $200 and can be accomplished on one of two grounds:

1. you have actually used the name in interstate commerce (that is, in two or more states) in connection with the marketing of goods or services; or

2. you intend to use the name in interstate commerce in connection with the marketing of goods or services.

If you specify the second ground in your trademark application, you must file an affidavit (sworn statement) within six months[4] stating that the name has been placed in actual use. This costs an additional $100. Simply stated, it is possible to reserve ownership of a trademark before actually using it, but you have to pay at least $100 extra for the privilege. Trademark application procedures are relatively simple and inexpensive and you may wish to tackle this task yourself—your local county law library should have practice guides available to help you handle state and federal trademark and service mark filing formalities.

Step 3. Prepare Your Articles of Incorporation

The next step in organizing your nonprofit corporation is preparing Articles of Incorporation. This is your primary incorporation document: your corporation comes into existence on the date you file your Articles document with your secretary of state.

Applying for a Federal Trademark

To apply for a federal trademark, call the Patent and Trademark Office (PTO) in Washington, D.C. and order a trademark application. Fill out the form following the instructions. A month or so after mailing the form, you should hear from the PTO. If there are any problems, you will receive a written list of questions together with the telephone number of a trademark examiner. The examiner should be able to address any questions and issues you can't handle yourself and should help you finalize your application without undue difficulty or delay.

A. Check Your Materials

Most secretaries of state provide sample or ready-to-use forms for Articles of Incorporation that meet the statutory requirements. Before you do anything else, go through your secretary of state materials and take out all forms and instructions related to preparing Articles of Incorporation. Look carefully—sample and tear-out Articles and instructions are occasionally hidden in the back of a general purpose publication (such as *Doing Business in the State of* _____). Here's what you can expect to find in your secretary of state materials:

Sample Forms and Instructions

Many secretaries of state provide a sample Articles form with instructions. You will need to re-type your final form using the format and content of the sample form.

Ready to Use Articles

Some states provide a printed form that you can fill in and file with the secretary of state. Instructions for filling in the blanks are often provided on the printed form.

Copy of Statutes

The contents of your Articles are determined by the nonprofit statutes of your state. Almost invariably there is a section called "Articles of Incorporation" that specifies the required and optional contents of this legal document. In the few states that do not provide sample or printed Articles, the secretary's office may include a copy of the state statute that lists the contents. If your state provides neither forms nor statutes, call the secretary's office and ask for a copy of the section(s) of the nonprofit corporation law governing the required contents of Articles of Incorporation [each State Sheet lists the Articles statute(s) for your state]. Most secretaries of state will be glad to comply with this request.

Filing Checklist

Some secretaries of state include a checklist showing both the filing requirements and common reasons for rejection of Articles. This information can help you comply with some of the less obvious substantive and formal requirements of the secretary of state's office (such as whether you can show a P.O. box as an address, how to properly sign and acknowledge the form, how much space to leave at the top of the first page for the secretary's file stamp, etc.).

Each State Sheet lists the Articles statute for the state and indicates whether your secretary provides sample or printed Articles and copies of your state's corporate statutes. In the few states where forms, guidelines and statutes are not provided, we point you to a commercial source for this material or tell you where to find your statutes in a state library.

B. Sample Articles of Incorporation

The basic clauses required in Articles of Incorporation in various states are similar. Below we provide sample language and explanations of the provisions you are likely to find in the Articles of Incorporation provided by your secretary of state (or in the article of incorporation provisions of your state's nonprofit corporation law). By following the material below and referring to the specific instructions for preparing Articles provided by your secretary of state, you should be able to prepare your form without undue difficulty. Here are some hints to make this job easier:

1. Scan the following information to get a general idea of the various types of clauses and provisions traditionally included in standard Articles of Incorporation. This information will help you understand the form and instructions provided by your secretary of state.

2. Make a copy of the form provided by your secretary of state to use as a draft. If your secretary provides a sample form which must be re-typed, type or write out a draft copy first.

3. Complete as much of the form as you can following your secretary of state's form and specific instructions. If you get stuck with a particular article or provision, refer to our instructions below.

4. To locate a particular incorporation requirement in your state (for example, the number of directors to be named in your Articles) see your State Sheet in the Appendix.

Sample article provisions and clauses are listed below, preceded by an article number and heading identifying the subject matter of the provision or clause. Blanks indicate information inserted in the text of the provision or clause. Explanatory text follows each sample article.

Typical Secretary of State Guidelines for Typing Articles

- All text must be in English (no foreign language characters, punctuation, or diacritical marks).
- If retyping the form, leave a small (2" x 2") blank area in the upper right of the first page of your Articles for the secretary's file stamp.
- Type your responses to blank items (or retype your form) using a black ink ribbon. Some secretaries may allow hand printed responses—check your secretary of state's instructions.
- Use letter-sized (8 1/2" x 11") paper.
- Fasten pages with staples, not rivet type fasteners.
- All typing and signatures (and any hand-printed responses) must be of sufficient contrast to be legibly photocopied by the secretary's office; black ink is usually specified.

Heading and Format of Articles

ARTICLES OF INCORPORATION

of

_____

a Non-Profit Corporation

Article 1.   ....

Article 2.   ....

Article 3.   ....

State law does not normally specify any format for the heading or body of the Articles. Typically, the name of the corporation is shown in the heading of the Articles and each provision is numbered sequentially. Your secretary of state's office may provide guidelines for preparing or typing Articles.

Statement of Statutory Authority

The undersigned incorporator(s), in order to form a corporation under the (name of state's nonprofit corporation law), adopt the following Articles of Incorporation:

Although not required in many states a statement of statutory authority is included at the beginning of the Articles stating the name or section numbers of the state's nonprofit corporation act under which the corporation is being formed. In some states it is customary to recite that the incorporators or the corporation meet specific statutory requirements (for example, that the incorporators are of legal age or that the corporation is not formed for pecuniary profit).

Here are examples of statutory authority clauses taken from the official forms of several states:

California   _This corporation is a nonprofit public benefit corporation and it is not organized for the private gain of any person. It is organized under the Nonprofit Public Benefit Corporation Law for _____ purposes._[5]

**Tips on Preparing a
Statement of Specific Purposes**

Make sure to keep your specific purpose
statement brief—one or two short
sentences is best (e.g., to set up a child
care center, home for the aged, AIDS
hotline, dance or musical troupe, to
provide scholarships to needy students,
establish a book fair, etc.). The secretary
of state usually doesn't want much detail
or narrative here. You will provide a fuller
description of your nonprofit purposes
and activities in your Bylaws and on your
federal tax exemption application).

If possible, describe the kinds of
activities you pursue in any one or more
of these categories with language that
will clearly identify them as ones which
the IRS considers to be tax-exempt.

For example, if your specific purpose
is to set up a hospital, indicate that you
are forming a *charitable* hospital; if
establishing a child care center, state
that *it is open to the general public and
will allow parents to be gainfully employed*; if setting up a scientific organization, that *scientific research will be
carried on in the public interest.*

Avoid using keywords, terms or
phrases associated with organizations
exempt from taxation under other [non-
501(c)(3)] sections of the Internal
Revenue Code, such as *social, fraternal,
recreational, social, political*, etc.

Florida   *The undersigned, acting as incorporator(s) of a Corporation
pursuant to Chapter 617, Florida Statutes, adopt(s) the following Articles
of Incorporation of such corporation:*

Illinois   *Pursuant to the provisions of "The General Not For Profit
Corporation Act of 1986," the undersigned incorporator(s) hereby adopt
the following Articles of Incorporation.*

Article 1. Name of Corporation

The name of this corporation is _____.

The heading to the Articles and the first article of incorporation normally specify the name of the corporation. See Step 2 above to select a
name for your corporation. If you have reserved a corporate name, make
sure to insert the exact spelling of the reserved name in your Articles.

Article 2. Registered Agent and Office

The name and address of the registered agent of this corporation are:

_____.

Most states require that Articles include the name and address of the
corporation's initial registered agent (or agent for service of process). The
agent is the person authorized to receive legal papers on behalf of the
corporation; the agent's office is also known as the registered office of the
corporation. Generally, the agent must be a resident of the state and at
least 18 years of age. Although the registered office may be different from
the principal office of the corporation in many states, most nonprofits
keep things simple and appoint one of the initial directors as the initial
agent, showing the principal address of the corporation as the registered
office of the corporation.

Note   A street address, not a post office box, is normally required
here. Also, some states require the filing of a separate Designation of
Registered Agent form with the Articles.

The State Sheets list any special requirements for registered agents and
indicate whether a separate registered agent form must be filed with the
Articles.

Article 3. Statement of Purpose

The purposes for which this corporation is organized are:

_____

A statement of purpose clause is a standard feature in nonprofit Articles of Incorporation. Your statement of purpose should be used to satisfy state corporate law and federal 501(c)(3) tax exemption requirements. Let's look at the federal requirements first.

Federal 501(c)(3) Tax Exempt Purpose Clause

The purpose clause in your Articles of Incorporation must include language stating that your corporation is organized for 501(c)(3) tax exempt purposes. We refer to this language in later discussions as your *statement of tax exempt purposes.*

Here is the standard IRS-approved language for this statement of tax exempt purposes (we show this language in italics below, inserted after the standard preamble to the purpose clause found in most Articles of Incorporation):

Article 3. The purposes for which this corporation is organized are: *This corporation is organized exclusively for one or more of the purposes as specified in Section 501(c)(3) of the Internal Revenue Code, including, for such purposes, the making of distributions to organizations that qualify as exempt organizations under section 501(c)(3) of the Internal Revenue Code, or corresponding section of any future federal tax code.*

This statement authorizes the corporation to engage in one or more 501(c)(3) tax exempt purposes, which include the making of distributions to other 501(c)(3) organizations.

The official form of Articles promulgated by your secretary of state may already contain this statement of tax exempt purposes (or a slight variation on the clause shown above). Some official forms include this clause in a statement of purposes article; others include it under a space set aside on the form for "additional provisions." In all cases, if this (or similar) tax exempt purpose language does not appear in your Articles, make sure to include it somewhere on the form.

If You Get Stuck on Your Statement of Nonprofit Purposes

We provide instructions for dealing with the types of purpose clauses required in the majority of states. However, if you encounter special language or special format requirements for this article not covered in our discussion, here are two suggestions:

- Rely primarily on the instructions to the sample and printed forms in your secretary of state materials—these will usually show you how to cope with any special state statutory requirements.
- For further assistance, check your state's Articles statute (listed in the Articles of Incorporation section on your State Sheet in the Appendix) for the special statutory language you must include or special requirements you must follow to complete your purpose clause.

Your secretary of state form may include other tax exemption provisions. See Article 8 below for a discussion of additional federal tax exemption language that is required, or may be included, in your Articles.

Additional Statements of Purpose Required Under State Law

In many states, a statement of 501(c)(3) tax exempt purposes will be all you need to satisfy the requirements for completing the purpose clause in your Articles. Some states, however, have their own unique requirements for purpose clause wording in the Articles. Below we look at the most common types of statements required under state statutes.

Remember These special statements of purpose will be included in your Articles to satisfy state law requirements. To satisfy the federal 501(c)(3) tax requirements, make sure to *also include a statement of your tax exempt purposes somewhere in your Articles.*

Statement of Lawful Purpose Some states require that the Articles contain specific statutory wording indicating that the corporation is formed for a lawful purpose under the laws of the state (we call this a *statement of lawful purposes*).

A typical statement of lawful purposes, taken from the Delaware form for Articles, reads as follows:

The purpose of the corporation is to engage in any lawful act or activity for which corporations may be organized under the General Corporation Law of Delaware.

Statement of Specific Purposes Some states require a brief, one or two sentence description of the purposes and activities of the corporation in the purpose clause of the Articles (we call this a *statement of specific purposes*). If you can't determine if your state requires a statement of specific purpose by reading your secretary of state materials, we suggest you include one just to be safe.

Examples of Specific Purpose Statements The following examples should give you an idea of how to draft a specific purpose statement.

Environmental Education Here is a sample statement of specific purposes for an environmental group:

Article 3. The purposes for which this corporation is organized are: *to publish a newsletter providing information to the public on preserving tropical rain forests.*

Publishing and Lectures Here is a sample specific purpose clause for a group that wishes to publish books and give public lectures.

Article 3. The purposes for which this corporation is organized are: *to develop an institution to teach and disseminate educational material to the public, including, but not limited to, material relating to __(the areas of instruction are mentioned here)__ , through publications, lectures, or otherwise.*

Dance Group The following sample clause is for a group that wishes to set up studios where it can teach dance and hold performances. The educational purposes of the group are clearly identified in the specific purpose clause and the general public is identified as the recipient of these services. For future flexibility, the group leaves itself open to teaching and promoting other art forms.

Article 3. The purposes for which this corporation is organized are: *to educate the general public in dance and other art forms. The means of providing such education includes, but is not limited to, maintaining facilities for instruction and public performances of dance and other art forms.*

Housing Improvement Here is a sample clause for a group planning to get grants and tax exemptions for improving housing conditions for low and moderate income people by organizing a housing information and research exchange. Note that the following example simply and succinctly states the group's specific purposes, characterizing them as charitable and educational purposes in the interests of the general public—no further embellishment or narrative in the specific purpose clause is needed here.

Article 3. The purposes for which this corporation is organized are: *to provide education and charitable assistance to the general public by organizing a housing information and research exchange.*

Medical Clinic This sample clause is for a community health care clinic for low-income individuals.

Article 3. The purposes for which this corporation is organized are: *to establish and maintain a comprehensive system of family-oriented health care aimed primarily at the medically underserved areas of ___(city and county)___ .*

Religious Teachings and Publishing Here is a statement that is appropriate for a religious group devoted to the teachings and works of a particular religious leader or religious order:

Article 3. The purposes for which this corporation is organized are: *to establish a religious organization to promote the teachings of, and publish materials of and concerning, (name of spiritual leader or religious order).*

Scientific Research Sometimes, the most general description of the tax-exempt purposes of the group will suffice, as follows:

Article 3. The purposes for which this corporation is organized are: *to engage in scientific research in the public interest.*

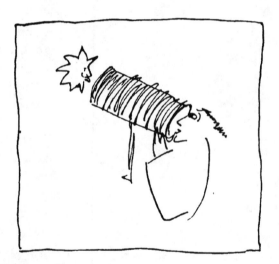

Article 4. Number, Names and Addresses of Initial Directors

The number of initial directors of this corporations is _____ .
Their names and address are as follows:

In many states the Articles must show the number of persons who will serve on the first board of directors, followed by their names and addresses. In some states, this information is not (or is only optionally) included in the Articles sent out by the secretary of state.

Each State Sheet indicates the minimum number of directors required in your state and any residency, age or other qualifications for directors imposed under state law.

To fill in this article, type the number of directors of your corporation, then list the names and (street, not P.O. box) addresses of the persons appointed to your initial board. Initial board members serve until the first meeting held to re-elect directors—the date of this meeting will be specified in your Bylaws.

Article 5. Names and Addresses of Incorporators

The names and addresses of the incorporators of this corporation are:

The incorporator is the person who forms the corporation by signing and filing Articles of Incorporation. Although more than one incorporator may be used, most nonprofits, if allowed, designate one person to assume this responsibility. Most Articles of Incorporation require the name and address of the incorporator of the corporation either in the body of the Articles or at the end of the document after the incorporator's signature line.

Although the incorporator is usually one of the initial directors of the corporation, normally any person may be designated the incorporator and prepare, sign and file Articles on behalf of your corporation.

Your State Sheet indicates if more than one incorporator is required in your state and lists any special incorporator requirements.

Article 6. Duration of Corporation

The period of duration of this corporation is:

In many states, the Articles include a provision specifying the duration of the corporation. Almost all nonprofit corporations wish to continue into the indefinite future and will insert the word "perpetual" in this provision. In the extremely rare circumstance that you wish to limit the duration of your corporation's existence, insert a specific period or date in this clause.

Article 7. Membership Provisions

The classes, rights, privileges, qualifications, and obligations of members of this corporation are as follows:

In a number of states, the Articles of Incorporation include a membership clause similar to the sample shown above.

As explained in Chapter 2, Section 4, most smaller nonprofit corporations will not wish to set up a formal membership structure and will indicate "No Members" if this clause appears in their Articles. If you do decide to adopt a formal membership structure, it's usually best to indicate here that "The membership provisions of this corporation shall be stated in the Bylaws of this corporation." This is the preferred approach since bylaw provisions may be repealed, changed and added with relative ease while amendments to Articles must be filed with the secretary of state.

Finally, if you wish to adopt membership provisions and your secretary of state materials indicate that you must do so in your Articles, here is some standard language you may wish to use that provides for one class of dues-paying membership in the corporation:

This corporation shall have one class of membership. Any person shall be qualified to become a member upon payment of the initial dues and shall continue as a member upon paying the annual dues. The amount, method and time of payment of dues shall be determined, and may be changed, from time to time, by the board of directors. Additional provisions specifying the rights and obligations of members shall be contained in the Bylaws of this corporation pursuant to, and in accordance with, the laws of this state.

For further information and suggested language to set up a formal membership structure, see Chapter 7.

Article 8. Additional Provisions

Insert additional provisions for operating the corporation in the space provided below:

[Insert required and optional 501(c)(3) tax exemption provisions, special language from state statutes for the operation of the corporation, etc.]

In many states, a blank article for additional provisions is included in the standard form sent out by the secretary of state. In some states, this blank article begins with wording similar to the language shown above (with suggestions for the types of optional clauses that may be inserted given in parentheses).

Below, we discuss some required and optional federal and state language you should include in this portion of your Articles if it is not already included on your state's form.

Additional Federal Tax Exemption Language

To be eligible for your 501(c)(3) tax exemption, your Articles must dedicate the assets of the corporation to exempt purposes. Technically, this dedication clause is not required in a few states—nonetheless, we recommend all incorporators make sure a dedication of assets clause appears in their Articles.[6] Here is a standard dedication of assets clause shown inserted in the space set aside in the Articles for additional provisions:

Article 8. Additional Provisions
Upon the dissolution of this corporation, its assets remaining after payment, or provision for payment, of all debts and liabilities of this corporation shall be distributed for one or more exempt purposes within the meaning of Section 501(c)(3) of the Internal Revenue Code or shall be distributed to the federal government, or to a state or local government, for a public purpose.

Make sure to include this dedication of assets statement in your Articles if one does not already appear on your form.

Alternative Wording for Dedication The sample dedication language above (from IRS publications) dedicates the assets of the nonprofit corporation to one or more allowable 501(c)(3) tax exempt purposes. The sample or printed language found in some state's Articles, however, may provide blanks for dedicating assets of the nonprofit corporation to a specific 501(c)(3) tax exempt purpose. Here is an example of a dedication clause of this type:

> *The property of this corporation is irrevocably dedicated to _____ purposes and no part of the net income or assets of this corporation shall ever inure to the benefit of any director, officer or member thereof or to the benefit of any private person. Upon the dissolution or winding up of the corporation, its assets remaining after payment, or provision for payment, of all debts and liabilities of this corporation shall be distributed to a nonprofit fund, foundation or corporation which is organized and operated exclusively for _____ purposes and which has established its tax exempt status under Section 501(c)(3) of the Internal Revenue Code.*

To fill in this dedication clause, insert the 501(c)(3) tax exempt purpose of your group in each blank (specify *charitable, educational, literary, religious* or *scientific*).

Optional 501(c)(3) Tax Exemption Language

Now let's look at optional federal tax exemption language which is commonly included in nonprofit Articles. If there is space, we suggest you include these provisions in your Articles. Note that many secretaries allow you to expand the portion of the Articles set aside for additional provisions by attaching a typewritten page to your form. Again, in some states these federal tax exemption provisions are already included on your secretary's sample or printed form.

Limitation on Political Activities   The following clause shows that your nonprofit group will comply with the 501(c)(3) limitation on political activities as discussed in Chapter 3, Section D3.

> *No substantial part of the activities of this corporation shall consist of carrying on propaganda, or otherwise attempting to influence legislation [except as otherwise provided by Section 501(h) of the Internal Revenue Code], and this corporation shall not participate in, or intervene in (including the publishing or distribution of statements), any political campaign on behalf of, or in opposition to, any candidate for public office.*

Limitation on Private Inurement (Private Benefits)   Below is standard IRS-approved language prohibiting private inurement. Generally, this term means providing private or personal benefits to individuals associated with the nonprofit corporation, such as directors, officers, employees, etc., as discussed Chapter 3, Section D2. The last portion of this clause indicates that reasonable compensation for services rendered is allowed under federal tax law.

No part of the net earnings of this corporation shall inure to the benefit of, or be distributable to, its members, directors, officers, or other private persons, except that this corporation shall be authorized and empowered to pay reasonable compensation for services rendered and to make payments and distributions in furtherance of the purposes set forth in these Articles.

General Limitation on Nonprofit Activities The statement below limits the activities of the corporation to those permitted to 501(c)(3) organizations and those allowed to corporations to which contributions are deductible under Section 170(c)(2) of the Internal Revenue Code.

Notwithstanding any other provision of these Articles, this corporation shall not carry on any other activities not permitted to be carried on (1) by a corporation exempt from federal income tax under Section 501(c)(3) of the Internal Revenue Code or (2) by a corporation contributions to which are deductible under Section 170(c)(2) of the Internal Revenue Code.

For a discussion of the deductibility of charitable contributions made to 501(c)(3) organizations, see Chapter 4.

Private Foundation Restrictions The following language relates to technical aspects of the 501(c)(3) tax exemption and states that the corporation will comply with all the operating restrictions that apply to private foundations if the corporation is classified as a private foundation by the IRS. You do not need to include this language in your Articles.[7] We mention it only because it may appear in the official form promulgated by your secretary of state.

In any taxable year in which this corporation is a private foundation as described in Section 509(a) of the Internal Revenue Code, the corporation 1) shall distribute its income for said period at such time and manner as not to subject it to tax under Section 4942 of the Internal Revenue Code; 2) shall not engage in any act of self-dealing as defined in Section 4941(d) of the Internal Revenue Code; 3) shall not retain any excess business holdings as defined in Section 4943(c) of the Internal Revenue Code; 4) shall not make any investments in such manner as to subject the corporation to tax under Section 4944 of the Internal Revenue Code; and 5) shall not make any taxable expenditures as defined in Section 4945(d) of the Internal Revenue Code.

Customizing Your Articles

Although the standard Articles discussed in this chapter and included in your secretary of state form will be sufficient for most incorporators, some may wish to adopt special operating rules or provisions. Although it is preferable to include these special rules in the Bylaws (which can be adopted and changed with relative ease), some special provisions must under state law be included in the Articles to be effective. For example, the following types of provisions, if adopted by the corporation, must often be included in the Articles:

- establishing different classes of membership (such as voting and non-voting members);
- allowing specific members of the board to be designated by individuals rather than elected by the board or voting membership;
- requiring a super-majority vote (such as 2/3 or 3/4) of directors or members for the approval of certain matters;
- providing for special indemnification or immunity for directors and officers.

Your state materials may indicate any special provisions that must be included in the Articles to be effective.

For a discussion of private foundation and public charity tax status, see Chapter 4.

Sample Completed Articles

We've covered a lot of ground in the individual sample Articles and explanations above. To help you tie all this information together, we include a sample completed form below together with our comments (which appear in boldface type).

ARTICLES OF INCORPORATION
of
The Bluegrass Music Society of the Appalachians, Inc.
A Nonprofit Corporation

Pursuant to the provision of the Nonprofit Corporation Act of this state, the undersigned incorporators hereby adopt the following Articles of Incorporation:

ARTICLE 1

The name of this corporation is: *The Bluegrass Music Society of the Appalachians, Inc.*

ARTICLE 2

The name and address of the registered agent and registered office of this corporation is: *Name of one of the initial directors, address of corporation.*

ARTICLE 3

The purposes for which this corporation is organized are: *To establish a musical society open to the general public to foster an appreciation of the American bluegrass music, through lectures, seminars, study groups, public and classroom performances, exhibits and any and all other appropriate means.* [**this is a statement of specific purposes requested by the secretary of state**]

This corporation is organized exclusively for one or more of the purposes as specified in Section 501(c)(3) of the Internal Revenue Code, including, for such purposes, the making of distributions to organizations that qualify as exempt organizations under section 501(c)(3) of the Internal Revenue Code, or corresponding section of any future federal tax code. [**this is a statement of tax exempt purposes required under IRC Section 501(c)(3)**]

ARTICLE 4

The number of initial directors of this corporation shall be *three* and the names and addresses of the initial directors are as follows:
Names and addresses of three initial directors

ARTICLE 5

The name and address of the incorporators of this corporation are:
Name and address of one of the initial Directors listed above

ARTICLE 6

The period of the duration of this corporation is: *perpetual.*

ARTICLE 7

The classes, rights, privileges, qualifications, and obligations of members of this corporation are as follows:

As stated in the Bylaws of this corporation

ARTICLE 8

Additional provisions (attach separate page if necessary):

Upon the dissolution of this corporation, its assets remaining after payment, or provision for payment, of all debts and liabilities of this corporation shall be distributed for one or more exempt purposes within the meaning of Section 501(c)(3) of the Internal Revenue Code or shall be distributed to the federal government, or to a state or local government, for a public purpose. **[this is the dedication of assets statement required under IRC Section 501(c)(3)]**

No substantial part of the activities of this corporation shall consist of carrying on propaganda, or otherwise attempting to influence legislation [except as otherwise provided by Section 501(h) of the Internal Revenue Code], and this corporation shall not participate in, or intervene in (including the publishing or distribution of statements), any political campaign on behalf of, or in opposition to, any candidate for public office. **[this is the optional limitation on political activities statement under IRC Section 501(c)(3)]**

No part of the net earnings of this corporation shall inure to the benefit of, or be distributable to, its members, directors, officers, or other private persons, except that this corporation shall be authorized and empowered to pay reasonable compensation for services rendered and to make payments and distributions in furtherance of the purposes set forth in these Articles. **[this is the optional limitation on private inurement statement under IRC Section 501(c)(3)]**

Notwithstanding any other provision of these Articles, this corporation shall not carry on any other activities not permitted to be carried on (1) by a corporation exempt from federal income tax under Section 501(c)(3) of the Internal Revenue Code or (2) by a corporation contributions to which are deductible under Section 170(c)(2) of the Internal Revenue Code. **[this is the optional general limitation on activities statement under IRC Section 501(c)(3)]**

The undersigned incorporators hereby declare under penalty of perjury that the statements made in the foregoing Articles of Incorporation are true.

Dated: _____

(signature of incorporator) _____

[Normally, the incorporator(s) must sign the Articles. Some states require initial directors, if named in Articles, to sign instead. If notarization is required, the signature(s) must be given in presence of notary.]

Name and Address of Incorporator:

_____

(signature) _____

Step 4. File Your Articles of Incorporation

File your Articles with your secretary of state following the instructions in your secretary of state materials. Filing is usually done by mail, although many offices will accept Articles in person.

In the Appendix we include a tear-out Articles filing letter you may wish to use (or modify) to submit your Articles of Incorporation to the secretary of state. Complete the tear-out form following the sample form and special instructions below.

Sample Articles Filing Letter

Address of Incorporator ①
Date

Corporate Filings Office
Secretary of State address

Corporate Filings:

I enclose an original and (number) ② copies of the proposed Articles of Incorporation of (name of corporation) .

Please file the Articles of Incorporation and return a Certificate of Incorporation (or file-stamped copy of the original Articles) to me at the above address.

A check/money order in the amount of $_____,③ made payable to your office, for total filing and processing fees is enclosed.

The above corporate name was reserved for my use pursuant to reservation # _____, issued on _____.④

Sincerely,

 (signature of incorporator)   ①
(typed name), Incorporator

Special Instructions

① A person who signs your Articles should prepare and sign this cover letter.

Note If you have reserved a corporate name, the person who reserved the corporate name should prepare and sign this letter, since the corporate name will be reserved for this person's use.

② In some states, you need only submit an original of the Articles—the secretary will file the original and send you a Certificate of Incorporation as proof of filing. In other states, you need to submit the original and one or more copies. The secretary will file the original and file-stamp and return one or more copies to you. In some states, an additional fee is charged for submitting more than one copy of your Articles for file-stamping. One copy should be sufficient—you can make copies of this file-stamped copy to send to financial institutions, grant agencies and others when necessary as proof of your incorporation.

③ Include a check for the total fees, made payable to the "Secretary of State" or other official title of the office that files Articles in your state. Check your secretary of state instructions carefully here to make sure your total fee payment is correct.

④ If you have reserved your corporate name, fill in the blanks here to show the certificate number and/or date of issuance of your reservation of corporate name. In some states, the secretary simply sends you a file-stamped copy of your reservation letter—if so, just show the file-stamped date on the letter in the second blank.

Your next step is to wait. The secretary of state will make sure your corporate name is available for use and that your Articles conform to law. If there are no problems, the secretary of state will mail you a Certificate of Incorporation (or file-stamped copy of your Articles). If there are any problems with your Articles, the secretary of state will usually return your Articles, indicating the items that need correction. Often the problem is technical, not substantive, and easy to fix. If the problem is more complicated (such as an improper or insufficient corporate purpose clause), you may be able to solve the problem by re-reading our examples and suggestions for completing the Articles. If you get stuck, you will need to do a little research or obtain further help from a nonprofit lawyer with experience in drafting and filing nonprofit Articles (see Chapter 11).

Congratulations! Once your Articles are filed, your organization is a legally recognized nonprofit corporation. Before rushing out to pursue your nonprofit objectives, we want to issue a few words of caution:

Whenever you sign a document, agreement, application or other financial or legal form on behalf of your corporation, be certain to do so in the following manner:

> *(name of corporation)* _____
>
> By   *(signature)* _____
>
> *(corporate title, e.g., director, president, staff position, etc.)*

If you fail to sign documents on behalf of the corporation in your capacity as a corporate director, officer, employee, etc., you are leaving yourself open to possible personal liability for corporate obligations. This is but one example designed to illustrate a basic premise of corporate life: From now on, it is extremely important for you to maintain the distinction between the corporation which you've organized and yourself. As we've said, the corporation is a separate legal "person" and you want to make sure that other organizations, businesses, the IRS and the courts respect this distinction.

Until you obtain your federal 501(c)(3) tax exemption and public charity status, your corporation will be unable to receive most public and private grant funds and will be unable to assure donors of the deductibility (for federal tax purposes) of contributions made to the corporation. Therefore, make sure to follow through with the procedures contained in the succeeding chapters—doing so is vital to the success of your new corporation.

Notes

1 Philharmonic is a musical term denoting the standard pitch of 440 cycles specifically, and an appreciation for music generally.

2 It is also possible to get ownership of a name by first registering it with the U.S. Patent and Trademark Office and then actually using it, provided that no one else actually used the name before your registration date. An assumed corporate name is one different from the name stated in an organization's articles—see Chapter 5 for further information.

3 An assumed corporate name is different from the name stated in an organization's Articles.

4 The six month period may be extended for additional six months periods (at a fee of $100 for each extension), for a total additional time of two and one half years . To obtain these extensions, you have to convince the Patent and Trademark Office that you have good cause for delaying your actual use of the name in interstate commerce.

5 California combines its statutory authority clause with its purpose clause. Note that California law places nonprofit corporations into one of three special classifications and requires a designation of the type of nonprofit being formed in the articles (the example applies to a California nonprofit public benefit corporation). We discuss purpose clauses and these special classifications of nonprofit corporations later in this section. Specific forms and instructions for forming a California nonprofit corporation are contained in *The California Nonprofit Corporation Handbook* by Mancuso (Nolo Press). If you are incorporating in California, use this more specialized book (a full refund is available from Nolo if you purchased this book by mistake).

6 IRS Revenue Procedure 82-2 lists the following states where a dedication of assets clause is not required in the articles: Arkansas, California, Louisiana, Massachusetts, Minnesota, Missouri, Ohio and Oklahoma. To avoid a delay in processing of your federal exemption application and to avoid problems that may arise if your state statutes change, we suggest you include a dedication of assets clause in your articles regardless of the state where you incorporate.

7 This language is only required to be included in the articles of a nonprofit 501(c)(3) private foundation formed in Arizona and New Mexico—see Revenue Ruling 75-38 (Volume 1975-1, IRS Cumulative Bulletin, page 161). Since you will wish your nonprofit corporation to be classified as a 501(c)(3) public charity, not as a private foundation, you have no need to include this language in your articles, no matter where you incorporate.

Prepare Your Bylaws

COMPANION COMPUTER DISK
FOR NONPROFIT INCORPORATORS

Included at the back of this book is a 3¹/₂" PC/MS DOS Nonprofit Corporation Computer Disk containing files for the tear-out incorporation forms
included in this book. These files are provided in standard file formats that
can be read into, completed, and printed with your PC wordprocessing
program. For specific instructions for using the forms on the disk, see the
README.TXT file included on the disk (insert the disk in your A: drive and
use the TYPE A:README.TXT or MORE <A:README.TXT command at the
DOS prompt to view this file on the screen).

Why Not Having Members Makes Sense

Here are some reasons why most nonprofit incorporators prefer a nonmembership corporation:

- Setting up a formal membership with voting rights dilutes directorship control over corporate operations.

- It isn't always easy to expel a member. State law may require that members only be expelled for good cause following a formal hearing.

- Non-membership groups can still receive support from subscribers, sponsors, patrons, friends, benefactors, etc. You can offer discounts or other benefits to outsiders who participate in the activities and programs of the corporation without giving them a legal right to participate in the management and other affairs of the corporation.

  Note: In some states you may even call these outside supporters "members" of the corporation without running the risk of entitling these persons to voting and other legal membership rights in the corporation. Nonetheless, to be safe and to avoid confusion and controversy later on, we suggest you use another term for persons who will not be legal members of your corporation but who will otherwise contribute to or participate in corporate affairs and activities.

Step 5. Prepare Your Bylaws

Your next step is to prepare your Bylaws. This document is, for all practical purposes, your corporation's internal affairs manual and contains the rules and procedures for holding meetings, electing directors and officers, and taking care of other essential corporate formalities. Before discussing specific bylaw provisions, let's look at an issue that is central to the preparation of your Bylaws: whether to adopt a membership structure for your nonprofit corporation.

A. Choose a Membership or Nonmembership Structure

Before deciding on whether to adopt a formal membership structure for your corporation, please review the discussion of membership rights and obligations in Chapters 1 and 2. To recap, members of a nonprofit corporation are given specific legal rights under state law to participate in corporate affairs. Such membership rights typically include the right to:

- vote for the election of the board of directors;

- approve changes to the Articles or Bylaws of the corporation;

- vote for a dissolution of the corporation;

- approve a sale of substantially all of the corporation's assets.

Most smaller groups will probably wish to form a nonmembership corporation. Why? Because a nonmembership corporation is simpler to establish and operate and does not result in the loss of any significant advantages. This is true because most supporters of the corporation aren't normally interested in obtaining the technical legal rights afforded members.

Some groups will conclude that the nature of their activities requires a membership structure. This might be a reasonable decision in the case of a group where a number of people want to formally participate in the legal and administrative affairs of the corporation. Some nonprofits may even decide to have a combination of a legal, voting membership structure together with a larger group of dues-paying supporters.

Example A large botanical society may have one class of formal members who elect the board of directors, as well as an informal group of dues-paying supporters who receive the society's magazine and attend special events sponsored by the society.

If you do decide to adopt a formal membership structure for your nonprofit corporation, we show you how to add basic membership provisions to your tear-out Bylaws in Section D below.

B. Purpose and Scope of Our Tear-Out Bylaws

The Appendix contains a tear-out Bylaws form which is suitable for all types of 501(c)(3) nonprofits, nonmembership and membership groups alike. The provisions contained in this document were drafted to serve the following purposes:

- they contain information central to the organization and operation of your corporation (time, place, date, call, notice and quorum requirements for meetings);

- they restate the most significant provisions applicable to tax-exempt nonprofit corporations, useful for your own reference and necessary to assure the IRS that your corporation is eligible for its tax exemptions;

- they provide a practical, yet formal, set of rules for the orderly operation of your corporation, to resolve disputes, to provide certainty regarding legal procedures, and to ensure at least minimum control over corporate operations.

How We Deal With State Law Differences

As you know, nonprofit corporation laws vary slightly from state to state. The provisions contained in our general-purpose Bylaws will conform to the statutory requirements of most states. In areas where state legal rules do diverge somewhat, our bylaw provisions simply refer to the laws of your state.

Example The indemnification provisions in the tear-out Bylaws illustrate the point. They state that your directors and officers are entitled to indemnification *to the fullest extent permissible under the law of this state.*

If a specific area of nonprofit law or procedure is particularly important to you or your legal advisor, you can easily replace the general-purpose provisions in the tear-out Bylaws with the exact provisions contained in your state's nonprofit corporation code. For a discussion on looking up the law yourself, see Chapter 11.

C. Prepare Your Bylaws

Tear-out Bylaws are contained in the Appendix. Make a photocopy of this tear-out form. Fill in the blanks on the form as you follow the instructions below. Instructions are provided for Bylaws containing blanks or for special bylaw provisions which warrant a further explanation.

Membership Provisions   There are certain provisions in the Bylaws which refer to "the members, if any," of the corporation or use other language making certain provisions applicable to the corporation only if the corporation has members. These provisions have no effect for nonmembership corporations using these Bylaws—they simply allow membership corporations to add membership provisions to the tear-out Bylaws as explained in Section D below.

Heading

Type the name of your corporation.

Article I, Section 1. Principal Office

Type the name of the county and state where the corporation's principal office is located—this is the corporate office where you will keep a copy of your Bylaws, records of meetings and other formal corporate records mentioned in various bylaw provisions. Customarily, the principal office designated here will be the same as the legal office of the corporation (the address specified in the Articles as the registered office of the corporation where legal papers must be served on the corporation).

Note   The blanks at the end of the Section 2 (Change of Address) should not be filled in at this time. Use these blanks later to change the principal office of the corporation to another location, within the same county, by showing the new address and date of the address change.

Article 2, Section 1. IRC Section 501(c)(3) Purposes

This section contains a standard statement of 501(c)(3) tax-exempt purposes (similar to the tax-exempt purpose clause discussed earlier for the Articles of Incorporation). We include this statement in the Bylaws to remind the IRS that your corporation is organized exclusively for a bona-fide 501(c)(3) purpose.

Should You Consult a Nonprofit Professional

The primary practical benefit of adopting the rules contained in the tear-out Bylaws is for the incorporators to arrive at a good, workable consensus regarding the ground rules of the corporation. However, these Bylaws may not meet all your needs or you may have questions about one or more of them. If so, check the provisions in our tear-out form against your state's nonprofit statutes or have them reviewed and customized by a lawyer with nonprofit experience.

Article 2, Section 2. Specific Objectives and Purposes

Use the space provided here to state the specific tax-exempt objectives and purposes of your nonprofit corporation. If you included a statement of specific purposes in your Articles of Incorporation, it should have been brief. Here you can go into as much detail as you want, describing the specific purposes and activities of your corporation. We suggest you list the major purposes and activities of your nonprofit organization, showing your nonprofit goals and the means by which you plan to achieve them. This is not only a useful exercise to help define and clarify your nonprofit objectives—this statement will also be helpful in giving the IRS additional information regarding the tax-exempt purposes and activities of your corporation.

Sample Response for a Dance Group

Here's an example of an expanded list of objectives and purposes which might be used by an educational-purpose, nonprofit dance group. It is illustrative of a large number of 501(c)(3) nonprofit corporations which will derive tax-exempt revenue primarily from the performance of services related to their exempt purposes, rather than from grants, contributions, etc.

SECTION 2. SPECIFIC OBJECTIVES AND PURPOSES

The specific objectives and purposes of this corporation shall be:

(a) to provide instruction in dance forms such as jazz, ballet, tap, and modern dance;

(b) to provide instruction in body movement and relaxation art forms such as tumbling, tai-chi and yoga;

(c) to give public performances in dance forms and creative dramatics;

(d) to sponsor special events involving the public performance of any or all of the above art forms as well as other performing arts by the corporation's performing troupe as well as by other community performing arts groups; and

(e) to directly engage in and to provide facilities for others to engage in the promotion of the arts, generally.

Making Modifications to the Tear-Out Bylaws

In the text, we discussed various reasons why some groups may wish to insert specific statutory rules from their state's nonprofit corporation law in the tear-out Bylaws. There are many good reasons why groups may wish to customize their Bylaws to add special language or provisions. Here are two examples:

If your 501(c)(3) nonprofit activities will consist of operating a formal "school," you will need to add an article to the Bylaws containing an IRS "nondiscriminatory policy statement." For information on the applicability of this statement to your group, see Chapter 3.

If your nonprofit corporation plans to receive federal or other public grants or monies, some funding agencies may require that you include special provisions in your Bylaws which state that no member of the board, officer or other person exercising supervisory power in the corporation or any of their close relatives can be individually benefited from the receipt of grant funds.[1] Generally, provisions of this sort are meant to prohibit board members, officers (President, Vice President, Secretary, Treasurer) and their families from being paid from, or directly benefited by, grant monies given to the organization.

Sample Response for a Nonprofit Book Festival

Here's a completed statement of specific objectives and purposes for a nonprofit educational purpose group that sponsors a book fair and promotes book reading and publishing in the local community.

SECTION 2. SPECIFIC OBJECTIVES AND PURPOSES

The specific objectives and purposes of this corporation shall be:

(a) to sponsor an annual book fair with an emphasis on exhibiting books created and published in our community;

(b) to sponsor other informational events open to the public which focus on books;

(c) to educate the public concerning our community's contributions to book creation, publication and distribution;

(d) generally, through educative and other efforts, to help make books and reading as inviting and accessible to as broad an audience as possible;

(e) to engage in other activities related to educating the public about book writing, publishing and distribution in our community.

Sample Response for a Women's Health Information Resource Center

Here's a completed statement for a women's health group.

SECTION 2. SPECIFIC OBJECTIVES AND PURPOSES

The specific objectives and purposes of this corporation shall be:

(a) to maintain a women's health library open to the public containing books, Articles and other material related to women's health issues;

(b) to maintain a physicians referral listing containing patient evaluations of physicians practicing in the community;

(c) to sponsor seminars and workshops open to the general public where ideas, opinions and writings relating to women's health issues and health concerns may be expressed and shared with others;

(d) to publish a monthly newsletter containing Articles informative of women's health issues;

(e) to engage in other activities related to educating the public concerning women's health issues and health concerns.

*Sample Response for an Environmental Conservation
and Protection Organization*

Here's a sample for an environmental group.

SECTION 2. SPECIFIC OBJECTIVES AND PURPOSES

The specific objectives and purposes of this corporation shall be:

(a) to educate the public concerning the necessity of preserving the nation's wetlands;

(b) to publish a newsletter which focuses on information related to wetlands preservation efforts and developments;

(c) to sponsor seminars and other educational events where community and environmental leaders, governmental, and organizational representatives, and other concerned members of the public and government may meet to exchange ideas, suggest solutions, and implement strategies to protect the nation's wetlands;

(d) to meet with governmental representatives; report to governmental committees, agencies and boards; and generally to attempt to help local, state and federal lawmakers establish enforceable legislation to help protect wetland areas;

(e) to expand and re-define our educational and environmental program from time to time as necessary to meet the continuing challenge of protecting the nation's wetland resources.

Sample Response for a Private College

Here's a completed statement for a private school.

SECTION 2. SPECIFIC OBJECTIVES AND PURPOSES

The specific objectives and purposes of this corporation shall be:

(a) to establish a private university, licensed by the state and accredited by a recognized regional accreditation organization;

(b) to maintain a regularly enrolled student body, an established curriculum and a full-time faculty;

(c) to participate in federal and state student loan and other student educational and financial incentive programs;

(d) to have the normal functions, operations, programs and pursuits incidental to a fully recognized and operational nonprofit center of learning and higher education.

A Suggestion   The last item in each of the above examples contains a clause which authorizes the corporation to engage in activities necessary or incidental to its main purposes and pursuits. We suggest you use similar language to allow your corporation to engage in activities related to its specific objectives and purposes.

Article 3, Section 1. Number of Directors

Insert the total number of directors who will serve on your board. Make sure the number of directors you specify here is equal to or greater than the minimum number required in your state as shown under the director qualifications heading in the Articles of Incorporation section on your State Sheet. Also, consider how many directors you will need to efficiently run your nonprofit corporation. We discuss this point further in Chapter 2.

Often, the number shown here will be the same as the number of initial directors specified in your Articles (if initial directors are listed in the Articles). However, you may state a greater number at this time if you wish to allow additional directors to be elected to your board.

Article 3, Section 2. Qualifications for Directors

Note that our Bylaws provide that directors must be of the age of majority in your state. Although not a legal requirement in every state, we think this is a sensible provision to avoid legal problems which can occur if minors conduct or manage business.

If the director qualifications information on your State Sheet indicates that any additional requirement applies to directors, such as a state residency requirement, insert the requirement in the space provided in this bylaw.

Unless required in your state, we suggest that you not add additional qualifications to limit the makeup of your board to a particular group individuals (for example, to educators or enrolled students of a school or to parents of children who attend a nonprofit day care center). The IRS likes to see various segments of the community represented on the board of a 501(c)(3) tax-exempt group, not just a select group with a singular nonprofit perspective or interest.

Instead of imposing a blanket qualification requirement on all board positions, it often does make sense to allocate a certain number of director positions to specific groups of individuals. This type of "selective diversity" is, in fact, encouraged by the IRS.

Sample Response

A nonprofit hospital wishes to set aside three board positions to physicians, three to health care administrators and three to community representatives. This section of the Bylaws is completed as follows:

SECTION 2. QUALIFICATIONS

Directors shall be of the age of majority in this state. Other qualifications for directors of this corporation shall be as follows:

Three board positions shall be filled by licensed physicians in private practice in Jefferson County; three board positions shall be filled by health care administrators of nonprofit hospitals in Jefferson County; three board positions shall be filled by representatives of the Jefferson County community who are not health care professionals.

Article 3, Section 5. Term of Office of Directors

Indicate the length of the term of office for directors in this blank.

We show the state requirements for directors' terms on the State Sheets. Many states require a one-year term for directors. A number of states allow longer terms. Others require an annual meeting for the election of directors only in the absence of a provision specifying a longer term of office in the corporation's Articles or Bylaws.

Although it is common for nonprofit Bylaws to provide for a one-year term of office for directors, you may wish (if permitted by your state statutes) to lengthen this period. By doing so, you increase the chances of assembling a seasoned board with practical experience in dealing effectively with corporate affairs. The first year or so for most nonprofit directors is an acclimation or initiation period, providing insight into nonprofit programs, problems and the decision-making process generally—the later years of nonprofit service are usually the most productive ones for any board member. Note also that while a single term may be limited to one year, a director may serve many consecutive one-year terms.

Sample Responses

> *Each director shall hold office for a period of <u>one year</u> and until his or her successor is elected and qualifies.*
>
> *Each director shall hold office for a period of <u>three years</u> and until his or her successor is elected and qualifies.*

Customizing Director Provisions   Some nonprofits with larger boards or other special requirements may wish to draft their own term of office or board election provisions. For example, some may wish to provide for a staggered board where only a portion of the full board is elected each term to guarantee that there will always be a majority of experienced members. Or some may want to allow certain members of the board to be appointed by specified individuals or organizations (such as a city council, board of directors of a hospital or a committee of an environmental organization). There are other possibilities as well. For example, you may wish to provide that a director can only serve two or three consecutive terms so as to bring in new directors periodically.

Are Staggered Boards Allowed In Your State?

The nonprofit laws of some states specifically allow staggered boards. In addition, staggered boards are allowable in a number of states whose nonprofit statutes are silent on this issue (for example, in states whose statutes only specify particular terms of office for directors). However, in states that are silent on this point and whose statutes specify that all directors must be elected at an annual (or other periodic) meeting for the election of directors, staggered boards may not be valid since the statutes can be read to require that all board members be elected at one time. Check with a nonprofit lawyer if you wish to authorize a staggered board and have a question regarding your state's statute on directors' terms of office.

In all cases, we suggest that you check your nonprofit corporation law to determine if the alternate provisions are permitted by your state's statutes.

Sample Staggered Board Provision

Here's an example of a substitute bylaw that provides for the election of a staggered board. A corporation with a twelve-person board, for instance, could use this provision to elect four directors each year:

> *Each year, one-third* [or some other percentage or number] *of the authorized number of directors shall be elected to serve on the board of directors. Each director shall hold office until his or her successor is elected and qualifies.*

The above provision can be used to elect a portion of the board each term. Of course, more complicated schemes are possible with different classes of directors serving for different lengths of time.

By the way, how do you tell which members of the initial board should first be selected to serve staggered terms? Here's one idea (simply a fancy way of saying that the corporate secretary can draw straws to make this selection):

> *If, at a meeting for the election of directors, more than one group of initial board members may be elected to serve for a first staggered term of office, then the Secretary of the corporation shall assign each director to a numbered group and shall make a chance selection between or among the numbered groups (by selecting among numbered lots or by some other chance selection procedure). The group corresponding to the number so chosen shall be subject to election to a staggered term at the meeting.*

Article 3, Section 6. Director Compensation

As we've said, nonprofit directors customarily serve without compensation since the IRS will probably view substantial payments to directors for performing director duties as instances of prohibited private inurement. This is the wise approach. This bylaw section, however, does allow the corporation to pay directors a reasonable fee for attending meetings as well as reasonable advancement or reimbursement for expenses incurred in performing director duties. In practice, many nonprofits do not pay directors even these lesser amounts except to reimburse directors who must travel a long distance to attend board meetings. However, some nonprofits may authorize minimal payments as incentives to individuals for serving on the board.

Article 3, Section 8. Regular Board Meetings

In the blanks in the first paragraph, specify the date(s) and time(s) when regular meetings of the board will be held. Many nonprofits with active agendas hold regular board meetings on a monthly or more frequent basis. Smaller or less active organizations may schedule a regular board meeting less frequently (quarterly, semi-annually, or even annually) and call special meetings during the year to take care of specific items of business.

We recommend that you use this bylaw provision to schedule regular board meetings on at least a monthly basis. The majority of nonprofit corporations, whether large, mid-sized or small, should keep their boards busy managing corporate projects and programs; setting up, supervising and hearing back from a number of corporate committees; and just generally taking care of business on an ongoing basis. And remember, to help avoid personal liability for management decisions, each board member should be able to show that she is as fully informed of, and actively involved in, corporate business as possible. Corporate records showing director attendance at, and participation in, regular meetings of the board are an excellent way of indicating that your directors meet this standard of corporate conduct.

Sample Response

> *Regular meetings of Directors shall be held on the second Tuesday of each month at 7:30 P.M.*

In the second paragraph of this section, nonmembership nonprofits should fill in the blank to indicate which one of the regular board meetings will be specified for election (or re-election) of corporate directors.

Membership Note The provisions in the second paragraph of this section only take effect for nonmembership corporations—membership corporations can leave this item blank since they will add provisions to their Bylaws which specify that the members, not the directors, elect directors of the corporation.

Note that in a nonmembership corporation, the directors vote for their own re-election or replacement. The frequency of this regular meeting to elect directors depends upon their term of office. If it is one year, then one regular meeting per year will be designated for election of the board. Likewise, if you have specified a three-year term for directors, then one regular meeting every third year will be designated as the meeting to elect directors. Under the terms of this bylaw, each director casts one vote for each candidate (up to the number of candidates to be elected) and the candidates receiving the highest number of votes are elected.

Sample Responses for Different Director Terms of Office

Directors elected annually:
If this corporation makes no provision for members, then, at the regular meeting of directors held on <u>*January 1st of each year*</u>*, directors shall be elected by the Board of Directors. Voting for the election of directors shall be by written ballot. Each director shall cast one vote per candidate, and may vote for as many candidates as the number of candidates to be elected to the board. The candidates receiving the highest number of votes up to the number of directors to be elected shall be elected to serve on the board.*

Directors elected every three years:
If this corporation makes no provision for members, then, at the regular meeting of directors held on <u>*the first Friday of July every third year*</u>*, directors shall be elected by the Board of Directors....*

Example Your nonprofit board consists of 15 members. The names of 20 candidates to the board are placed in nomination at the beginning of the regular meeting for election of the board. Pursuant to this bylaw provision, each director casts one vote for 15 (of the 20) candidates. The 15 candidates receiving the highest number of votes are elected to the board. Of course in smaller nonmembership nonprofits it's common to hold uncontested elections in which each director simply places himself in nomination and the board votes itself in for another term.

State Law Note If you wish to add special nomination, balloting or other director election procedures to your Bylaws in place of this standard provision, check your nonprofit statutes before doing so (look for a section heading entitled "Election of Directors").

Article 3, Section 10. Notice of Board Meetings

Section (a) of this Bylaw dispenses with notice of all regular meetings of directors (this includes the regular meeting for the election of directors). This is a standard provision codified in the nonprofit statutes of most states. It is assumed that directors will keep track of, and attend, regular meetings, once they have been given the schedule. As a practical matter, you may wish to call and remind less active directors of all upcoming meetings of the board.

Section (b) requires that the date, time, place and purpose of special director meetings be communicated to each director at least one week in advance. Our bylaw specifies that notice may be given in person, by mail, by telephone or fax machine. Since fax messages may go unnoticed or unread (or occasionally be eaten by the machine), they must be acknowledged by a return fax or telephone call within twenty-four hours.

Section (c) allows the corporation to obtain a written consent from a director prior to or after a meeting. Written consents and waivers of this sort are specifically authorized under the nonprofit statutes of many states and are a good way to ensure that a director is informed of the meeting. Also, this avoids having to worry about complying with any special statutory rules that may exist for calling, noticing or holding the meeting. If a director consents in writing to the meeting, she cannot register a protest later for a failure of the corporation to comply with a formality contained in your nonprofit corporation code.

Customization Note We think these are reasonable notification provisions which keep all directors informed of special business while eliminating pre-meeting preliminaries and delays for all regular meetings. You may wish to adopt provisions that match exactly any special requirements in your state or you may wish to customize these provisions to suit your own needs or circumstances. For example, you may wish to mail written notice and agendas of all regular and special board meetings to each director one week prior to the meeting date.

Article 3, Section 11. Quorum for Board Meetings

Indicate the percentage of the full board (or the number of directors) who must be present at a directors' meeting to constitute a quorum so that business can be conducted. The percentage or number shown here must be at least equal to any minimum quorum rule for directors established in your state. State director quorum requirements are listed on the State Sheets.

Sample Responses

Quorum Specified as Percentage of Full Board:
A quorum shall consist of <u>a majority</u> of the members of the Board of Directors.

Quorum Specified as Number of Directors:
A quorum shall consist of <u>three</u> of the members of the Board of Directors.

Most corporations specify a majority of the board as the director quorum requirement here, even if state law allows a smaller percentage or number of directors to be specified. Of course, you can set a larger quorum requirement if you wish. Whatever you decide, you should realize that this section of the Bylaws concerns a quorum, not a vote requirement. Under the provisions of the next section in the Bylaws, normal board action can be taken by a majority of directors at a meeting at which a quorum is present.

Example If a six-director corporation requires a majority quorum and a meeting is held at which a minimum quorum (four) is present, action can be taken by the vote of three directors, a majority of those present at the meeting.

Article 3, Section 13. Conduct of Board Meetings

Use this blank to specify the rules of order which will be used at directors' meetings. Some larger nonprofits will wish to specify Roberts' Rules of Order (major editions change every 10 years or so) here but you may indicate any set of procedures for proposing, approving, and tabling motions that you wish. If you will have a small informal board, you may wish to leave this line blank if you see no need to specify formal procedures for introducing and discussing items of business at board meetings or you may wish to specify "such procedures as may be approved from time to time by the board of directors" in this blank to allow your board to develop its own set of procedures for the conduct of meetings.

Article 4, Section 1. Designation of Officers

This section provides for the four standard officer positions of President, Vice President, Secretary and Treasurer and allows the board to designate and fill other corporate officers positions as needed. In most nonprofits, directors are appointed to serve as the unpaid officers of the corporation. The officers, in turn, oversee the salaried staff. For a list of the formal duties and responsibilities associated with each officer position, see Sections 6 through 9 of this article in the tear-out form.

In most states, one or more corporate officer positions cannot be filled by the same person. Commonly, the same person cannot serve as both the corporate President and corporate Secretary. The State Sheets include the rules for filling officer positions in your state.

Even if you set up a small nonprofit run by just a few individuals, it is customary to fill these four primary officer slots. You will elect officers when you hold your first meeting of directors. Under this bylaw provision, your board may designate and fill other officer titles and positions whenever it wishes to do so.

Article 5, Section 1. Executive Committee of the Board

This section allows the board to appoint an executive committee of directors to make management decisions for the corporation. If you wish to use this provision, insert the number of directors who will serve on this committee. Note that this provision requires that the designation of an executive committee be approved by a majority of directors.

The State Sheets list the number of directors required on an executive committee and lists the major corporate actions which cannot be taken by the executive committee, typically the amendment of Articles or Bylaws or the approval of director compensation. Full board approval (and, when appropriate, membership approval) must be obtained for these larger corporate decisions.

While we do not necessarily recommend that board authority be delegated, the establishment of an executive committee of directors may be advisable in certain nonprofits where action must routinely be taken in between formal board meetings or where distance, time or other constraints sometimes make it difficult to achieve a quorum for board meetings. In all cases, the executive committee should keep Minutes of its meetings and document all formal action. Regular and timely reports of executive committee actions should be presented to the full board.

Under state law and court decisions, less active board members (those who sit on the full board and approve actions taken by the more active executive committee members) can be held personally accountable (and, in extreme cases, personally liable) for executive committee decisions. Mostly, such personal liability can occur if members of the full board are willfully or grossly negligent in carrying out their duties, which includes reasonably monitoring executive committee action.

Article 7, Sections 3 and 4. Director and Member Inspection Rights

These provisions provide for broad director and membership inspection rights of the corporation's properties and financial and corporate records. State law may impose additional inspection rights and obligations (or may allow you to restrict these rights). For the details of any additional inspection provisions which may apply in your state, see your nonprofit corporation law.

Article 7, Section 6. Periodic Report Requirements

In most states, nonprofit corporations must file an annual or other periodic report form with the secretary of state, the attorney general's office, or some other state office or agency, showing the names and addresses of the corporation's directors and officers and other information. Standard corporate financial statements and reports of charitable solicitation programs and finances may also be required.

Special Membership Reports

Your nonprofit corporation act may also require the furnishing of annual corporate financial statements to members. In addition, it may require an annual written report to members detailing specific transactions, such as the making of loans or guarantees to directors or officers. Your state nonprofit law will contain any special membership reporting requirements that apply in your state.

The Bylaws section of the State Sheets list the basic corporate report requirements in your state. Your secretary of state materials should contain—or show you how to order—a copy of your state's corporate report form.

Article 8. 501(c)(3) Tax Provisions

The various sections in this article contain language which will help show the IRS and, if applicable, your state revenue or tax department, that you qualify for tax-exempt status. Here is a short discussion of the purpose of each section:

- Section 1 contains specific and general limitations on your nonprofit activities. The first paragraph indicates that you will comply with the specific 501(c)(3) prohibitions against substantial lobbying activities and involvement with political campaigns for public candidates [the reference to IRC Section 501(h) is a reminder that you may elect to fall under the alternative political expenditures test available to 501(c)(3) public charities—see Chapter 3, Section D3]. The second paragraph limits the activities of the corporation, generally, to those permitted to 501(c)(3) organizations and to organizations that qualify for tax deductible charitable contributions [under IRC §170(c)(2)].

- Section 2 restates the 501(c)(3) prohibition against private inurement (against benefiting individuals associated with the nonprofit organization). Payments made to individuals as reasonable compensation for services rendered and to further the tax-exempt purposes of the group are specifically authorized.

- Section 3 irrevocably dedicates the assets of the organization to another 501(c)(3) group or to a governmental office or agency for a public purpose. The last sentence is a reminder that any such distribution of assets must be accomplished in accordance with state law.

- Section 4 contains technical language restating the requirements applicable to 501(c)(3) organizations classified as private foundations. These provisions state that for any year the corporation is classified as a 501(c)(3) private foundation, it will operate in such a way as to avoid all private foundation excise taxes imposed under various sections of the Internal Revenue Code. Since you will not want to be classified as a private foundation (but, rather, as a public charity), why do we include these provisions in the tear-out Bylaws? Simply to show the IRS that you mean business (in a nonprofit sense of course) and will comply with any and all 501(c)(3) restrictions (whether your organization is classified as a public charity or as a private foundation).

Adoption of Bylaws

Use the Adoption of Bylaws page as the last page of your completed Bylaws. In the blank, specify the number of preceding pages in your Bylaws. Fill in the date and have each of the persons named as initial directors in your Articles sign on a blank line below the first paragraph. If directors were not named in your Articles then have each of your incorporators (the person or persons who signed your Articles) sign here.

D. Prepare Membership Provisions

This section shows how to add membership provisions to the tear-out nonprofit corporation Bylaws prepared in the preceding section.

Note If you have decided to form a nonmembership corporation (as most nonprofits will), this section does not apply to you and you should skip ahead to Chapter 8.

To add membership provisions to your Bylaws, fill in the blanks in the tear-out membership provisions in the Appendix, following the instructions below.

Heading

Type the name of your corporation in this blank.

Article 11. Membership Provisions

The membership provisions start with Article 11 since the basic tear-out Bylaws end with Article 10. You will include these membership provision pages at the end of the tear-out basic bylaw pages as explained below.

Article 11, Section 2. Qualifications of Members

Use this blank to indicate any special qualifications required of members in your corporation. We suggest you do not limit or qualify membership in your corporation unless the qualification is of obvious utility (members must be of the age of majority) or is clearly related to the tax-exempt purposes or activities of your organization.

Example A nonprofit private college decides to limit membership to alumni because the founders wish to confer legal membership power only on those who have attended and completed the educational program. Since any person may enroll in the school, the IRS should have no objection.

Another Example A specialized philanthropic and fundraising newsletter only admits as members persons who can show a few years' prior experience working with or for nonprofit organizations. This selection criterion is intended to select for a membership that is involved in the organization's areas of interest and should be acceptable to the IRS.

Sample Response

 If you do not wish to limit or qualify membership in your corporation, complete this blank as follows:

> *The qualifications for membership in this corporation are as follows:* <u>*Any person is qualified to become a member of this corporation.*</u>

Dues Note Do not use this blank to limit your membership to those who pay membership fees or dues—you will specify any initial and ongoing payments required of members in separate membership provisions as explained below.

Article 11, Section 3. Admission of Members

Most smaller nonprofit corporations do not require formal application for membership in the corporation. A few, however, may do this to determine if prospective members meet the qualification requirements set forth in Article 11, Section 2 as discussed above. Others will use this bylaw to indicate that members must pay an admission fee and/or annual dues prior to acceptance as a member in the corporation.

Note The actual amounts paid by members will be specified in the following sections of this bylaw.

Sample Response

> *Applicants shall be admitted to membership on making application therefor in writing and upon approval of the application by the membership committee of this corporation [and/or] upon payment of the application fee and first annual dues, as specified in the following sections of this bylaw   .*

Article 11, Section 4. Membership Fees and Dues

Use these blanks to authorize or specify any application fee or annual dues charged to members.

> *(a) The following fee shall be charged for making application for membership in the corporation: (state specific admission fee or leave to discretion of board, e.g., "in such amount as may be specified from time to time by resolution of the Board of Directors charged for, and payable with, the application for membership," or, if no fee, type "None")   .*

> *(b) The annual dues payable to the corporation by members shall be   (state amount of annual dues, leave to discretion of board, e.g., "in such amount as may be determined from time to time by resolution of the Board of Directors," or type "None")   .*

Article 11, Section 9. Termination of Membership

The termination of membership provisions here are basic ones. Membership can be terminated voluntarily by a member or by the corporation if the member fails to pay dues. The corporation may also terminate a member for cause if the member is provided written notice and an opportunity to be heard.

State Law Note The statutes and court decisions of your state may contain specific substantive and procedural rules for terminating membership in a nonprofit corporation. If you do need to expel a member, we suggest you do so only after checking the latest annotated nonprofit

Customizing Your Membership Provisions

The statutes of each of the states contain significant differences with respect to membership rules and procedures. In drafting the tear-out membership provisions, we have specified general membership rules which avoid areas subject to significant state differences and provide a skeletal membership structure for your corporation to help you complete your Bylaws and continue with your incorporation process (apply for your tax exemptions, etc.).

Particular areas of customization may be warranted—for example to provide for different classes of membership, proxy voting, special director nomination or selection procedures, additional grounds and procedures for terminating memberships, etc. Drafting extra membership provisions of this sort pursuant to the specific nonprofit statutes in your state will require legal research or a consultation with a nonprofit lawyer.

statutes[2] in your state (look under Membership Provisions in your state's nonprofit corporation act).

Article 12, Section 2. Regular Meetings of Members

In the blanks in the first paragraph of this section, indicate the date and time of the regular meeting of members held to elect the board of directors. Many membership nonprofits will specify an annual meeting to elect the board here. The frequency of this meeting will, of course, depend on the length of the term of office for your directors (see the instructions for Article 3, Section 5 above).

Sample Responses for Different Director Terms of Office

Directors elected annually:
A regular meeting of members shall be held on <u>January 2nd of each year</u>, at <u>1</u> PM, for the purpose of electing directors and transacting other business as may come before the meeting…

Directors elected every three years:
A regular meeting of members shall be held on <u>the first Friday of July every third year</u>, at <u>9</u> AM, for the purpose of electing directors and transacting other business as may come before the meeting…

In the second paragraph, type the date and time of any *additional* regular meetings of members which you wish to schedule. Although we encourage frequent membership meetings, some smaller membership nonprofits may not wish to provide for regular meetings (other than the regular meeting to elect directors as specified in the preceding paragraph of the Bylaws) and will leave these items blank. Others with a more active membership will use these blanks to specify frequent or occasional (e.g., monthly or semi-annual) regular meetings of members.

Note Your nonprofit membership corporation can also call and hold special meetings of members during the year—see the discussion below.

Article 12, Section 3. Special Meetings of Members

This provision allows special meetings of members to be called by the board, the Chairperson of the Board, or the President of the corporation—this represents standard practice (and the standard state rule) for most nonprofits. Your nonprofit corporation law may allow other special meetings to be called by a specified percentage of the membership of the corporation—see your nonprofit corporation law if you wish to allow members to call special meetings (look under "Special Meetings of Members").

Article 12, Section 4. Notice of Members' Meetings

Our notice provisions for members' meetings are, for the most part, standard provisions found in state nonprofit statutes, requiring personal or mailed notice for regular and special membership meetings. If you wish to extend or shorten the notice period (10 to 50 days), dispense with notice for regular meetings or make other changes, check that your language conforms to your state's nonprofit law before making your changes.

As with the director notice provisions, members can waive notice of a meeting in writing—this procedure can come in handy if you don't have time to give formal notice to members of a meeting.

Telephone and Fax Machine Notice Our bylaw permits personal notification by telephone or fax machine. Again, a fax notice must be personally acknowledged by a return fax message or telephone call within twenty four hours.

Article 12, Section 5. Quorum for Members' Meetings

Most smaller nonprofits indicate a majority quorum rule here (a majority of the members must be present to hold a members' meeting). The nonprofit corporation laws of a number of states are flexible on this point and allow the corporation to set its own member meeting quorum requirement. In the absence of a specific provision in the Articles or Bylaws, many states set this quorum requirement at one-tenth of the membership. This is reasonable for larger membership nonprofits whose members are spread over a large geographical area.

See your State Sheet for the specific membership quorum rules in your state.

Sample Response

> *A quorum shall consist of   a majority   of the voting members of the corporation.*

Remember For membership approval at a meeting, the vote of a majority of those present is required (see Article 12, Section 6 of the membership provisions). For example, in a corporation with 50 members and a majority-quorum rule for membership meetings, a quorum for meetings consists of 26 members. If 26 members attend a meeting, action can be approved at the meeting by 14 members, a majority of those present.

Article 12, Section 8. Action By Written Ballot

To make membership provisions more applicable and realistic, we have included this written ballot procedure to allow members to elect directors and transact other membership business by mail. These are standard, workable provisions but may not cover all the technical requirements found in your state's nonprofit statutes.[3] To be certain, check our provisions against the membership written consent or written ballot procedures in your nonprofit code or check with a lawyer.

Article 12, Section 9. Conduct of Members' Meetings

Indicate, if you wish, the sets of rules which will govern the proposing and taking of action at your membership meetings. Roberts' Rules of Order is the standard, of course, but you may specify another set of procedures if you wish or leave this item blank if you see no reason to adopt formal rules for conducting membership meetings.

Completion of Membership Bylaws

Assemble your membership Bylaws by adding the completed membership provision pages to the end of your completed bylaw pages. Then use the Adoption of Bylaws page as the last page of your Bylaws—this page is included as the last page of the tear-out basic Bylaws in the Appendix. Fill in this page according to the Adoption of Bylaws instructions given earlier.

Notes

1   Section 8.13 of the Model Nonprofit Corporation Act contains "disinterested director" provisions that prevent more than 49% of the board (or their relatives) from being paid in a non-director capacity by the corporation. In other words, a majority of the directors cannot also be paid as salaried officers or staff of the nonprofit corporation. If a state adopts this provision of the Model Act (California has done so—see §5227 of the California Nonprofit Corporation Law), the corporation will be bound by this disinterested director rule as a matter of state law. As a reminder to the group, the incorporators in these states may wish to include the appropriate disinterested director language in the bylaws.

2   Annotated codes list the statutes plus any court decisions interpreting and applying the statute. Court decisions which discuss termination of membership provisions can be helpful in showing permissible and impermissible grounds and procedures when expelling a member from a nonprofit organization.

3   Many states authorize membership action by written consent but require the giving of notice to any non-consenting members. If you follow our provisions and mail a written ballot to each member, you should satisfy this notice requirement.

Apply for Your Federal 501(c)(3) Tax Exemption

Now that you've filed your Articles and prepared your Bylaws, it's time to prepare your federal 501(c)(3) tax exemption application. This is a critical step in the formation of your nonprofit organization since most of the real benefits of being a nonprofit flow from 501(c)(3) tax-exempt status. The time and effort devoted to this task will be well worth it.

Remember We assume that your organization is a nonprofit corporation formed for a Section 501(c)(3) religious, educational, charitable, scientific or literary purpose which will qualify for 501(c)(3) public charity status as explained in Chapters 3 and 4.[1]

How Much Time and Effort? The IRS estimates that it takes the average person 4 hours, 41 Minutes to learn about the form and 9 hours, 22 Minutes to prepare and send it to the IRS. Hopefully, by reading and following our line-by-line instructions below, you will accomplish this task in substantially less time.

How to Handle the Technicalities This is not an easy form, particularly for nonprofit corporations that have been in existence for eight months or more—for these groups, a number of questions are quite technical and require attention to the fine print in the specific instructions. So, a suggestion: If you get stuck on a difficult question or run low on energy, take a break and return to this task when you feel better able to follow and absorb this material.

Step 6. Prepare and File Your Federal Tax Exemption Application

You will need the following federal tax forms and publications:

Form 8718	User Fee for Exempt Organization Determination Letter Request
Package 1023	Application for Recognition of Exemption with instructions
Form SS-4	Application for Employer Identification Number
Publication 557	Tax-Exempt Status for Your Organization
Publication 578	Tax Information for Private Foundations and Foundation Managers

Note If you plan to elect the political exepnditures test for your organization as explained in Chapter 3, Section D, also order IRS Form 5768, Election by an Eligible Section 501(c)(3) Organization to Make Expenditures to Influence Legislation.

√ Call your local IRS forms request telephone number (or the national IRS forms and publications request number, 1-800-TAX-FORM) or stop by your local IRS office in person to obtain these forms and publications. If you ordered a Nolo corporate kit (see Chapter 9, Step 8), IRS Form 8718, Form SS-4 and Package 1023 are included as part of your kit.

Preliminary Reading As a first step in preparing your federal tax exemption application, read the General and Specific Instructions to Package 1023 [again, this is the federal 501(c)(3) tax exemption application package]. Also read through the information in IRS Publication 557 before filling out your federal exemption application.

Don't get bogged down in this technical material. The information in this book relating to the requirements for obtaining your federal tax exemption and achieving public charity status, together with the line-by-line instructions below should be enough to get you through. If you need to, you can always refer to the IRS publications and instructions later in responding to particular questions, or to fill out specific schedules.

1023 Schedules and Attachments Form 1023 contains several schedules designed to be used only by certain types of nonprofit corporations (schools, hospitals, etc.). Don't include any schedule with your application unless it specifically applies to you. Some items will require the preparation of an attachment page or pages. Use letter-sized (8 1/2" x 11") paper and make sure each attachment page contains the following information:

- a description of the information on the attachment (specify Form 1023 and identify the part and line item number); and

- the name and address of your corporation.

Example

GoodWorks, Inc.
1220 Buena Vista Avenue
Glendora, California 94567
EIN _____

Attachment To Form 1023
Continuation of Response To Part II, Line 1

Page 1

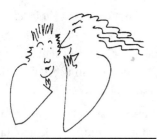

How to Keep Form 1023 Information Confidental

Generally, any information submitted with your 1023 is open to public inspection. However, if any attachment or response to your application contains information regarding trade secrets, patents or other information which would adversely affect your organization if released to the public, you should clearly indicate "NOT SUBJECT TO PUBLIC INSPECTION" next to the material and include your reasons for requesting secrecy. If the IRS agrees, the information will not be open to public inspection.

A. Do You Need to Apply for Your 501(c)(3) Tax Exemption?

Form 1023 serves two purposes:

1. It is used by nonprofit organizations to apply for 501(c)(3) tax-exempt status; and

2. It serves as your notice to the IRS that your organization is a public charity, not a private foundation. Remember, as discussed earlier, 501(c)(3) nonprofit groups are presumed to be private foundations unless they notify the IRS that they qualify for public charity status.

A few groups, technically, are not required to file Form 1023:

- a group which qualifies for public charity status and which normally has gross receipts of not more than $5,000 in each tax year;[2]

- a church, interchurch organization, local unit of a church, convention or association of churches, or an integrated auxiliary of a church; or

- a subordinate organization covered by a group exemption letter (if the parent organization timely submits a notice covering the subordinate organization—see the group exemption letter requirements in IRS Publication 557).

Even if one of the above exception applies to you, we recommend filing Form 1023 anyway. Why? First, because its risky to second guess the IRS. If you're wrong and the IRS denies your claim to 501(c)(3) tax status several years from now, your organization may have to pay substantial back taxes and penalties. Second, because the only way, on a practical and legal level, to assure others that you are a bona-fide 501(c)(3) group is to apply for an exemption. If the IRS agrees and grants your tax exemption, then, and only then, can you assure contributors, grant agencies, and others that you are a qualified 501(c)(3) tax exempt, tax-deductible organization listed with the IRS.

What if You File Late?

In our experience, the single most common problem faced by nonprofits is a failure to file their Form 1023 on time. Your 1023 application is timely filed if it is postmarked within 15 months after the end of the month in which your Articles were filed. Note that you can request an extension of time to file your 1023 package if you submit your request within this 15 month period—see IRS Publication 557. If you file on time (or within the extension period approved by the IRS), the tax exemption is effective retroactively to the date on which your Articles were filed. If you file late, it is effective from its postmark date.

If you're just now getting around to filing your 1023 Form several years after the initial organization of your nonprofit, don't despair; you've got plenty of good company. The important point here is to persevere, complete your application and mail it to the IRS as soon as possible.

B. Prepare User Fee Form 8718

Form 8718, *User Fee for Exempt Organization Determination Letter Request*, must be completed and submitted with your tax exemption application. This form is used to compute and pay the fees due for applying for your federal tax exemption. Fill in the 8718 form as you follow these instructions:[3]

Line 1   Type the name of your corporation.

Line 2   Groups which qualify for a reduced user fee of $150 check box a. Your organization qualifies for this reduced fee if it is submitting its initial exemption application and:

1. it is a new organization (not in operation for four years) and it anticipates gross receipts of not more than $10,000 during each of its first four tax years; or

2. it has been in operation for four tax years or more and has had annual gross receipts averaging not more than $10,000 during the preceding four years.[4]

If you check box a to qualify for the lower $150 fee, complete the Certification section in the middle of item 2. Type the name of your corporation in the blank and have the person who signs your exemption application sign on the line below the certification, showing this person's title in the blank to the right.[5]

Other nonprofit groups (except those seeking a group exemption letter) should check box b—the user fee in this case is $465 (don't complete the certification section if you check this box).

Ignore box c—this box doesn't apply to groups using this book.

Box d only applies to special organizations seeking an exemption for a group of nonprofits (such as an association of churches—see Publication 557 and check with a nonprofit advisor for more help; you can't use Form 1023).

How to Pay   Write a check made payable to the Internal Revenue Service for the amount of the user fee and staple your check to the 8718 form (place the check in the box at the bottom of the form). The check does not have to be an organizational check. The person preparing the application or any other incorporator may write a personal check in payment of this fee.

What to Send   After completing your 1023 application, attach Form 8718 together with your user fee check to the front page.

Where to File   Mail your completed exemption application package to the appropriate IRS District office listed on the User Fee Form. These addresses are the most current and supersede the IRS addresses listed in the 1023 application package and in other IRS forms and publications.

Completing the SS-4 Form

The date you started your business is the date your Articles were filed with your secretary of state. Use the file-stamped date on your certificate of incorporation or the copy of your Articles returned by the secretary of state's office. You can indicate that the date you will pay wages is "unknown." Have an incorporator or initial director sign the form, indicating his or her title as incorporator or director.

If another federal form asks for your EIN prior to your receipt of this number, indicate "Applied For" followed by the date of mailing of your 1023 tax exemption application.

C. Prepare Your Tax Exemption Application

Now it's time to get out your pencil and go through Form 1023, line by line. The IRS 1023 package includes two copies of the form. Use one as a draft. When you are satisfied with your draft responses, type or neatly print your final answers on the second copy of the form.

Note   The information presented in this section is based upon the most current revision of the IRS 1023 package (July 1993) at the time of printing of this edition. The IRS often revises its exemption application, but future changes shouldn't present problems. Revised forms may contain different line numbers or ordering of questions, but should not differ significantly in terms of the information requested.

Part I. Identification of Applicant

Lines 1a-d Show the name of your corporation exactly as it appears in your Articles of Incorporation. If you have operated (or plan to operate) your corporation under an assumed or fictitious corporate name, show this name in parenthesis after your formal name in item 1(a).

Provide the address of the corporation in blanks 1(c)-(d). If you have designated one person to receive tax information and forms from the IRS (usually your corporate Treasurer), show this person's name as the "c/o name" in item 1(b).

Line 2 All nonprofit corporations (with or without employees) must obtain a federal Employer Identification Number (EIN)—you will use this identification number on all your federal tax returns and reports. Even if your organization held an EIN prior to incorporation, it must obtain a new one for the corporate entity. Most new groups will not have obtained their EIN yet and should do so now.

The easy way is to complete the SS-4 form, "Application for Employer Identification Number," then to call the IRS Tele-TIN number for your state listed in the SS-4 instructions. Type in the EIN number assigned to your organization over the phone in Line 2 of your 1023 form, then mail or fax a copy of your completed SS-4 form to the IRS as explained in the SS-4 instructions.[6]

Note You can get an EIN the slow way by mailing your SS-4 form to the IRS without calling. Expect to wait at least four weeks. In this case, type the following in Line 2: "Applied for: [insert date of mailing of SS-4 form] ."

Line 3 Provide the name and telephone number of a director or other person to be contacted regarding your application and the phone number where this person can be reached during business hours. We suggest you show the name and telephone number of the person who is preparing your tax exemption in this blank.

Line 4 Specify the month your accounting period will end in this item. The accounting period must be the same as the tax year selected for your corporation. Most nonprofits use a calendar year as their accounting period and tax year and specify December here.

If you anticipate special seasonal cycles for your activities or non-calendar year record keeping or grant accountability procedures, you may wish to select a non-calendar accounting period for your corporation. For example, a federally funded school may wish to specify June in this blank to indicate an accounting period of July 1 to June 30th.

If you have any questions regarding the best accounting period and tax year for your group, check with your (probable) funding sources and consult your accountant or bookkeeper for further guidance.

Line 5 Show the date your Articles were filed by your secretary of state.

Line 6 Indicate up to three IRS activity codes, obtained from the inside back of the 1023 Schedule I form, that best describe your tax-exempt primary purposes, activities or type of organization. Enter these codes in order of importance. For example, a non-institutional educational group which plans to provide seminars and lectures, publish materials, and engage in non-scientific research would indicate numbers 123 (discussion groups, forums, panels, lectures), 120 (publishing activities), and 124 (study and research—non-scientific), in order of importance. If you don't find three codes which apply to you, list only one or two.

Line 7 The boxes that appear here will not apply to most incorporators and should be ignored by most groups:

- 501(e) applies to organizations which perform cooperative services for hospitals;

- 501(f) applies to groups that perform collective investment services for educational organizations;

- 501(k) applies to child care organizations. Certain child care groups will be treated as 501(c)(3) educational organizations if they meet special requirements contained in this IRC section—see Chapter 3C5, "Child Care Centers," and IRS Publication 557, page 8, "Child Care Organizations."

Line 8 Naturally, we assume this is your first application for your federal tax exemption and that you will check "No" here. If your organization has previously applied for its federal tax exemption (perhaps because it incorrectly applied under another section of the code), check "Yes" and attach a letter explaining the status or determination of the previous application.

Line 9 Some nonprofits using this box will be exempt from filing IRS Form 990, the annual information return for nonprofits or the shorter 990EZ form for smaller groups—see Chapter 10, Section B1. If you expect to be exempt—the most common exemptions apply if you are forming a church or plan to have gross receipts of less than $25,000 per year—mark "No" and state the reason why you are exempt. All other nonprofits using this book should mark "Yes" here. Only 501(c)(3) private foundations can check the not applicable ("N/A") box—as

Submitting a Conformed Copy of Your Articles to the IRS

An important technical IRS requirement is that you submit with your exemption application a *conformed copy* of your Articles. A conformed copy is one that agrees with the original, shows the signatures of your initial directors or incorporators and the acceptance of your secretary of state. Therefore make sure to submit a copy of your Articles which bears a file stamp, certification or other evidence that it is a copy of a document filed with your secretary of state's office. Don't submit a copy of unfiled Articles with your 1023 application—the IRS wants proof that your organization is incorporated in your state.

explained in Chapter 4, we're sure most incorporators will not want to form a private foundation.

Note For more information on the specific exemptions from the annual information return filing requirements, see Publication 557 and obtain and look at the instructions to the 990 form (call 1-800-TAX-FORM for a copy of this and the 990EZ tax form).

Line 10 If your corporation has previously filed regular income tax returns or tax-exempt information returns, check "Yes" and provide the information requested. Most groups should be able to indicate "No" to this question. If you indicate "Yes" to either of these questions, you're probably converting a profit corporation to a nonprofit corporation or are late in submitting your exemption application—in this case, be sure to specify the form number of each return filed, the year covered by the return, and the IRS office where it was filed.

Important Note If the deadline for filing the annual information return for a tax-exempt organization (IRS Form 990 and Form 990 Schedule A) occurs while your federal exemption is pending, you are required to file the return. Indicate that your 1023 is pending on the return.

Line 11 Check box (a) to indicate that your group is a corporation and attach copies of your Articles and completed Bylaws to your application. Make sure your Articles are a *conformed copy* of the original Articles filed with your secretary of state's office (see sidebar). Make sure you have filled in all the blanks in the tear-out Bylaws and have completed the adoption of Bylaws section at the end of this form. Since you are enclosing your Bylaws, do not check the box at the right of the last line of this item.

Part II. Activities and Operational Information

Note The answers to the next series of questions will require a thorough familiarity with the material in Chapters 3 and 4. Here is where terms such as "public charity" and "private foundation" start to become important. We will make specific cross-references as we go along, but it would be wise to look over Chapters 3 and 4 again before you proceed.

Line 1 Provide a narrative description of *all* your organization's activities—past, present and those you plan to conduct in the future—in their order of importance. For each activity note in detail:

- its purpose;
- when it was initiated (or, if it hasn't yet begun, when it will);

Public Inspection Requirements

Your federal 1023 tax exemption application, any papers submitted with the application and your tax exemption determination letter from the IRS must be made available for public inspection during regular business hours at your organization's principal office (any information which has been approved as confidential need not be disclosed). If your organization regularly maintains one or more regional or district offices having three or more employees, copies of these documents must also be made available for public inspection at each of these offices.

Copies of your organization's three most recent annual information returns must also be available for public inspection at your principal office (and, if applicable, your regional or district office).

The names and addresses of contributors do not have to be disclosed.

Members of the public can also obtain copies of these documents at any IRS office by paying a small fee. These public inspection requirements apply to 501(c)(3) public charities, not to 501(c)(3) private foundations—again, we expect most incorporators to qualify as public charities.

Failure to permit public inspection carries a $10 per day penalty. An automatic $1,000 additional penalty is imposed if any failure to comply is willful. These penalties are not imposed on the organization—they are applied against "the person failing to meet [these] requirements." See IRS Publication 557 and IRC §§ 6104(e), 5562(c)(1)(C) and (D) and 6685 for further information on these rules.

- where and by whom it will be conducted.

Many new groups will be describing proposed activities which are not yet operational, but you must still be very thorough in providing information about the activities that will be engaged in.

If appropriate, include a description of any unrelated business you plan to engage in. At this point of course, most nonprofits will not have formulated specific plans for unrelated business activities. If they have, they will not want to stress the importance or scope of these incidental unrelated activities—see Chapter 3D1 for further information.

Using Purpose Clause Language The IRS does not want to see general language repeated here which has been taken from the purpose clause in your Articles. If you wish, you may include a reference or repeat the language of the more expanded statement of specific objectives and purposes included in Article 2, Section 1 of your Bylaws. However, unless your bylaw language includes a detailed narrative of both your activities and purposes, we suggest you use it only as a starting point for a fuller response here. Generally, we recommend starting over with a fresh, straightforward statement of your group's nonprofit activities in this response.

Example A response by an environmental organization might read in part as follows:

The organization's purpose is to educate the public on a variety of environmental issues with special attention to educating the public on how to use less energy. Since January, 1990 the organization has published informational brochures explaining how to implement solar energy heating systems as an alternative to traditional energy sources. Publications are provided to the public at a fee slightly above cost—see copies of educational material enclosed, Attachments A-D. The brochures are published in-house at (address of principal office). Both paid and volunteer staff actively contribute to the research, writing, editing and production process. In addition to publishing, the organization's other activities include the following [list in order of importance other current, past or planned activities]:

Another Example A nonprofit organization plans to sponsor special activities for the purpose of supporting other nonprofit charities. It should describe both its activities to obtain revenue at special events and the manner in which this money will be spent to support other groups.

If you are forming an organization which automatically qualifies for public charity status (a church, school, hospital or medical research organization) or has special tax exemption requirements, you will want to show that your organization meets the criteria which apply to your type of organization (see Chapter 4, Section F1 and the instructions to the appropriate schedule in the 1023 package).

Type of Organization	See Schedule
Church	A
School, College or University	B
Hospital and Medical Research Organization	C
Home for the Aged or Handicapped	F
Child Care Organization	G
Student Aid or Scholarship Benefit Organization	H

Line 2 Briefly indicate the anticipated sources of financial support of your organization in the order of their magnitude (most money to least money). Here are a few additional points to help you complete your response to this item:

• Your sources of support should be related to your exempt purposes, particularly if you plan to be classified as a public charity under the support test described in Chapter 4, Section F3, where the group's primary support is derived from the performance of tax-exempt activities.

• If you plan to qualify as a publicly supported public charity described in Chapter 4, Section F2, your responses here should show significant support from various governmental grants, private agency funding or individual contributions.

• If you expect your principal sources of support to fluctuate substantially, attach a statement describing and explaining anticipated changes—see the specific instructions to Part II, Line 2 in the 1023 package.

There is not much room in this item to list your anticipated sources of financial support. Although your response should be as brief as possible, if it won't fit in the allotted space, continue it on an attachment page.

Line 3 This question asks how the corporation will go about obtaining revenues from the sources of expected support which you have just set out in your answer to the preceding question. If you've provided the details of your fundraising activities in the previous response, simply indicate "Fundraising activities are described in Part II, No. 2, above."

Otherwise, indicate how you will go about implementing your fundraising activities. For example, if you will give classes to obtain revenue, indicate how instructors will be recruited and students attracted; or if you will rely on grants, how grant funds will be solicited and the particular or general categories of grant agencies you plan to ap-

Who Are Disqualified Persons?

The concept of disqualified person is an important one for 501(c)(3) private foundations and public charities alike. The IRS uses the word "disqualified" only in a tax sense, which does not necessarily mean that these persons are disqualified from participating in the operation of the 501(c)(3) nonprofit corporation. If the corporation is classified as a 501(c)(3) private foundation, the corporation and the individual can be held liable for certain private foundation excise taxes. If the corporation is classified as a 501(c)(3) public charity (we assume yours will be), it is prevented in some cases from counting contributions received from disqualified persons as public support.

Disqualified persons include:

1. Substantial contributors: donors of more than $5,000 if the amount contributed is more than 2% of the total contributions and bequests received by the organization from the date it was created up to the end of the year in which the donation was made by the individual.

2. All foundation managers: directors, trustees and officers (or people with similar powers or responsibilities), or any employee with final authority or responsibility to act on the matter in question. Officers include persons specifically designated as such in the Articles, Bylaws or Minutes and persons who regularly exercise general authority to make administrative and policy decisions. Officers do not include independent contractors such as accountants, lawyers, financial and investment advisors and managers, nor, generally, any person who

proach. The question also requests information regarding the extent to which these fundraising activities have been implemented. For newly-incorporated groups, most fundraising activities will not yet be operative and you should so indicate, perhaps including a general indication of what set-up work and initial operations will be entered into during your first year.

Include any literature you plan to distribute to solicit support and indicate that this material is attached in your response to this item.

Unrelated Business Activities As explained in the 1023 instructions for this line, fundraising activities include unrelated business activities. If you have concrete plans to engage in unrelated activities (which, of course, will be clearly characterized as an insubstantial part of your overall activities), include the details here.

Reality Note At this point, most nonprofits will not have formulated specific plans for unrelated business activities. If they have, they will not want to stress the importance or scope of these incidental commercial activities—see Chapter 3, Section D1 for further information.

Lines 4(a) and 4(b) Provide the names and addresses of the initial directors named in your Articles. If directors were not named in your Articles, show the names of the persons who will be appointed by your incorporator to serve on the initial board. Show the residence or business address of each director—do not show the address of the corporation for any person listed here. Since directors will not be paid a salary, you may wish to reply: "Pursuant to Article 3, Section 6 of the corporation's Bylaws, directors will not be paid a salary but may be paid a reasonable fee for attending meetings of the board and may be allowed reasonable reimbursement or advancement for expenses incurred in the performance of their duties."

Since you will formally elect officers (President, Vice-President, Secretary, and Treasurer) and provide for any officer salaries later as part your first board meeting, you may wish to insert the following in your response to this item: "The persons who will serve as officers, and the compensation they will receive, if any, has not been determined as yet by the board of directors. Any such compensation will be reasonable and will be paid in return for the performance of services related to the tax-exempt purposes of the corporation."

Alternatively, if you have decided who will be elected to serve as officers (and the amounts of any salaries to be paid), you can provide the details of these officer arrangements.

simply makes recommendations for action, but who cannot implement these recommendations.

3. An owner of more than 20% of either the total combined voting power of a corporation, the profits' interests of a partnership or the beneficial interest of a trust or unincorporated enterprise, if any of these entities is a substantial contributor to the foundation.

4. A member of the family—this includes ancestors, spouse, lineal descendants such as children and grandchildren, but not brothers and sisters—of any of the individuals described in 1, 2 or 3 above.

5. Other business entities (e.g., corporations, partnerships, trusts, etc.) in which the persons described in 1-4 above have at least a 35% ownership interest.

For example, Ms. X makes a gift of $20,000 to your nonprofit corporation. If this gift exceeds 2% of all contributions and bequests made to your organization from the time it was created until the end of the corporate tax year in which Ms. X made the contribution, Ms. X is a substantial contributor.

For purposes of this test, gifts and bequests made by an individual include all contributions and bequests made by the individual's spouse. Once a person is classified as a substantial contributor, he generally remains classified as one (regardless of future contributions made, or not made, by the individual or future support received by the organization). However, if other conditions are met, a person will lose his status as a substantial contributor if he makes no contribution to the organization for ten years.

For further information on disqualified persons, see Chapter V of IRS Publication 578.

Line 4(c) Check "Yes" or "No." Although not necessary, the IRS likes to see public officials, or people appointed by public officials, on your board when they consider whether or not you have a representative governing body, particularly if you are seeking public charity status as a publicly-supported organization (as discussed in Chapter 4, Section F2). If you check "Yes," provide the information requested.

Line 4(d) Before answering this question, read the definition of disqualified persons in the sidebar (a shortened explanation is contained in the 1023 specific instruction for this line). Basically, the IRS is trying to determine whether your directors are disqualified persons for any reason other than the fact that they are directors (directors are disqualified persons, by definition, as foundation managers), or are related to, or have a business relationship with, disqualified persons.

The answer to this question is not critical to most groups planning to qualify as 501(c)(3) public charities. Receiving money from disqualified persons only serves as a minor limitation if you seek public charity status under the support test described in Chapter 4, Section F3, in that money received from disqualified persons can't be included as public support. Since these groups will be relying primarily on payments from outsiders (not directors) in return for services as their primary source of qualifying public support, there should be little problem.[7]

Of course, the IRS would like to see people on the board who are not disqualified persons since they are likely to have less personal and self-interested motives in carrying out the public purposes of the organization. Don't worry, though—it's quite common for directors or officers to be disqualified in a tax sense either because they are members of the family of a disqualified person (e.g., directors related to each other or to officers) or for some other reason.[8]

So, indicate whether any of the directors are disqualified persons (other than by virtue of the fact of being directors), or are related to or have a business relationship with disqualified persons. If so, describe how each director is disqualified in the space indicated.

Line 5 Indicate "Yes" or "No" as appropriate to these two questions. If you answer "Yes" to the first question because your nonprofit controls, or is controlled by, another organization, your operations are more complex than usual and you should consult a lawyer before applying for your federal exemption.

Check "Yes" to the second question if you have incorporated a pre-existing organization such as an unincorporated association and provide a short statement to this effect in your response.

Sample Response

> *"The Better Living Center, Inc." is an outgrowth of, and successor to, the operations of an unincorporated association, "The Better Living Association."*

If you check "Yes" to the second question because of shared directors, officers, employees or office space (or other special relationships) with another group, the IRS will wish additional information on the purposes and activities of the other group. Again, consult a lawyer for help with this complex incorporation scheme.

Line 6 You should be able to answer "No" to this item. Only unique groups, such as those which will set up, share facilities with, or support another politically active affiliate organization, will answer "Yes" here. A "Yes" response means that you should be applying for your tax exemption with the help of an experienced nonprofit professional.

Line 7 You should be able to indicate "No" to this question unless you are financially accountable to another organization (if you must report income and expenses to another tax-exempt, or taxable, organization). If so, you will need to provide the information requested and should check with a tax advisor or lawyer to make sure you will qualify for your 501(c)(3) tax exemption.

Line 8 Indicate what assets you have obtained since your incorporation, or at the time of your incorporation from a pre-existing unincorporated organization (such as land, buildings, equipment and publications—don't include cash and income producing property). Indicate if your assets are not fully operational, as would be the case if a building is under construction.

Most newly formed nonprofit corporations will have few, if any, operational assets unless they have incorporated an existing organization. Some may have made arrangements for acquiring assets or putting them into use. If so, you should provide this information.

If you have not acquired assets or made arrangements for the acquisition of assets, you need only indicate that the question is not applicable.

Sample Response

The corporation has the following operational assets:

Brand Name Computer System consisting of 1 file server and 4 workstations. Once the main system hub is connected to the 4 workstations in approximately 1 month, system will be fully operational and will be used to maintain organizational mailing lists, keep corporate books, generate organizational invoices and purchase orders, make and record payroll transactions and pay ongoing bills.

Line 9 Frankly, we're not sure why the IRS is asking this question, but most groups will check "No" here anyway. If you answer "Yes" because your organization to receive tax-exempt bond financing in the next two years, the IRS may have a few extra questions about this item when it responds to your tax exemption application.

Line 10(a) Indicate if any of your facilities will be managed by another organization or individual under the terms of a contract, explaining the relationship of the parties involved. What the IRS is looking for here is whether some person or organization closely associated with your nonprofit corporation will be unduly benefited by this type of managerial contract. If, for instance, a day care center plans to hire a director, officer or other person who is closely associated with the corporation to manage the center, the IRS will want to make sure that the corporation is not paying more than fair value for these services (of course, it helps if some portion of these services is volunteered by the director or officer). If you have reduced the terms of this type of management agreement to writing, include a copy of the contract as an attachment.

Line 10(b) If your nonprofit corporation leases property (as the landlord or tenant), check "Yes" here, attach a copy of the lease or rental agreement and explain the relationship of the parties to the lease in your response.

Mostly, the IRS is looking here for lopsided or special-interest rental agreements, as would be the case where a director leases space in his home to the nonprofit for an excessive rent payment. Although not required in situations of this sort, it helps if the director or officer donates the use of a portion of the space or rents the premises to the nonprofit at a substantial discount so that it's clear that no self-dealing is involved.

Line 11   Indicate whether or not you are a membership organization. If you have adopted a formal membership structure by including membership provisions in your Bylaws, you should check "Yes" and answer questions 11(a), (b) and (c). If you have not formed a formal membership organization, check "No" and go on to question 12.

Line 11(a)   Indicate any membership qualifications you've decided on and attach a schedule of fees and dues to be charged to members. If the amount for such fees hasn't been determined, you should so indicate and state that "the amounts shall be reasonable and as specified from time to time by resolution of the Board of Directors."

Line 11(b)   In all cases, the IRS likes to see you actively solicit the general public to become members of the corporation, so describe your present and proposed efforts to attract members. If you have final or draft copies of literature for soliciting members, indicate that they are enclosed and include them as attachments. If you haven't prepared (but plan to distribute) such literature, indicate that "promotional literature to attract members of the general public to become members of the corporation is not yet prepared, but will be prepared and distributed to members of the general public" (or of the "community served by the corporation").

Line 11(c)   Certain membership groups solicit the general public to become members and give them exclusive rights to participate in the activities and events of the corporation in exchange for payment of dues. This is acceptable in most cases provided you allow members of the general public, or a broad cross-section of the community, to become members and actively solicit public or community membership in your corporation.

If corporate programs, activities and benefits are available to members and non-members alike, indicate this in your response. If members are given special discounts or preferences, list these differences in your answer. Use an attachment page to continue your response if you run out of room on the application form.

Line 12(a)   It's a common (and completely permissible) practice to charge members of the public for services related to your exempt functions. (Of course, it helps overall with your tax exemption application if you charge less than commercial enterprises for goods or services, but this is not a tax requirement.) Many groups will derive income primarily from these services. This might be the case for a performing arts group, a dance studio, a health clinic or a nonprofit school. If your group is in this category, indicate "Yes," also stating, if appropriate, that benefits, services and products will be available to the "general public." A "Yes" response requires a statement as to what specific services you will charge for, and the amount of such charges. Usually, at this point, groups have not fully determined the amount of payment to be charged for services. If this is the case, first list the services and benefits which will be provided to the public and explain how the fees for them will be determined. Indicate that "charges for the above benefits, products or services, although at present undetermined, will be reasonable and related to the cost of the service to be provided." If you already know what the charges are, attach a copy of your fee schedule as requested.

Line 12(b) Most groups will indicate "No" to this question since the IRS frowns upon the limitation of benefits or services to a specific class of individuals. However, if the class of people benefited by the corporation is broad, not limited to specific individuals, and related to the exempt purposes of the nonprofit group, the IRS should have no objection.

Example A nonprofit musical heritage organization plans to provide programs and benefits to needy musicians residing in the community. If the overall tax-exempt purpose of the organization is allowed, this limitation of benefits will be permitted by the IRS.

Line 13 Most groups will indicate "No" to this question. If you plan to engage in efforts to influence legislation, check "Yes" and read the discussion in Chapter 3, Section D3. You should indicate in your response here that you will engage in efforts to influence legislation either "to an insubstantial degree" or, if you plan to elect to fall under the political expenditures test, "within the limits allowed under Section 501(h) of the Internal Revenue Code." Be sure to provide an estimate of the percentage of your organization's time and funds that will go into activities to influence legislation. Keep in mind that if the IRS considers the percentages "substantial," you risk putting your 501(c)(3) status in jeopardy (see Chapter 3, footnote 6).

Line 14 A 501(c)(3) nonprofit organization may not participate in political campaigns. Participation in or donations to a campaign can result in denial or revocation of tax-exempt status. Most groups should answer "No" here.

If you must answer "Yes" to this question, your activities should be strictly limited to nonpartisan voter education work and statements—see Chapter 3, footnote 4, and check with a nonprofit lawyer or tax consultant to make sure you are on safe ground before proceeding with your exemption application

If You End Up on Part III, Line 5, Should You Ask for Relief?

Most groups will not end up on Line 5 in Part III because even those that file late (beyond 27 months of incorporation) qualify for an automatic extension of time to file unless they have been contacted by the IRS—see the Line 4 instructions in the text. If your group does end up here, you may decide not to bother with seeking an extension to file and simply check "No" here. This means that your 501(c)(3) exemption, if granted, will only be effective from the date of its receipt by the IRS, not from the date of your incorporation. Is this so terrible? Often, it isn't. Here's why: many nonprofits will not have any taxable income and will not have received contributions from donors during these early startup months (the 27-plus months of operation prior to filing their 1023 application). Consequently, obtaining a tax exemption for these early months will not normally provide a tax benefit. However, if your group is facing tax liability for early operations, needs to provide donors with tax deductions for gifts contributed during the first 27-plus months, or needs to obtain 501(c)(3) tax-exempt status from the date of its creation for some other pressing reason, then it makes sense to prepare a special statement under Line 5 as explained in the text. If you are unsure, check with your tax advisor.

Part III. Technical Requirements

Line 1 Most new groups will be able to answer "Yes" to indicate that they are mailing their exemption application within 15 months from the end of the first month in which their Articles of Incorporation were filed. If you answer "Yes," skip Lines 2-7 and go on to Line 8.

Lines 2(a)-(c) If you are filing your application late (you answered "No," to Line 1), you may qualify for one of the three exceptions to the 15-month filing deadline listed here (other extensions to the normal filing deadline are covered in later Lines of this part). These are the groups not required to file Form 1023: churches; public charities that normally have gross receipts of not more than $5,000 in each year; and subordinate organizations exempt under a group exemption letter. If you are mailing your exemption application late (after 15 months from the end of the month of incorporation) and feel that you are one of these groups, check the box that applies to you and go on to Line 8 (if you are filing within 27 months of your incorporation date, you may prefer to ask for one of the other automatic late-filing extensions available under Lines 3 or 4 instead—see below). If the IRS agrees that you qualify under one of the three special tests listed here, your federal exemption will be effective retroactively from the date of your incorporation.

A Common Exception to the 15-Month Deadline Under Line 2
The 2(b) exception is often applicable to new nonprofits.[9] This applies to your group if: (a) Your organization is a public charity (not a private foundation—since one of the purposes of completing your 1023 applica-

tion is to establish that you are eligible for public charity status, we assume you meet this requirement); and (b) Your organization "normally" has gross receipts of not more than $5,000 in each tax year. For groups that have been in existence for two tax years, under the regulations this means gross receipts of $12,000 or less during the first two years (we assume you are into your second tax year at this point since you missed the 15-month filing deadline). Many new groups without outside sources of support can meet this gross receipts test during their beginning tax years.[10]

Line 3 If you will not mail Form 1023 within the 15-month limit and you are unable—or don't wish—to qualify under the exceptions discussed in Lines 2 (a)-(c) above, you automatically qualify for an extension of time to file as long as you submit a completed 1023 application to the IRS within 12 months from the end of the normal 15-month period—in other words, before the end of the 27th month following the date of your incorporation. This is a handy extension and allows you to apply within two years plus from your date of incorporation—ample time for most groups (just don't miss this extended 27-month deadline—finish your application and mail it to the IRS pronto). This means your tax exemption, if granted, will apply retroactively to the date of your incorporation. If you are filing your application late and qualify for this extension, check "Yes" and go on to Line 8. If you don't qualify for this automatic extension, check "No" and go on to Line 4.

Line 4 This line asks you if the IRS has contacted you about your failure to file your 1023 application within 27 months of your incorporation. If they haven't, check "No" and go on to Line 8. You qualify for another extension to the normal 15-month filing deadline.[11] If the Service has contacted you, you must check "Yes," then go on to Line 5.

Line 5 Here is where you end up if your group is filing the 1023 application more than 27 months from the date of your incorporation, and the IRS has contacted you about your failure to complete your application within 27 months of incorporating. This doesn't happen too often—most groups are not notified unless they fail to respond to questions posed by the IRS in response to the filing of a prior 1023 application.

To qualify for late filing under these circumstances, check "Yes" and attach a statement giving the reasons why you failed to complete the 1023 application process within 27 months of your incorporation. Revenue Ruling 92-85 contains a list of the reasons that are normally acceptable to the IRS, as well as ones that aren't. This ruling is summarized in the 1023 instructions for this Line. If you want more informa-

501(c)(4) Organizations

IRC Section 501(c)(4) provides a federal corporate income tax exemption for nonprofit social welfare groups and civic leagues (see Table 3.1 in Chapter 3). Since the promotion of public welfare is defined as "… promoting the common good and general welfare of the people of the community," many 501(c)(3) nonprofits also qualify as 501(c)(4) social welfare organizations. Although 501(c)(4) nonprofits are exempt from federal corporate income taxation, they are not eligible to receive tax deductible contributions from donors and do not enjoy many of the other advantages associated with 501(c)(3) tax-exempt status, such as eligibility to receive public and private grant funds, to participate in local, state and federal nonprofit programs, to obtain county real and personal property tax exemptions, etc. But 501(c)(4) organizations do enjoy one advantage not available to 501(c)(3) groups: they may engage in substantial legislative activities and may support or oppose candidates to public office. For further information on 501(c)(4) tax-exempt status, see IRS Publication 557.

tion, you can look this ruling up at the law library—see the 2nd volume of the 1992 IRS Cumulative Bulletin, starting at page 490—or check with your tax advisor. After attaching your statement, go on to Line 8.

If you don't think you can qualify for an extension under this Revenue Ruling (or if you decide not to bother—see the sidebar), check "No" and go on to Line 6.

Line 6 If you checked "No" to Line 5 (you don't want to qualify for an extension under revenue Ruling 92-85, you end up here and should check "Yes," then go on to Line 7. This means that you agree that your 501(c)(3) exemption can only be recognized from the date of its receipt by the IRS, not retroactively to the date of your incorporation. By the way, we don't know what happens if you check "No" here—literally, this response means that you are not asking for an extension to file your application late, but don't agree that it should be treated as late. Such stubbornness is to be commended, but the Service probably will not be impressed and probably will hold up the processing of your application until you give in and answer "Yes" to this question in later correspondence with the IRS (or the Service may deny your exemption outright).[12]

Line 7 If you end up here (your application for 501(c)(3) status will only be considered from the date of its receipt by the IRS), you may wish to check the box in this question. If you do, you are asking the IRS to grant your group tax-exempt status as a 501(c)(4) organization—a social welfare group or a civic league—during your late filing period. This is the 27-month plus period from the date your Articles were filed up to the date your 1023 application is received by the IRS. What does this do for you? If your request for 501(c)(4) status is approved, your organization will be exempt from paying federal corporate income taxes (as a 501(c)(4) organization) from the date of its formation until the date of approval of your 501(c)(3) tax-exempt status. For most newly-formed groups without taxable income during this initial period, obtaining this extra tax exemption will not be necessary and this box can be ignored.

However, if you or your tax advisor determine that your organization is subject to tax liability for this initial period, check this box and call 1-800-TAX-FORM to order IRS Publication 1024. Fill in the first page of Form 1024 and submit it with your exemption application. If you qualify as a 501(c)(4) social welfare group (as many 501(c)(3)s do—see the sidebar), your 501(c)(3) tax determination letter will indicate that you qualify as a 501(c)(4) organization during your initial late filing [your pre-501(c)(3)] period.

Table 8.1
IRS Line 8 Instructions
Covered in Chapter 4

Groups listed in Line 8 instructions	
(1), (2), (3), (6) and (7)	Section F1
Groups listed in (4)	Section F2
Groups listed in (5)	Section F3

Table 8.2
IRS Line 10 Public Charities
Covered in Chapter 4

Line 10 (a)	Chapter 4, Section F1
Line 10 (b)	Chapter 4, Section F1
Line 10 (c)	Chapter 4, Section F1
Line 10 (d)	Chapter 4, Section F1
Line 10 (e)	Chapter 4, Section F1
Line 10 (f)	Chapter 4, Section F1
Line 10 (g)	Chapter 4, Section F1
Line 10 (h)	Chapter 4, Section F2
Line 10 (i)	Chapter 4, Section F3
Line 10 (j)	Chapter 4, Sections F2 and F3

Line 8 Lines 8 though 15 relate to whether or not you are seeking to be classified as a 501(c)(3) public charity or as a 501(c)(3) private foundation. In Chapter 4, we discussed the distinction between these two classifications and why you should wish to meet one of the three primary tests for being classified as a public charity.

The 1023 instructions for Line 8 provide a brief explanation of the differences between public charity and private foundation status and the types of organizations that qualify as public charities. Table 8.1 shows how the organizations listed under the IRS instructions to Line 8 fit in with our organizational scheme in Chapter 4.

Check "Yes" or "No" on Line 8 to indicate whether or not you are a private foundation. Hopefully, as we've said, you will expect to qualify as a public charity and will mark "No" to this question. If your response is "No," go on to Line 10. If you are forming a 501(c)(3) private foundation, check "Yes" and go on to Line 9.

Line 9 If you've checked "Yes" to Line 8 indicating that you are a private foundation and you believe you can obtain the benefits of being a private operating foundation as explained in Chapter 4, Section D1 (also see the heading "Private Operating Foundations" in IRS Publication 557 and IRS Publication 578), check this box and complete Schedule E of the application. To understand the technical requirements of this special classification, you will need to refer to various subsections of Federal Income Tax Regulation 53.4942 and will probably wish to consult a tax advisor for help in preparing this schedule.

If you are forming a 501(c)(3) private foundation but do not seek to be classified as a private operating foundation, check "No" here and go on to Part IV.

Sample Responses to Line 10

The First Fellowship Church, a religious organization which plans to maintain a space to provide weekly religious services to its congregation, checks box (a) to request automatic public charity status as a church.

The Workshop for Social Change, an educational group which plans to receive support from public and private grant funds and from individual and corporate contributions checks box (h) to request public charity status as a publicly supported organization.

Everybody's Dance Studio and Dinner Theater, a group which expects to derive most of its operating revenue from student tuitions, special workshops, and ticket sales (as well as from other exempt purpose activities), selects box (i) to be classified as a group which meets the public charity public support test discussed in Chapter 4, Section F3.

Line 10 Check the box [letters (a)-(j)] that corresponds to the basis of your claim to public charity status. First, absorb what you can of the technical material given in the 1023 Line 10 instructions. Then reread Chapter 4, Sections F1, F2 and F3—these sections provide the names of these public charity organizations, the requirements they must meet, and the Internal Revenue Code sections that apply to them. Note that Letter (j) is a special case that allows certain groups to have the IRS determine which public charity support test best suits their activities and sources of revenue—more on this special choice later in this discussion.

After checking the appropriate public charity classification box for your organization under Line 10, make sure to go on to the next question on the 1023 that applies to your organization.

Table 8.2 shows how the different types of groups listed in this part of the application fit within the three different categories of public charity status discussed in Section F of Chapter 4. If you concentrate on our basic division of these different groups into the three public charity categories rather than focusing on the individual Internal Revenue Code sections, we think this part will go smoothly.

Let's look a little more closely at each of the lettered boxes in Line 10:

Box (a) If you are seeking to qualify automatically for public charity status as a church, also see the instructions to Schedule A in the 1023 package and our discussion of this schedule in the Line 15 instructions below. Go on to Part III, Line 15.

Box (b) Groups seeking to qualify as private schools should refer to the IRS instructions to Schedule B and see our discussion of this schedule under the Line 15 instructions below. Go on to Part III, Line 15.

Boxes (c)-(g) Few groups will choose one of these boxes since each applies to a special type of organization such as a hospital, public safety organization or government agency.

Box (c) Hospitals and medical research groups will need to complete Schedule C and should refer to the 1023 instructions for this schedule before checking this box.

Box (e) Organizations operated solely for the benefit of, or in connection with, any of the other public charity organizations (except one testing for public safety) must complete Schedule D. This information helps the IRS determine whether this type of organization supports other qualified public charities. For further information, refer to the 1023 instructions and Publication 557, "Section 509(a)(3) Organizations."

Groups checking boxes (c) through (f) go on to Part III, Line 15. Governmental organizations checking box (g) go on to answer questions 12 and 13 in Part III.

For More Help If you do check one of the (c)-(g) boxes, the lawyer, accountant or other advisor who is helping you organize one of these special corporations should help you with your application. Again, we don't expect many nonprofit groups to be seeking public charity status under these IRC provisions.

Box (h) This box is for organizations that receive a substantial part of their support from government agencies or from the general public. These are the publicly supported groups discussed in Chapter 4, Section F2. If you believe this is the public charity best suited to your organization's sources of support, check the box on this line. If you are unsure whether this is the best support test to use for your group (if you think that the public charity support test listed in box (i) also may apply to your organization), you may wish to let the IRS make this decision for you as explained in the box (j) instructions below.

As discussed in Chapter 4, Section F2, many groups will not want to fall under this public charity test since it does not allow receipts from the performance of services related to the corporation's exempt purposes to be included as "qualified public support."

Groups checking box (h) go on to Part III, Line 11.

Box (i) This box is for organizations that normally receive 1/3 of their support from contributions, membership fees and gross receipts from activities related to the exempt functions of the organization (subject to certain exceptions) but not more than 1/3 from unrelated trades and businesses or gross investment income. The support test applicable to this means of achieving public charity status is discussed in Chapter 4, Section F3—this is the most common and often the easiest way of qualifying a new nonprofit organization as a public charity. So reread the requirements of this test and the definition of terms associated with it in Chapter 4. If you believe this public charity test best suits your expected sources of support, check this box. If you are unsure, see the instructions to box (j) just below.

Groups checking box (i) go on to Part III, Line 11.

Box (j) If you feel that your group may qualify as a public charity either under box (h) or box (i) but aren't sure which, then you can check this box. The IRS will decide which of these two public charity classifications best suits your organization based upon the financial data and other financial support information included in your 1023 application. For

**More Sample Responses
to Line 10**

The School for Alternative Social Studies, an accredited private post-graduate school with a formal curriculum, full-time faculty and regularly enrolled student body, checks box (b) to request automatic public charity status as a formal private school.

The Elder Citizens Collective and Information Exchange, which plans to derive support from contributions and grants as well as subscriptions to its weekly newsletter (and other exempt-purpose services and products made available to members and the public at large), checks box (j) to have the IRS decide whether box (h) or box (i) is the appropriate public charity classification.

many new groups, box (j) is the best way to go. Rather than work through the math and technical definitions necessary to approximate whether you will qualify as a public charity under box (h) or box (i), checking this box lets the IRS do the work for you.

Groups checking box (j) go on to Part III, Line 11.

Line 11 Groups that checked Line 10 boxes (h), (i) or (j) must answer this question (we refer to these groups as "Line 11 groups"). All other groups should ignore this question and should go on to Line 15.

Your responses in Line 11 will indicate whether your group is requesting an advance or definitive IRS ruling as to its public charity status and whether you must go on to answer additional questions 12 through 14 in Part III. Note that the IRS automatically makes a definitive ruling as to the public charity status of groups that are not required to fill in Line 11. In other words, the only groups allowed to request an advance ruling on their public charity status are some Line 11 groups.

Advance vs. Definitive Rulings We've already discussed the basic differences between advance and definitive public charity rulings in Chapter 4, Sections F2 and F3. Here we discuss these differences in more detail.

If your group has not been in existence for one tax year consisting of at least eight months, it must request an advance public charity ruling by checking the fourth Line 11 box (the "No" box). Your group must complete two copies of Form 872-C and attach them to your application (see the instructions for this form below). Go on to Question 15—you do not have to answer Lines 12 through 14.[13]

Example The Nonprofit Center, Inc., filed its Articles with the secretary of state on September 1st and closed its first tax year on December 31st (it specified December as the ending month of its accounting period in Part I, Line 4 of the 1023 application). The corporation is a Line 11 group and is preparing its 1023 tax exemption application during October of the following year. The group must check the "No" box here and request an advance ruling period since it has completed one tax year consisting of less than eight months. Its first and only completed tax year was a "short year" running from September 1st to December 31st of the previous calendar year. For further tax year examples, see the back of IRS Form 872-C.

If your group has been in existence for one tax year consisting of at least eight months, check the first Line 11 box (the "Yes" box). Your group has the option of requesting a definitive or an advance ruling by checking the second or the third Line 11 box respectively.

Sample Responses to Line 11

Remember the Workshop for Social Change from the earlier example? This is a group that plans to qualify for public charity status as a Line 10 box (h) publicly supported organization. If the group has not completed one tax year of at least eight months, it must request an advance ruling by checking the Line 11 "No" box and going on to Line 15. Everybody's Dance Studio and Dinner Theater is seeking public charity status as a Line 10 box (i) group. It has completed its first tax year consisting of 11 months and checks the Line 11 "Yes" box. It decides to check the third Line 11 box to request an advance ruling of its public charity status and goes on to Line 12.

Which Type of Ruling Should Your Line 11 Group Request? Most nonprofits given a choice opt for an advance public charity ruling. If you request a definitive ruling on your public charity status, the IRS will look at the actual support received to-date by your group. If this support is not sufficient to qualify your group under the applicable public charity category, your public charity status will be denied or the IRS will issue an advance, not a definitive, public charity ruling anyway. Further, requesting a definitive ruling may take extra time and could involve responding to additional IRS questions before your tax exemption is approved.

Obtaining an advance public charity ruling is easier. The IRS will approve an advance ruling if it appears from the financial statements and other information contained in and submitted with the 1023 application that the group's anticipated sources of support will qualify the organization for public charity status. At the end of a five-year advance ruling period, the IRS will look at the annual information returns of the organization. If actual support meets the requirements of the selected public charity category, the group will then receive final approval of its 501(c)(3) public charity status. If the group does not qualify for public charity status at the end of this period, it will be classified as a 501(c)(3) private foundation during succeeding tax years.

Two related points:

- If the organization does not qualify as a public charity at the end of its advance ruling period, it is subject to excise taxes on investment income (only if it has not met the private foundation investment income rules during this period). The group is not, however, retroactively liable for other private foundation excise taxes during its advance ruling period.

- Even if public charity status is denied at the end of the advance ruling period, contributions made during the advance ruling period by individual donors will still be treated as having been made to a valid public charity.

In our opinion, it is usually best to request an advance ruling period for your public charity status. Of course, if your group is the exception and you can reasonably predict that its past support qualifies it for public charity status, go ahead and request a definitive ruling.

- Remember to check the second or third Line 11 box to specify the type of public charity ruling you are requesting. Check the second box to request a definitive ruling (and go on to answer Lines 12 through 15). To request an advance ruling, check the third box, then go on to answer questions 12 and 15 (skip questions 13 and 14), and make sure to attach two completed 872-C forms to your application.

Line 12 This line applies only to Line 11 groups that have checked the first Line 11 box (the "Yes" box) indicating that they have completed a tax year consisting of at least eight months.

Government Groups Note Government groups that have checked Line 10 box (g) must also complete Line 12. Again, few readers will be applying on behalf of this special sort of group.

Complete the Financial Data in Part IV-A First To answer this question, you must first supply the financial data (statement of revenue and expenses) requested in Part IV-A. If you have listed any unusual grants on Line 12 of any of the financial statements prepared in Part IV-A, list them here along with the donor's name, date and amount and the nature of the grant (was it general, restricted to a specific use, etc.).

Have You Received Sums Large Enough to Need Classification as Unusual Grants? Unusual grants are large contributions, bequests or grants received by the organization that are attracted by the publicly supported nature of the organization. The benefit of having a large grant qualify as an unusual grant is that it does not jeopardize the group's public charity status (as do other large sums received from a single source). It is unlikely that your beginning nonprofit has received sums that need classification as unusual grants. For further information on this technical area, see the 1023 instructions to Line 12 of Part IV-A; the discussions and examples of unusual grants in Chapter 4, Sections F2 and F3; and the specific rules on unusual grants contained in IRS Publication 557.

Line 13 This item should be filled out only if *both* the following conditions apply:

1. Your group checked Line 10, box (g) or (h); and

2. You checked the first and second Line 11 boxes indicating that your organization has completed a tax year consisting of at least eight months and you wish to obtain a definitive ruling as to its public charity status.

If both conditions apply, check the box in Line 13 and answer sections 13(a) and 13(b) following the instructions below after completing Part IV-A (statement of revenue and expenses) of the exemption application.

What About Line 10, Box (j) Groups? If condition 2 applies to you [you have completed one tax year of at least eight months and you are requesting a definitive ruling, but you checked Line 10, box (j)], does Line 13 apply to you? This is a good question, not covered by the current 1023 instructions. Remember: Line 10, box (j) groups have asked the IRS to decide whether they are a Line 10 box (h) or box (i) public charity. If the IRS decides that the group is a box (h) public charity, it may request that Line 13 be answered before the 501(c)(3) tax exemption is approved. So a suggestion: If condition 2 above applies to you and you checked Line 10, box (j), try to answer this question. If this seems too much trouble just now, fine—the IRS will ask for this information later if it is determined that this question does apply to your group.

Line 13(a) Enter 2% of the amount shown in Part IV-A, Line 8, column (e)—this is 2% of your organization's total support received over the tax years shown in Part IV.

Line 13(b) If any individual or organization—other than a government unit or another 501(c)(3) public charity described in Line 10, boxes (h) or (i)—has contributed more than the amount shown in Line 13(a) during the tax years covered in Part IV-A of your application, supply the name(s) of the contributor(s) and the amount(s) contributed on an attachment page.

Why the IRS Wants This Information For Line 10(h) public charities, amounts that exceed 2% of the group's total support generally are not counted as qualified public support (see Chapter 4, Section F2, and IRS Publication 557, "Support from the General Public").

Line 14 This line should be filled out only if both the following conditions apply:

1. Your group checked Line 10, box (i); and
2. You checked the first and second Line 11 boxes indicating that your organization has completed a tax year consisting of at least eight months and wishes to obtain a definitive ruling as to its public charity status.

If both conditions apply to you, check the box in Line 14 and answer sections 14(a) and 14(b) following the instructions below after completing Part IV-A (statement of revenue and expenses) of the exemption application. Again, if condition 2 above applies to you, but you checked Line 10 box (j), we suggest you act as though this line applies to your organization. By doing this, you'll avoid a delay later if the IRS concludes you are a Line 10, box (i) public charity and must answer this question.

Why the IRS Wants This Information Both questions here are intended to get you to disclose sources of support that are not considered qualified public support for groups in this public charity category: contributions from disqualified persons or gross receipts from other individuals that exceed $5,000 in any tax year.

Line 14(a) For a definition of disqualified persons, see the earlier sidebar above titled "Who Are Disqualified Persons?" If a disqualified person provided gifts, grants or contributions; membership fees; or payments for admissions or other exempt-purpose services or products (these are the categories listed in Lines 1, 2 and 9 of Part IV-A) during any tax year shown in Part IV-A, provide the names of the disqualified persons and amounts contributed or paid on an attachment page.

Line 14(b) If any person (other than a disqualified person), has paid more than $5,000 to your organization for admissions or other exempt-purpose services or products (these payments are reported in Part IV-A, Line 9) during any tax year shown in Part IV-A, provide the information requested on an attachment page. Payments by government agencies and other public charities described in Line 10, boxes (a)-(c), (d) and (g) must also be disclosed here.

A Reminder Coming to terms with these (and other Part III) questions can be a trying experience. So relax and take your time. If you get stuck on these technical questions, seek out a nonprofit legal or tax person to help you get through this material, or come back to this material in a day or two when you're not feeling so overwhelmed.

Line 15 All groups seeking 501(c)(3) public charity status should answer "Yes" or "No" to each question listed here. If you answer "Yes" to any question, fill out the schedule indicated. The following information is furnished to help you determine whether or not you need to fill out a particular schedule and, if you do, to help you do it. For the most part, these schedules are required to ensure that particular types of organizations are "charitable" in nature, meet special 501(c)(3) exemption requirements applicable to their activities or meet special requirements associated with the Part III, Line 10 public charity classification they are seeking. For further help in following this material, see the 1023 instructions to Line 15 and any specific instructions included on the schedules.

Churches If you checked Line 10, box (a) to seek automatic public charity status as a church or an association of churches, check this "Yes" box and complete Schedule A. We've already discussed requirements for churches in Chapter 3, Section C2. Questions 1 through 15 seek to determine if your organization possesses conventional, institutional church attributes. Questions 16 through 19 relate to whether your organization unduly benefits, or was created to serve the personal needs of, your pastor or the pastor's family and relatives. You can use the information completed for Line 11(e) of your California tax exemption application (see Chapter 7) in your response here

Schools Check the "Yes" box and fill in Schedule B if you checked Line 10, box (b), to seek automatic public charity classification as a formal private school. Make sure to check "No" to Line 2 on Schedule B—only state schools answer "Yes" to this question. A school is defined as an educational organization that has the primary function of presenting formal instruction, normally maintains a regular faculty and curriculum, normally has a regularly enrolled body of students and has a place where its educational activities are carried on (e.g., private primary or secondary schools, colleges, etc.). Your responses to this schedule should show that your operations are nondiscriminatory and in accordance with a statement to this effect included in your Bylaws that has been published in the community that you serve (you must attach this bylaw resolution to Schedule B). For information on drafting and publishing this statement of nondiscrimination, see IRS Publication 557, "Private Schools."

Hospitals and Medical Research Organizations If your activities will consist of operating a hospital or medical research organization [and you checked Line 10, box (c)], check the "Yes" box and complete Schedule C. Make sure to check the appropriate boxes at the top of the schedule and to fill out the appropriate section of the form. Generally this schedule seeks to determine two things: (1) whether the hospital is charitable in nature and qualifies for 501(c)(3) tax-exempt status (see IRS Publication 557, "Hospitals"); and (2) whether the hospital or medical research organization qualifies for automatic public charity status (see the Schedule C instructions and IRS Publication 557, "Hospitals and Medical Research Organizations".)

If you are submitting your 1023 on behalf of a cooperative hospital service organization under IRC Section 501(e)—you checked the box in Part I, Line 7a—do not complete Schedule C. Your tax advisor can help you obtain an exemption for this special type of organization.

A 501(c)(3) charitable hospital normally has many of the following characteristics:

- doctors as part of its courtesy staff who are selected from the community at large;
- a community-oriented board of directors;
- emergency room facilities open on a community-access basis;
- admission of at least some patients without charge (on a charity basis);
- nondiscrimination with respect to all admissions and particularly Medicare or Medicaid patients;
- a medical training and research program that benefits the community.

If You're Feeling Woozy

We know completing the Part III Technical Requirements section of the federal tax exemption application can be tricky. If you're feeling lost, overwhelmed or just plain disgusted, take a break. After coming back and reading our instructions to this part one or two more times, most groups will be able to successfully tackle this material and move on to the next (and last!) part of this federal form. If you do get stuck choosing the proper public charity classification or responding to special questions that apply to your group, ask a board member, friend, or friend of a friend with some legal or tax background to give you a hand getting over this incorporation hurdle.

The IRS frowns upon nonprofit hospitals that rent office space to individual physicians to allow them to engage in their individual practices, unrelated to the community service programs of the hospital, particularly if such physicians are prior tenants and present members of the board of the nonprofit hospital whose rent is below fair market value. Question 6 of Schedule C addresses this issue.

Supporting Organizations If you have checked Line 10, box (e), complete Schedule D. This is a complicated schedule and a number of special tests must be met. Your nonprofit legal or tax advisor can help you qualify this special type of 501(c)(3) public charity classification.

Private Operating Foundations See our instructions to Part III, Line 9, and complete Schedule E if you are applying for a tax exemption for a private foundation that qualifies as a "private operating foundation." Again, we expect your organization to qualify as a 501(c)(3) public charity, not as this special type of 501(c)(3) private foundation.

Homes for the Aged or Handicapped If you are forming a 501(c)(3) charitable organization that is a home for the aged or handicapped, check "Yes" and fill in Schedule F. This schedule attempts to determine whether or not the home is charitable in nature, looking to see if the facilities are available to members of the public or the particular community at reasonable rates, whether provision is made for indigent residents, whether health care is adequate and whether facilities are adequate to house a sufficient number of residents. For further information on IRS Guidelines, see Chapter 3, Section C1, "Assistance to the Aged," and IRS Publication 557, "Home for the Aged."

Child Care Organizations If you are forming a child care organization—you have checked the box under Part I, Line 7c—check "Yes" and complete Schedule G. This schedule is used by the IRS to see if you qualify as a 501(c)(3) educational organization providing child care under IRC Section 501(k). See our instructions to Part 1, Line 7, above for further information. If your child care center also may qualify under 501(c)(3) as a private school, complete Schedule B—see our instructions for schools above.

Scholarship Benefits Organizations Whether you are a formal "school" or not, if you provide or administer scholarship benefits, student aid, etc., check "Yes" to this question and fill out Schedule H. Of course, it's unlikely that you will be able to administer any private or public student aid funds unless you have set up a school with institutional attributes. The basic intent of Schedule H is to ensure that you administer or provide financial aid on a nondiscriminatory basis to recipients. For further information on IRS guidelines, see IRS Publication 557, "Charitable Organization Supporting Education" and "Organization Providing Loans."

Lines 1(b)-(c) allow your 501(c)(3) organization to apply for approval of your grant procedures in the event that your organization is classified as a private foundation (in the event that your request for public charity classification under Part III, Line 10, is denied). If you wish to plan for this contingency, consult your tax advisor to help you select the appropriate IRC section on Line 1(c).

Successors to Profit-Making Organizations If you are incorporating a pre-existing profit organization (for instance one that has been doing business and filed tax returns for prior tax years) check the "Yes" box and fill in Schedule I. If you have incorporated an unincorporated association or similar nonprofit organization in which no person was allowed a propriety (monetary or property) interest, this question does not apply to you.

The IRS intent behind Schedule I is to see if the activities, principals or policies of the pre-existing group and the newly-formed nonprofit corporation are the same or different. The IRS wants to know whether the former profit-making enterprise that served the needs of a few individuals is now truly directed by, and serving the interests of, the community or general public. Yes, you may engage in the same activities as those of the pre-existing organization and still obtain your tax exemption (if the activities qualify for tax-exempt status), but the more differences, the better. You should not, of course, still be serving the interests of, or providing special benefits to, the major figures of the former for-profit business.

You'll notice that question 4(a) on the schedule asks that you attach a copy of an agreement of sale or other contract relating to the transfer of the assets of the predecessor organization to the corporation. We provide instructions for preparing an Offer for the transfer of assets to the nonprofit corporation in Chapter 10, Step 13. You may, at this time, prepare this Offer and attach it to your application or, in the alternative, state that no agreement has been formalized, stating, if applicable, the general nature of the terms of the agreement you will prepare later for the sale of the assets of the predecessor organization to the nonprofit corporation.

Question 4(b) of this schedule requests that you have an independent qualified expert attach an appraisal of the facilities or property interest sold, showing the fair market value at the time of sale. Have an accountant prepare this statement. At the same time, seek the accountant's advice with respect to the preparation of the Offer of Sale, if appropriate.

If your nonprofit corporation will lease property or equipment used by the predecessor organization, include an explanation and copies of any leases as required by question 5. The IRS will scrutinize a lease to ensure that it does not provide for excessive rent payments to the principals of the former business. It's usually best, if possible, simply to assign such leases to the nonprofit corporation without payment and have the corporation deal with the landlord directly (or have the corporation renegotiate the lease with the landlord), rather than have the former business owners retain the lease and require rent payments from the nonprofit corporation. See Chapter 7, instructions to Item 7(i), for a sample assignment of lease form and further information.

Part IV. Financial Data

All groups should complete the financial data sheets (Statement of Revenue and Expenses and the Balance Sheet) contained in Sections A and B in this part.

Statement of Revenue and Expenses

The number of columns you use in Section A depends on how long your group has been in existence. Use column (a) to show revenues and expenses for the current tax year. The ending date for this period must be within 60 days of the mailing date of the application.

If your group has been in existence in prior tax years, use the remaining (b)-(d) columns to show revenues and expenditures for the corporation's previous tax years. In other words, go back three tax years if your corporation has been in existence that long.

If your group has not been in existence for any prior tax year, use column (b) and (c) to show proposed revenues and expenditures for your next two years (indicate the future year each column applies to in the blank at the top of each column).

Remember, your corporation's first tax year begins on the date when your Articles of Incorporation were filed with the secretary of state.

New Corporations If you are a new group applying for your tax exemption during the corporation's first tax year, the beginning date of the period shown at the top of column (a) is the date when your Articles were filed. The ending date for this period must be within 60 days of the date you expect to mail your application to the IRS. Use columns (b) and (c) to show projected figures for your next two tax years. Many new groups will repeat much of the information from their first tax year for the next two proposed tax years unless they anticipate a major change in operations or sources of support.

The IRS will use this financial data for a few purposes:

- to make sure your group's receipts and expenses correspond to the exempt purpose activities and operational information you've supplied in Part II of the application;

- to make sure you do not plan to substantially engage in unrelated business activities;

- to make sure you meet the appropriate public charity support test if you checked Part III, Line 10, box (h), (i) or (j)

- to make sure you meet the appropriate public charity support test if you checked Part III, Line 9, box (h), (i) or (j).

How to Fill in the Items   Read the 1023 instructions describing the various items included on the Section A statement. Don't expect to fill in all the items. The IRS knows you've just commenced operations and expects to see a few blank lines. In fact, the bulk of the revenues and expenses shown by many new groups for their first tax year and the two proposed tax years do not neatly fit the categories shown in Section A. Rather, this information is often attached as schedules in response to revenue item 7 (other income) and expense item 22 (other expenses). If you do attach these schedules of other income and expenses, make sure to break down the amounts as much as possible—the IRS does not like to see large lump-sum amounts.

Balance Sheet

Prepare the balance sheet to show assets and liabilities of your corporation as of the last date of the tax year period covered by column (a) of your statement of revenues and expenses in Part IV-A.

Example   You have organized a new nonprofit corporation, formed on April 1. You are preparing your 1023 application in November. The current tax year period covered by column (a) of your Statement of Revenue and Expenses is April 1, 19___ to October 31, 19___. Your balance sheet ending date will be October 31, 19___. This date should appear in the blank at the top-right of the balance sheet page.

Its not uncommon for a small starting nonprofit without liabilities and accounts receivable to simply show a little cash as its only reportable balance sheet item. The other most common items reported are Line 8 depreciable assets—equipment owned by the corporation and used to conduct its exempt activities.

File Your Annual Information Returns

Make sure to file annual federal and state information returns for your organization while your federal tax exemption is pending (see Chapter 10). Indicate that your federal 1023 application is pending on these federal and state tax returns.

If you experience any difficulty in preparing the financial information under this part, get the help of a tax or legal advisor.

Form 872-C

If you request an advance ruling of your public charity status by checking the first and third—or just the fourth—box of Part III, Line 11, you must complete and file *two* copies of Form 872-C with your 1023 application. The 1023 package from the IRS contains three copies of this form.

By completing and filing this form, you allow the IRS one year longer than normal to assess the excise taxes on investment income if your group is not granted public charity status at the end of its advance ruling period. By signing this form you're not signing your life away. You are letting the IRS collect one excise tax from you for a limited, but longer than usual, period of time, only if you are determined not to be a public charity at the end of the extended advance ruling period and only if you are then liable for this particular excise tax because of your operations during the extended advance ruling period. The IRS can assess this tax for any of the five years in the advance ruling period any time up to 8 years, 4 months and 15 days after the end of the first tax year in the advance ruling period.

If this form applies to you, complete it by typing the name of the corporation and the address of its principal office in the items at the top of the form. Show the ending date of your first tax year in the last paragraph (the month when your accounting period and tax year ends is given in Part I, Line 4, of Form 1023). Finally, fill in the bottom portion of the form. Type in the name of the corporation and the name of one of your directors, indicating this person's title as Director. Have the director sign and date the form. This person should sign your exemption application and User Fee form (Form 8718) as well. Do not fill in the items under "For IRS use only" at the bottom of the form.

Sign Your Federal Exemption Application

The final step in preparing your federal exemption application is to have a director sign and date the application at the bottom of the first page. Show the person's title as Director in the blank provided.

D. Mail Your Tax Exemption Application to the IRS

Now gather up your application papers and do the following:

√ Organize your federal tax exemption materials. These will include your original Form 1023 application papers as well as any necessary attachments (copies of your Articles and Bylaws, etc.). All groups should submit pages 1 through 9 of the form. Also submit any schedules (A-I) you may have prepared under Part III, Line 15 of the application. Don't include blank schedules that do not apply to your organization. Also include two completed Form 872-C Consent forms if you have requested an advance public charity ruling period. Make sure to include a completed 8718 User Fee form.

√ Make sure you have dated and signed your 1023 application, 8718 User Fee form and, if applicable, the two completed copies of the 872-C Consent form.

√ Make out a check payable to the IRS in the amount of the user fee.

√ Make one photocopy of all pages and attachments to your application and file them in your corporate records book.

√ Staple the pages of your completed original 1023 application together. Remember to staple your check to the space provided at the bottom of the completed User Fee form and staple this form to the front of your exemption application.

√ Mail your exemption application papers to the IRS District Office for your area shown on the 8718 User Fee form. These addresses are the most current and supersede the addresses shown in the 1023 package. If you're not sure which address applies to you, call your local IRS office.

Your next step is to wait. Although the IRS turnaround time is often two months, you may have to wait three to six months before receiving a response to your exemption application.

E. What to Expect From the IRS

The IRS will respond to your application in one of the following ways:

• grant your federal tax exemption;

• request further information; or

• issue a proposed adverse determination—this is a denial of tax exemption which becomes effective 30 days from the date of issuance.

If the IRS asks for more information and you feel the issues are too complex or are not sure what the IRS is getting at, you may wish to consult a nonprofit attorney or tax advisor. If you receive a proposed denial and you wish to appeal, see a lawyer *immediately*. For further information on appeal procedures, see the general instructions to the 1023 package and IRS Publication 892, *Exempt Organization Appeal Procedures for Unagreed Issues*—this publication should be mailed to you with the denial letter.

The Federal Determination Letter

When you receive a favorable determination letter from the IRS indicating that you are exempt from federal corporate income taxes, read it carefully. It contains important information regarding the basis for your exemption and the requirements for maintaining it.

Briefly, the information in the determination letter will state that you are tax exempt under Section 501(c)(3) of the Code and will indicate under what section of the Internal Revenue Code you qualify as a 501(c)(3) public charity. Check to make sure that the section listed by the IRS corresponds to the kind of public charity status you have sought for your nonprofit corporation. You will find the various public charity code sections listed in Part III, Line 9 of your copy of the 1023 form. Remember: Some groups will have checked Part III, Line 9(j) to let the IRS determine the proper public charity category for the organization.

The determination letter will indicate if you are required to file a federal annual information return, IRS Form 990. Most 501(c)(3) groups must file this form (see Chapter 10). Unless you filed your application late and were not entitled to an extension, your tax exemption and public charity status should be effective retroactively to the date when your Articles were filed with your secretary of state.

The determination letter should also state that you are not liable for excise taxes under Chapter 42 of the Internal Revenue Code. These are the taxes applicable to private foundations. With the exceptions noted below for groups which have requested an advance public charity ruling, these excise taxes do not apply to you. The letter also refers to other excise taxes for which you may be liable. These are the regular excise taxes applicable to all businesses which engage in certain activities, such as the sale of liquor, the manufacturing of certain products, etc. For further information, see IRS Publication 510, *Excise Taxes*.

Your letter will also provide information on the deductibility of charitable contributions made to your organization and will provide technical IRC section references as to the deductibility of such donations. It should also indicate (for most groups) that you are exempt from Federal Unemployment (FUTA) taxes and that you are subject to filing nonprofit unrelated business income tax returns (Form 990-T).

Remember 501(c)(3)s and their employees are subject to Social Security (FICA) taxes—see Chapter 10, Section D.

If you have requested an advance ruling period for determining your public charity status, the letter will indicate that a final determination of your status will be made 90 days after the end of your advance ruling period. Check to make sure that the IRS has the correct ending date of your annual accounting period. At the end of this period, the IRS will review your past annual information returns and determine whether you have, in fact, met the public charity support requirements during the advance ruling period. Although the determination letter indicates that you must submit information to the IRS, this is not normally necessary. You need submit additional information only if you want to, or are asked to do so later, to help the IRS determine that you have qualified as a public charity during the advance ruling period.

The determination letter may also refer to IRC Sections 507(d) and 4940—these sections will apply to you if you are found to be a private foundation, not a public charity, at the end of your advance ruling period. We have already mentioned the Section 4940 tax on investment income which may apply to you in such a case. Section 570(d) refers to an extra tax imposed on private foundations if they repeatedly (at least two times) engage in activities that give rise to the private foundation excise taxes discussed in Chapter 4.

If the IRS determines that you are not a public charity, but rather a private foundation, both your current and previous corporate activities will be scrutinized and may be subject to private foundation excise taxes. Don't be alarmed by this. These taxes don't normally apply to newly-formed nonprofits. Again, your organization should be able to meet the support requirements of its public charity category during the advance ruling period.

Congratulations! You've just finished the most complicated, and indeed most crucial, part of your nonprofit incorporation process. The remaining formal incorporation steps are explained in the next chapter.

Notes

1 Special purpose nonprofit groups, exempt under other subsections of Section 501(c), must use IRS Form 1024 to apply for their federal tax exemption. Technical Exception: Certain cooperative hospital service organizations and cooperative educational service organizations can use Form 1023 (see the General Instructions to Form 1023, Section A3).

2 A special formula is used to determine if a group "normally" has annual gross receipts of not more than $5,000. For specifics, see IRS Publication 557, page 9, "Gross Receipts Test."

3 If the 8718 Form which you ordered from the IRS is more current than the tear-out form, make sure to use the more recent form. Also note: It is possible that future 1023 forms will incorporate the User Fee form into the 1023 application. If this is the case, you do not need to submit a separate 8718 form.

4 For the full text of the regulations which explain these user fees, see Revenue Procedure 88-8.

5 What if you incorrectly guess that gross receipts will be no more than $10,000 during each of your first four tax years and actual gross receipts during this period exceed this amount in one or more years? We don't know the answer, although it seems reasonable to assume that the IRS may monitor your annual information returns and ask you to pay the remaining balance on the full Form 8718 fee if you make more than this threshold amount. Of course, if the financial information submitted with your 1023 exemption application shows that your group has, or expects to have, average gross receipts exceeding $10,000 for its first four years and you check the wrong box here, expect the IRS to return your exemption application due to insufficient payment.

6 If you are located in a special IRS test area (such as San Francisco), one of the organizers of your corporation (not the lawyer or accountant for the corporation) may call a special IRS telephone number for your district to obtain your EIN over the phone (you should have a completed SS-4 form in front of you when you make the call). Call your local IRS office to find out if you are located in one of these special IRS districts.

7 Of course, if your 501(c)(3) nonprofit is classified as a private foundation (a classification you will try to avoid), the significance of being a disqualified person becomes more substantial.

8 Don't forget that putting people on the payroll who are related to directors may create a conflict of interest problem for government-funded organizations.

9 Again, a safer way to qualify for an exception to the normal filing deadline is to ask for the automatic extension available under Line 3 of this part. If you submit your application within 27 months of the end of the month of your incorporation, you will qualify for late filing without having to take your organization's gross receipts or activities into account.

10 Even if your group files its 1023 application late and cannot meet this gross receipts test for all initial tax years, it may still be eligible for this exception

if gross receipts did not exceed these amounts. See IRS Publication 557, Chapter 3, "Gross Receipts Test," for further information on this point.

11 Although we call this another "automatic" extension, it really isn't: technically, you are qualifying for an extension under grounds listed in Revenue Ruling 92-85.

12. It's also possible that a "No" response here simply makes you ineligible to move ask for 501(c)(4) tax status during your late-filing period. Not such a terrible fate, really, but we've speculated enough on these technical niceties—let's get back to more important questions.

13 As often happens with technical tax forms, explicit instructions to guide some groups (in this case, Line 11 "No" groups) to the next question are missing. Our directions here (to skip Lines 12, 13 and 14 and go on to Line 15) are based on our interpretation of the questions and instructions on this form and a comparison of this material with similar material on previous 1023 application forms.

Final Steps in Organizing Your Nonprofit Corporation

**COMPANION COMPUTER DISK
FOR NONPROFIT INCORPORATORS**

Included at the back of this book is a 3^1/$_2$" PC/MS DOS Nonprofit Corporation

Computer Disk containing files for the tear-out incorporation forms included in this

book. These files are provided in standard file formats that can be read into,

completed, and printed with your PC wordprocessing program. For specific

instructions for using the forms on the disk, see the README.TXT file included on

the disk (insert the disk in your A: drive and use the TYPE A:README.TXT or MORE

<A:README.TXT command at the DOS prompt to view this file on the screen).

Most of the hard work is over, but there are still some important incorporation details to attend to. Don't be overwhelmed by the number of steps that follow—many will not apply to your particular nonprofit corporation and others are very simple.

Again, we recommend you use the Incorporation Checklist included in the Appendix to chart your way through these steps by checking off the box in the "Done" column for each step you complete.

Step 7. Obtain State Corporate Income Tax Exemption

Most states impose an annual corporate income, franchise or other tax based upon the net earnings of the corporation. In these states, your corporation must obtain an exemption from payment of these corporate taxes. In many cases, obtaining this state tax exemption is a formality and is based exclusively or primarily upon filing nonprofit Articles in your state and having obtained a federal 501(c)(3) tax exemption.

Your State Sheet indicates if your state imposes a corporate income or other type of tax and, if so, the name and address of the state agency from which your state corporate tax exemption must be obtained. The general requirements and procedures for obtaining this exemption are also shown (whether the state tax exemption is based upon filing Articles of Incorporation, obtaining a federal 501(c)(3) exemption or upon a separate state tax exemption application). We suggest you call your state corporate tax agency now and request all information and forms necessary for you to apply for your state exemption from corporate taxes.

The state tax exemption application process will be simple and self-explanatory in most cases. In the few instances where you must answer detailed questions or submit separate financial data, the responses and attachments to your federal 1023 package should serve as sufficient responses on the state form.

Make sure to take care of your state tax exemption in a timely fashion (usually by the end of your first tax year). As with the federal form, if you reach the deadline date for your annual state tax return and your state tax exemption is pending, make sure to file your required annual state return, indicating that the state tax exemption application is pending. Remember, like the IRS, state tax departments can impose severe fines and penalties for a failure to file required tax returns, whether or not your corporation is subject to, or liable for, any corporate taxes.

Note Unlike stock certificates in profit corporations, membership certificates in nonprofit 501(c)(3) corporations do not represent an ownership interest in the assets of the corporation and serve only as a formal reminder of membership status.

Step 9. Prepare the Minutes of Your First Board of Directors Meeting

Your next step is to prepare Minutes of your first board of directors meeting. The initial board of directors named in your Articles of Incorporation attend this meeting. If you did not name an initial board in your Articles, see the sidebar for instructions on having your incorporator(s) appoint the initial board. The purpose of this meeting is to transact the initial business of the corporation (elect officers, fix the legal address of the corporation, etc.) and to authorize the newly elected officers to take actions necessary to get your nonprofit corporation going (set up bank accounts, admit members if appropriate, etc.). Your directors should also discuss any other steps necessary at this point to get your nonprofit activities and operations started.

Prepare the Minutes by filling in the blanks on the tear-out Minutes of the First Meeting of Board of Directors included in the Appendix as you follow the instructions below.

Note Optional resolutions are flagged in the special instructions below. If an optional resolution does not apply to you, do not include the optional resolution page in your final Minutes.

Instructions to Prepare Your Minutes

Waiver of Notice Form This form in included preceding the tear-out Minutes in the Appendix. The purpose of this form is to obtain the prior written consent of each initial director to your first board meeting. Under the statutes of many states, the written consent of directors may be obtained to dispense with special notice procedures that would otherwise apply to this first unscheduled meeting of the board. Even if this written consent procedure does not apply in your state, it makes sense to use this form to notify each of your directors of the upcoming first meeting of the board.

Fill in this form showing the name and address of your corporation and the date, time and place of the meeting. Date the form and have each initial director sign.

If You Have Not Named Initial Directors in Your Articles

In some states, initial directors need not be named in the Articles. If this is the case, then the incorporators (the person or persons who signed the Articles) must appoint the initial board of directors. To do this, type the following form, fill in the name of the persons appointed to the board, and have each incorporator sign the form. Then prepare the Minutes of your first board meeting as explained in the text. Make sure to place a copy of this form in your corporate Minutes.

MEETING OF INCORPORATORS

On _____, 19__, at _____ o'clock, a meeting of the incorporator(s) of (name of corporation) was held to elect the initial members of the board of directors. After nomination and discussion, the following persons were unanimously voted to serve on the board of directors of this corporation, and until their successors shall be elected and qualified:

_____

_____

_____

_____

There being no further business, the meeting was adjourned.

Dated: _____

[signature(s) of incorporator(s)]

Preamble to Minutes   The first page of the Minutes contains several standard paragraphs reciting facts necessary to hold a meeting of directors. Type the name of your corporation, the date and time of the meeting and show the address of the corporation in the first few blanks. Next, show the names of the initial directors present at and, if applicable, absent from, the meeting. Remember, a quorum of the board, as specified in the Bylaws, must be shown in attendance. Name one of the directors Chairperson, and another Secretary of the meeting. You will elect permanent officers later in the meeting.

Articles of Incorporation   Indicate the name of the state corporate filings office (usually the secretary of state) where the Articles were filed and the date of this filing.

Bylaws   This resolution shows acceptance of the contents of the Bylaws by your directors.

Corporate Tax Exemptions   This resolution shows that your organization has obtained a favorable IRS determination of its 501(c)(3) tax-exempt status and is exempt from any applicable state corporate income taxes as well. Show the date of your federal determination letter in the blank in the first paragraph.

Election of Officers   Type the names of the persons you elect as officers of your corporation. Most nonprofits will wish to fill each of the four officer positions listed in this resolution. In many cases, particularly in larger nonprofits, officers are selected from among the board of directors.

Your State Sheet indicates the officer positions required to be filled in your state and any special requirements for filling these positions. Often, the same person may not be elected to serve as President and Secretary.

Principal Office   Article 1, Section 1 of the tear-out Bylaws indicates the county of the principal office of your corporation. Here you should provide the street address and city of this office. You should not show a post office box.

Bank Account   It is important to keep corporate funds separate from any personal funds by depositing corporate funds into, and writing corporate checks out of, at least one corporate checking account.

Step 8. Set Up a Corporate Records Book

A. Corporate Records Book

You will need a corporate records book to keep all your papers in an orderly fashion. These documents include Articles of Incorporation, Bylaws, Minutes of your first board meeting and ongoing director and shareholder meetings, tax exemption applications and determination letters, membership certificates, etc. You should keep your corporate records book at the principal office of your corporation at all times.

To set up a corporate records book, you can simply place all your incorporation documents in a three-ring binder. If you prefer, however, you can order a custom designed corporate records book as part of one of the Nolo corporate kits described below.

B. Nolo Corporate Kits

If you wish to order a Nolo corporate kit, you can do so by completing the order form contained at the back of this book. Nolo corporate kits include:

- a corporate records book with minute paper and index dividers for Articles of Incorporation, Bylaws, Minutes and Corporate Certificates;

- a metal corporate seal designed to emboss your corporate name and year of incorporation on important corporate documents;

- IRS nonprofit tax forms: IRS Package 1023—the 501(c)(3) tax exemption application—plus IRS Forms 8718 and SS-4;

- 20 Director Certificates are included with each kit acknowledging the services of members of the board of directors. Additionally, you may order 20 Sponsor Certificates which recognize the contributions made by individuals to your nonprofit corporation's program and purposes;

- an option to order a membership materials is also included, conisting of a Membership Index and Roll Sheets to keep a consolidated record of the names and addresses of your corporation's members plus 40 printed Membership Certificates.

The basic difference between the Nolo kits offered is the style of the corporate records binder. Here are brief descriptions of each kit:

The Ex Libris®

features a higher quality brown vinyl binder with an integrated slipcase with your corporate name embossed on the spine.

The Centennial

features a handcrafted, simulated red and black leather binder with your corporate name embossed in gold on the spine. If you are willing to pay for a fancier binder, this kit is definitely worth it.

C. Corporate Seals

A corporation is not legally required to have or use a corporate seal, but many find it handy to do so. A corporate seal is a formal way of indicating that a given document is the duly authorized act of the corporation. It is not normally used on everyday business papers (invoices, purchase orders, etc.) but is commonly employed for more formal documents such as leases, membership certificates, deeds of trust, certifications of board resolutions, and the like. As indicated above, a good quality, reasonably-priced metal pocket seal is available as part of the Nolo corporate kits described above. Embossed and stamped seals are also available separately through legal stationers (for approximately $40). Most seals are circular in form and contain the name of the corporation, the state, and year of incorporation.

D. Corporate Certificates

Each Nolo corporate kit includes 20 Director Certificates to distribute to your board members. You may also wish to order 20 Sponsor Certificates. These contain language recognizing the contributions of benefactors, patrons, volunteers and friends of your nonprofit. We also include an option on the order form at the back of the book for you to order membership materials consisting of 40 printed Membership Certificates, a Membership Roll and Index. If you have set up a formal membership corporation by including membership provisions in your Bylaws, you may wish to order these membership materials.

Indicate the bank and branch office where you will maintain corporate accounts in the first blank. In the second blank, indicate the number of persons (one or more) who must co-sign corporate checks. In the remaining blanks, show the names of individuals allowed to co-sign checks. Normally, officers or paid staff of the corporation are designated. The names of the President and Treasurer are often listed among those who can sign corporate checks.

Optional Compensation of Officers Indicate any salaries to be paid to the officers in the blanks in this resolution. Type a zero to show unpaid officers' resolutions. Most nonprofits do not compensate officers, or do so only minimally. If you do provide for real officer salaries, make sure they are reasonable and are related to payment received for similar services in the nonprofit sector.

Optional Corporate Seal If you've ordered a corporate seal, impress the seal in the space to the right of this resolution.

Optional Corporate Certificates This is an optional resolution. Include this page in your final Minutes if you have ordered director, sponsor, membership or other certificates for your corporation and attach a sample of each certificate to your completed Minutes. Director, sponsor, and membership certificates may be ordered as part of each of the Nolo corporate kits.

Secretary Certification Page Your Secretary should date and sign the blanks on the last page of the Minutes.

Step 10. Place Minutes and Attachments In Corporate Records Book

You are now through with the preparation of your Minutes. Place your Minutes and all attachments in your corporate records book. Your attachments may include the following forms or documents:

- Waiver of Notice and Consent to Holding of the First Meeting;

- Copy of your Articles, or Certificate of Incorporation, file-stamped or certified by the secretary of state;

- Copy of your Bylaws;

- Federal 501(c)(3) tax exemption determination letter;

- Copy of state tax exemption application determination letter, or other correspondence;

- Sample director, sponsor or membership certificates.

Remember, you should continue to place an original or copy of all formal corporate documents in your corporate records book (including Minutes of director, committee and membership meetings) and keep this book at your principal office.

Step 11. File Assumed Business Name Statement

If your nonprofit corporation is to do engage in activities (raise funds, apply for grants, advertise, sell goods or services, etc.) under a name other than the exact corporate name given in your Articles of Incorporation, you will need to file an assumed or fictitious business name statement with your secretary of state and/or county clerk's office.[2]

Example If the name stated in your Articles is "THE ART WORKS, INC." and the corporation plans to continue using the name of the pre-existing organization which was incorporated, "THE ART STUDIO, " (or chooses another name different from the one set out in the Articles), you should file an assumed corporate name statement

Your secretary of state materials should contain information on assumed corporate name statements. If not, call your secretary of state or other corporate filings office and ask if this filing is made at the state or county level (or both). Order the form from the appropriate office and prepare and file the statement. In most cases, a small fee is charged for this filing. Also, the statement may need to be published locally in a legal newspaper and a proof of publication filed with your county clerk. Check the instructions to the form for the requirements in your state.

Step 12. Apply for a Federal Nonprofit Mailing Permit

Most 501(c)(3) tax-exempt nonprofit corporations will qualify for and wish to obtain a third-class nonprofit mailing permit from the U.S. Post Office. This permit entitles you to lower rates on mailings, an important advantage for many groups since the nonprofit rate is considerably lower than the regular third-class rate.

To obtain your permit, bring the following papers to your local or main post office branch:

- file-stamped or certified copy of your Articles;
- a copy of your Bylaws;
- a copy of your federal (and, if applicable, state) tax exemption determination letter; and
- copies of program literature, newsletters, bulletins and any other promotional materials.

The post office clerk will ask you to fill out a short application and take your papers. If your local post office branch doesn't handle this paperwork, the clerk will send you to a classifications office at the main post office branch. You will have to pay a one-time fee and an annual permit fee. The clerk will take your papers and forward them to the regional post office classification office for a determination. In about a week or so you will receive notice of the post office's determination.

Once you have your permit, you can mail letters, parcels, etc., at the reduced rate by affixing stamps to your mail; taking the mail to your post office and filling out a special mailing form; or by using the simpler methods of either stamping your mail with an imprint stamp (made by a stampmaker) or leasing a mail stamping machine that shows your imprint information. Ask the classifications clerk for further information.

Step 13. Apply for Property Tax Exemptions

We've already discussed state tax exemptions for real and personal property taxes in Chapter 5. Now is the time to apply for any property tax exemptions available to your group. Remember:

- Most groups will wish to apply for an exemption from local personal property taxes if real property is owned or leased by the corporation.

- Establishing an exemption on leased premises should result in a corresponding reduction in rent payments from your landlord.

- Even if your federal tax exemption is pending, you may want to submit your application for a property tax exemption as soon as possible and forward a copy of your federal tax exemption to the taxing agency later. This way, you may be able to obtain at least a partial exemption for the current property tax year.

The procedure for applying for local personal and real property taxes varies. Often you will need to submit a completed application form, copies of your Articles and Bylaws, and current and projected financial statements. The initial financial statements may often be copied from, or based upon, the financial statement information submitted with your federal 1023 form.

Call your county tax assessor or collector and determine what property tax exemptions are available for your tax-exempt 501(c)(3) nonprofit corporation and the procedures for applying. In some cases, application is made to an office in the state capitol; in others, all papers are processed locally by the county office. There may be multiple exemption categories to choose from. For example, a religious group may qualify for a church property tax exemption and for a separate property exemption available to 501(c)(3) nonprofit organizations. The county office should be able to advise you as to the most appropriate property exemption available to your group.

Step 14. File a Corporate Report Form

In most states, a periodic nonprofit corporate report form or statement must be filed with the secretary of state's office. Most often, this form must be filed annually.

Your State Sheet lists the corporate report requirements in your state. Your secretary of state materials should contain further information on any periodic corporate report requirements.

While the nature and extent of the information required in each state varies, certain basic organizational information is usually required, such as the address of your principal office, the names and addresses of your directors and officers, your registered agent and office, etc. In some cases, financial information must also be submitted, such as directors' and officers' salaries, officer and supervisory staff compensation, fundraising receipts, etc. Usually, this information is made available to the public by the secretary of state.

Since a failure to file a periodic report may lead to a fine or, for repeated failures, a suspension or forfeiture of corporate powers, make sure to file your corporate reports on time.

Step 15. Register with the Attorney General

In some states, nonprofit corporations must register and report to the state attorney general's office. The general focus of the attorney general's scrutiny of nonprofit activities is to make sure that the assets of the 501(c)(3) organization are being used for valid charitable or public purposes, not private purposes.

The information sought on attorney general reporting forms varies, but most commonly the financial reporting requirements seek to determine if funds solicited from the public are being used for their stated purpose and whether any of the principals of the nonprofit (directors, officers, staff) are being unduly benefited by nonprofit funds or programs.

In some states, an initial registration form must be filed by the nonprofit organization, with a periodic report required each succeeding year or so. We suggest you check with the attorney general's office by calling the main office in your state capitol. Ask if your 501(c)(3) tax-exempt nonprofit corporation must register or report to this office. In many states, this reporting function is handled by the charitable trusts division or department. Ask if your state has a similar division or department in the attorney general's office.

Step 16. Comply with Political Reporting Requirements

If your nonprofit corporation plans to lobby for legislation, hire a lobbyist, or otherwise be politically active (for example, by supporting or opposing state, county or city measures to be voted on by the public), we suggest you check to see if your state imposes political registration or reporting requirements.[3] Often, a Fair Political Practices Commission or similar body in the state capitol oversees and administers these requirements. Another politically active nonprofit organization in your community should have experience with these requirements and should be able to direct you to the proper state office.

Note The final three steps of this chapter below apply only to groups that have incorporated a pre-existing organization.

Step 17. Prepare Assignments of Leases and Deeds

If you have incorporated a pre-existing organization, you may wish to prepare an assignments of lease or deed if real property interests are being transferred to the corporation. Here is a basic Assignment of Lease form you can use, or modify for use.

Check Local Ordinances

If you plan to solicit contributions locally (for example, as part of a door-to-door fundraising drive), make sure to comply with all local solicitation ordinances and regulations. Some counties and cities enforce local registration and reporting requirements. Other localities require the furnishing of specific statements and disclosure information to persons solicited by the nonprofit corporation.

Sample Assignment of Lease

    (Name of original lessee, e.g., the unincorporated nonprofit organization) , _Lessee of those premises commonly known as_ __(address of leased property)__ , _hereby assigns the attached Lease relating to the above premises, executed_ __(date original lease was signed)__ , _and all rights, liabilities and obligations thereunder to a proposed corporation,_ __(name of corporation)__ . _This Assignment is given without consideration and no consideration will be required to effectuate this Assignment._

Dated:

(name of Lessee)

_By:_ _(signature of Lessee representative)_
    (typed name of representative)

    The undersigned Lessor of the above premises hereby assents to this Assignment of Lease.

Dated:

(signature of Lessor)
(typed name of Lessor), Lessor

Reality Note Of course, assignments can be dispensed with if rental agreements or leases are simply renegotiated between the landlord and the new corporation. Even if you do prepare an assignment, the terms of the lease itself will normally require you to get the landlord's consent (the sample assignment of lease form above includes a clause showing the lessor's consent to the assignment). It is particularly important to communicate with the landlord if the nonprofit corporation expects to obtain an exemption from local real property taxes on the leased premises. Nonprofit groups in this situation will want to insert a clause in their new lease allowing them a credit against rent payments for the amount of the decrease in the landlord's property tax bill as a result of obtaining their real property tax exemption.

A real estate broker or agent can help you obtain and prepare new leases and deeds. If a mortgage or deed of trust is involved, you may need the permission of the lender.

Step 18. File Final Papers for Prior Organization

If you have incorporated a pre-existing group, you may need to file final sales tax, employment tax and other returns for the prior organization. You will also want to cancel any permits or licenses issued to the prior organization or its principals, obtaining new licenses in the name of the nonprofit corporation.

Step 19. Notify Others of Your Incorporation

If a pre-existing group has been incorporated, notify creditors and other interested parties, in writing, of the termination and dissolution of the prior organization and of its transfer to the new corporation. This is advisable as a legal precaution and as a courtesy to those who have dealt with the prior organization.

To notify past creditors, suppliers, organizations and businesses of your incorporation, send a friendly letter which shows the date of your incorporation, your corporate name and its principal office address. Retain a copy of each letter for inclusion in your corporate records book.

Note for Prior Partnerships Although not common, if the prior group was organized as a partnership, some states require the publication of a Notice of Dissolution of Partnership in the county or judicial district where the partnership office or property was located. To do this, call a local legal newspaper and ask if this notice form is published by the paper. If so, the newspaper will charge a small fee to publish the statement the required number of times and send you a proof of publication form for your files. If required, the newspaper should also file the proof of publication with the county clerk, the county recorder, or other appropriate county office.

Notes

1 Black Beauty® and Ex Libris® are registered trademarks of Julius Blumberg, Inc.

2 The filing of an assumed or fictitious business name statement does not authorize the use of a name which is already in use by another business or organization as a trademark, service mark or tradename. See Chapter 6, Step 2F.

3 For a discussion of political activities permitted to 501(c)(3) nonprofit groups, see Chapter 3D.

After Your Corporation Is Organized

The incorporation and initial organizational business of your nonprofit corporation are now complete. But before you close this book, read just a little more. After incorporating, you need to become familiar with the formalities of corporate life. These include preparing minutes of formal corporate meetings, filing tax returns and paying employment taxes.[1] The information presented here is not meant to tell you everything you will need to know about these subjects but simply to provide some of the basics and indicate some of the major areas which you (or your tax advisor) will need to go over in more detail.

A. Piercing the Corporate Veil— If You Want to Be Treated Like a Corporation, It's Best to Act Like One

After you've set up a corporation of any kind, your organization should act like one. Although filing your Articles of Incorporation with the secretary of state brings the corporation into existence and makes it a legal entity, this is not enough to ensure that a court or the IRS will treat your organization as a corporation. What we are referring to here is not simply maintaining your various tax exemptions or even your nonprofit status with the state—we are talking about being treated as a valid corporate entity in court and for tax purposes. Remember, it is your legal corporate status which allows your organization to be treated as an entity apart from its directors, officers and employees and allows it to be taxed (or not taxed), sue or be sued, on its own. It is the corporate entity that insulates the people behind the corporation from taxes and lawsuits.

Courts and the IRS do, on occasion, scrutinize the organization and operation of a corporation, particularly if it is directed and operated by a small number of people who wear more than one hat (fill director and officer positions, etc.). If the corporation doesn't have adequate money to start with, making it likely that creditors or people who have claims against the corporation won't be able to be paid; if corporate and personal funds are commingled; if the corporation doesn't keep adequate corporate records, such as Minutes of meetings, or generally doesn't pay much attention to the theory and practice of corporate life, a court may disregard the corporate entity and hold the principals (directors, officers, etc.) personally liable for corporate debts. Also, the IRS may assess taxes and penalties personally against those connected with managing the affairs of the corporation if they conclude that the corporation is not a valid legal or tax entity. In legal jargon, this is called "piercing the corporate veil."

To avoid problems of this type, be careful to operate your corporation as a separate legal entity. This includes holding regular and special meetings of your board and membership as required by your Bylaws and as necessary to take formal corporate action. It is critical that you document formal corporate meetings with neat and thorough Minutes. Also, it is wise to have enough money in your corporate account to pay foreseeable debts and liabilities which may arise in the course of carrying out your activities—even nonprofits should start with a small cash reserve. Above all, keep corporate funds separate from the personal funds of the individuals who manage or work for the corporation.

B. Federal Corporate Tax Returns

1. Annual Exempt Organization Return for Public Charities

Nonprofit corporations exempt from federal corporate income tax under Section 501(c)(3) and qualified (under an advance or definitive ruling) as public charities must file IRS Form 990, annual Return of Organization Exempt From Income Tax (together with Form 990, Schedule A), on or before the 15th day of the fifth month (within four and a half months) following the close of their accounting period (tax year). This return should be filed even if your 1023 federal application for exemption is still pending.

IRS Form 990-EZ This is a short form annual return which can be used in place of Form 990 by smaller tax exempt public charities—those with gross receipts of less than $100,000 and total assets of less than $250,000.

Note Your first 990 return deadline may come upon you sooner than you expect if your first tax year is a "short year"—a tax year of less than 12 months.

Example If your accounting period as specified in your Bylaws runs from January 1 to December 31 and your Articles were filed on December 1, your first tax year consists of one month, from December 1 to December 31. In this situation, your first Form 990 would have to be filed within four and a half months of December 31 (by May 15th), only

For More Information

We suggest all nonprofits obtain IRS Publication 509, *Tax Calendars*, prior to the beginning of each year. This pamphlet contains tax calendars showing the dates for corporate and employer filings during the year.

Further information on withholding, depositing, reporting and paying federal employment taxes can be found in IRS Publication 15, *Circular E, Employer's Tax Guide* and the Publication 15 Supplement, as well as IRS Publication 937, *Employment Taxes*. Further federal tax information can be found in IRS Publication 542, *Tax Information on Corporations* and Publication 334, *Tax Guide for Small Business*.

Helpful information on accounting methods and bookkeeping procedures is contained in IRS Publication 538, *Accounting Period and Methods* and Publication 583, *Information for Business Taxpayers*.

These publications can be picked up at your local IRS office (or ordered by phone—call your local IRS office or try the toll-free IRS forms and publications request telephone number 1-800-TAX-FORM).

five and a half months after your Articles were filed. It is likely that your federal tax exemption application would be pending at this time.

Exemptions   The Internal Revenue Code exempts certain public charities from filing this return, including the following: certain churches, schools, mission societies, religious activity groups, state institutions, corporations organized under an Act of Congress, tax-exempt private foundations, certain trusts, religious and apostolic organizations and public charities, generally, whose gross receipts are "normally" not more than $25,000 in each taxable year.[2]

Your federal exemption determination letter should indicate whether you must file Form 990. Most public charities will be publicly supported organizations or receive a majority of their support from exempt-purpose revenue (see Chapter 4, Sections F2 and F3). Since these groups are not institutional public charities falling under one of the automatic exemptions to filing listed above, they will have to file Form 990 unless they meet the "normally" not more than $25,000 gross receipts exemption. To rely on this exemption, fill in the top portion of the 990 form and check the box which indicates you are eligible for this exemption.

IRC § 501(h) Political Expenditures Test   If your nonprofit corporation has made the political expenditures election discussed in Chapter 3, Section D3 by filing the Federal Election Form 5768, indicate on Form 990, Schedule A that you have made this election and fill in the appropriate part of this schedule showing actual lobbying expenditures made during the year.

Note   If you are required to report annually to your secretary of state or attorney general, you may be allowed or required to submit a copy of your federal 990 return to meet your state's annual financial disclosure requirements.

2.   Annual Exempt Organization Return for Private Foundations

Although we don't expect many nonprofit 501(c)(3) tax-exempt corporations to be classified as private foundations, if this is the case, you must file a Federal Annual Return of Private Foundation Exempt From Income Tax, Form 990-PF, instead of the 990 discussed above, within four and half months of the close of your tax year. This return requests specific information relevant to determining whether you are liable for private foundation excise taxes, as well as the usual information on receipts and expenditures, assets and liabilities, etc. This form and separate instructions for completing it should be mailed to you close to the end of your accounting period. Again, watch out for a first short year and an early deadline for filing your 990-PF.

The foundation manager(s) must publish a notice of availability of public inspection of this annual report form in a local county newspaper by the filing date for the 990-PF. This notice must indicate that the annual report is available for public inspection, at the principal office of the corporation, within 180 days after the publication of notice of availability. A copy of the published notice must be attached to the 990-PF.

3. Annual Exempt Organization Unrelated Business Income Tax Return

Section 501(c)(3) federal tax-exempt corporations, with a few minor exceptions, having gross incomes of $1,000 or more during the year from an unrelated trade or business must file an Exempt Organization Business Income Tax Return (Form 990-T), within two and a half months after the close of their tax year. For a definition and discussion of unrelated trades and businesses, see Chapter 5, Section C and obtain Federal Publication 598, *Tax on Business Income of Exempt Organizations*. Use booklet 598 and the separate instructions to Form 990-T in preparing this form.

The taxes imposed on unrelated business income are the same as the normal federal corporate income tax rates. Remember: Too much unrelated business income may indicate to the IRS that you are engaging in non-exempt activities to a "substantial" degree and may jeopardize your tax exemption.

C. State Corporate Tax Returns and Reports

Make sure to file your state corporate tax returns on time. In many states, the state forms incorporate, are based upon, or follow the federal non-profit corporate tax returns discussed above and are due on the same date. Your state tax corporate forms may be included in your secretary of state materials. If not, make a call to your state department of taxation and revenue (or similar state tax agency or department) and order your annual nonprofit corporation tax forms, schedules and instructions.

File Tax Returns on Time

The IRS and the state are notoriously efficient in assessing and collecting late filing and other penalties. So, while it's generally true that your nonprofit corporation normally does not have to worry about paying taxes, you should worry a little about filing your annual information returns (and employment tax returns and payments). Too many nonprofit corporations have had to liquidate when forced to pay late filing penalties for a few years' worth of simple informational returns that they inadvertently forgot to file.[3]

Another important aspect associated with the assessment of late filing penalties and delinquent employment taxes is that the IRS (and state) can, and often do, try to collect these often substantial amounts from individuals associated with the corporation if the corporation doesn't have sufficient cash to pay them. Remember, one of the exceptions to the concept of limited lability is liability for unpaid taxes and tax penalties. The IRS and state can go after the person (or persons) associated with the corporation who are responsible for reporting and/or paying taxes.

The State Sheets list state corporate income tax departments. Call this office for further information.

D. Federal and State Employment Taxes

Federal and state employment (payroll) taxes must be withheld and paid on behalf of the people who work for the nonprofit corporation. Directors, with certain exceptions, are not considered employees if they are paid only for attending board meetings. However, if they are paid for other services or as salaried employees of the corporation, they will be considered employees whose wages are subject to employment taxes. Check with the IRS and your local state employment tax office for further information.

501(c)(3)s are exempt from paying federal unemployment insurance (FUTA) taxes but normally are subject to collecting, withholding, reporting and paying federal social security (FICA) and individual income taxes on employees' salaries. Your tax-exempt nonprofit may be exempt from having to pay some state employment taxes as well. For information and help in computing your federal withholding and employer contribution payments, obtain the IRS publications listed in the first sidebar in this chapter. To register as an employer in your state and for information on meeting state payroll tax requirements, call the state employment tax office in your vicinity.

E. Employee Income Tax Returns

Corporate staff and other compensated corporate personnel must report and pay taxes on employment compensation on their individual annual federal income tax returns (IRS Form 1040). If your state imposes a personal income tax, then state income taxes are computed and paid with the employee's state personal income tax return.

F. Sales, Use, Excise and Other State Taxes

Your corporation may be required to charge and collect state, county and city sales, use, transit, excise and other state taxes from customers or clients. In some cases, nonprofit exemptions from one or more of these state taxes may be available to your 501(c)(3) nonprofit corporation. Contact your state department of revenue, taxation or similar state agency to register your corporation and obtain any exemptions to which you may be entitled.

G. Licenses and Permits

Many businesses, whether operating as profit or nonprofit corporations, partnerships or sole proprietorships are required to obtain state licenses and permits before commencing business. So, while you may not be subject to the usual kind of red tape applicable to strictly profit-making enterprises (such as contractors, real estate brokers or engineers), you should check with your state department of consumer affairs (or similar state licensing agency or department) for information concerning any state licensing requirements for your activities or type of organization. Many nonprofit institutions, for example schools or hospitals, will need to comply with a number of registration and reporting requirements administered by the state and, possibly, county government. A local business license or permit may also be required for your activities—check with your city business license department.

H. Workers' Compensation

Workers' compensation insurance coverage compensates workers for losses caused by work-related injuries and protects the corporation from lawsuits brought to recover these amounts. In some states, this coverage is mandatory; in others it is optional. Specific exemptions from coverage may be available to directors and officers in some instances. Make sure to check with your insurance agent or broker, or call your state compensation insurance commission, for names of carriers, rates and extent of required coverage in all cases.

**Independent Contractors
and Payroll Taxes**

Generally, independent contractors, such as consultants, who are not subject to the control of the corporation—both as to what shall be done and how the work is to be performed—are not considered employees. Wages paid to these people are not subject to payroll tax withholding or payment by the nonprofit corporation.

Be careful when trying to avoid the payment of employment taxes by classifying people as independent contractors. The law in this area is fuzzy and the IRS and the employment tax agency in your state are usually obstinate in maintaining that outsiders really work for the corporation (and must be covered by payroll taxes).

I. Private Insurance Coverage

Nonprofit corporations, like other organizations, should carry the usual types of commercial insurance to prevent undue loss in the event of an accident, fire, theft, etc. Although the corporate form may insulate directors, officers, and members from personal loss, it won't prevent corporate assets from being jeopardized by such eventualities. Coverage for general liability, product liability, and fire and theft should be examined. Liability insurance for directors and officers should also be examined, particularly if your nonprofit corporation wants to reassure any passive directors on the board that they will be protected from personal liability in the event of a lawsuit.

To take advantage of special state statutes immunizing volunteer directors and officers from personal liability (see Chapter 2, Section H), adequate director and officer liability insurance coverage may be required, or must be shown to be unobtainable or unaffordable.

Notes

1 The information regarding taxes (return deadlines, tax rates, penalties, etc.) is subject to change. Make sure it's current when you attend to your taxes.

2 See the official instructions to IRS Form 990 for the details of these exemptions.

3 Although the IRS regulations state that late filing penalties won't be assessed if you can show "reasonable cause" for the delay, don't count on this provision. The IRS can be quite unreasonable here.

Lawyers and Accountants

While we believe you can take care of the bulk of the work associated with organizing and operating your nonprofit corporation, you may need to consult a lawyer or accountant on complicated or special issues.

We think it makes sense to have a lawyer experienced in forming nonprofits within your state look over your Articles and Bylaws to make sure your forms contain all special state-specific provisions applicable to your group. Also, having a nonprofit lawyer or tax advisor review your federal (and, if applicable, state) tax exemption application may be a good idea. Besides, making contact with a legal and tax person early in your corporate life is often a sensible step. As your group grows and its programs expand, you'll be able to consult these professionals for help with ongoing legal and tax questions.

The professionals you contact should not only have experience in nonprofit incorporations and the 501(c)(3) tax exemption application process. They should be prepared to help you help yourself—to answer your specific, informed questions and review, not rewrite, the forms you have prepared.

The next sections provide a few general suggestions on finding the right lawyer or tax advisor and, if you wish to do your own legal research, how to find the law in your state statutes.

A. Lawyers

Finding the right lawyer is not always easy. Obviously, the best lawyer to choose is someone you personally know and trust and who has lots of experience advising smaller nonprofits. This, of course, may be a tall order. The next best is a nonprofit advisor whom a friend, another nonprofit incorporator, or someone in your nonprofit network recommends. A local nonprofit resource center, for example, may be able to steer you to one or more lawyers who maintain an active nonprofit practice. With patience and persistence (and enough phone calls), this second word-of-mouth approach almost always brings positive results.

Another approach is to locate a local nonprofit legal referral panel. Panels of this sort are typically run by a local bar association or another nonprofit organization. One in your area may be able to give you the names of lawyers who are experienced in nonprofit law and practice and who offer a discount or free consultation as part of the referral panel program. Ask about and try to avoid referral services which are operated on a strict rotating basis. In this case you'll get the name of the next lawyer on the list, not necessarily one with nonprofit experience. Also watch out for private (and highly suspect) commercial referral services that often refer lawyers to themselves—you'll want to avoid these.

When you call a prospective lawyer, speak with the lawyer personally, not just the reception desk. You can probably get a good idea of how the person operates by paying close attention to the way your call is handled. Is the lawyer available, or is your call returned promptly? Is the lawyer willing to spend at least a few minutes talking to you to determine if she is really the best person for the job? Does the lawyer seem sympathetic to, and compatible with, the nonprofit goals of your group? Do you get a good personal feeling from your conversation? Oh, and one more thing: Be sure to get the hourly rate the lawyer will charge set in advance. If you are using this book, you will probably want to eliminate lawyers who charge $250 per hour to support an office on top of the tallest building in town.

What About Lost-Cost Law Clinics?

Law clinics advertise their services regularly on TV and radio. Can they help your form a nonprofit organization? Perhaps, but usually at a rate well above their initial low consultation rate. Since the lawyer turnover rate at these clinics is high and the degree of familiarity with nonprofit legal and tax issues is usually low, we recommend you spend your money more wisely by finding a reasonably-priced nonprofit lawyer elsewhere.

B. Legal Research

Many incorporators may wish to research legal information on their own. In most states, county law libraries are open to the public (you need not be a lawyer to use them) and are not difficult to use once you understand how the information is categorized and stored. They are an invaluable source of corporate and general business forms, federal and state corporate tax procedures and information, etc. Research librarians will usually go out of their way to help you find the right statute, form or background reading on any corporate or tax issue.

If possible, we recommend that incorporators obtain (purchase if necessary) a copy of their nonprofit corporation code from their secretary of state or a commercial publisher. Your State Sheet lists the publisher of your state's nonprofit corporation law and, if applicable, the price for this publication. Remember, in some states the nonprofit statutes are included as part of the state's regular business corporation act.

Whether you are leafing through your own copy of your state's nonprofit corporation law or looking up corporate statutes at your local county law library, finding a particular corporate provision is usually a straightforward process. First define and, if necessary, narrow down the subject matter of your search in terms of essential keywords associated with your area of interest. For example, if one of the directors on your board resigns and you wish to determine whether your state has any statutory rules for filling vacancies on the board, you will define and restrict your search to the key areas of "directors" and "vacancies." Look up these keywords in the index to your state's nonprofit corporation law (in multi-volume sets, the index is found at the back of the last volume). In this case, any special section on "vacancies" should be listed under the major heading of "directors" in the index.

If your index search does not yield results, then search for your key topics in the main and subsidiary table of contents contained in the corporations act. For example, at the beginning of your corporation law, a main table of contents will show headings for the major headings covered in the corporation law. One of these major headings will probably be labeled "Directors," followed by a range of code sections devoted to this subject area. Just before the first of these code sections in the corporation code, a subsidiary table of contents should be included showing individual headings for each code section in this code section range. In this mini table of contents for the "Directors" code sections, one heading may be listed for a code section devoted to "Vacancies."

If your table of contents search is unsuccessful, another search strategy is to start at the beginning of the corporation law and leaf through all the major and minor headings. Eventually—usually after just a few minutes or so—you will hit upon your area of interest or will satisfy yourself that the area in question is not covered by your corporate statutes. By the way, after going through your nonprofit law this way once or twice, you should become acquainted with most of its major headings. This, in turn, will help you locate specific nonprofit subject areas and statutes quickly when performing future searches of this material.

Legal Shorthand and Definitions   A number of the rules contained in the corporate statutes are often given in legal shorthand—in short legal catchwords and phrases that are defined elsewhere in the code. For example, a common requirement contained in corporate statutes is that a matter or transaction be "approved by the board" or "approved by a majority of the board." Each of these phrases is defined in separate sections of the corporations code. [By the way, the first phrase usually means approval by a majority of directors present at a meeting at which a quorum of directors is present; the second usually means approval by a majority of the full board.] Special definitions of this sort are usually listed at the beginning of the state's nonprofit corporation law—read this starting definition section first to understand any special rules and legal shorthand used throughout your nonprofit corporation statutes.

Using the Internet   Many states provide all or some state statutes on their web site. While some states have all their statutes on the Internet, along with keyword searching, others have nothing at all. The address for your state's home page should be www.state.[*postal abbreviation*].us.

If you are interested in doing self-help legal research, an excellent source of information is *Legal Research: How to Find and Understand the Law* by Elias (Nolo Press). Nolo also publishes *Legal Research Made Easy: A Roadmap Through the Law Library Maze* by Berring, a 2 1/2-hour videotape (with manual) by University of California law librarian Bob Berring which explains how to use the law library. If you are interested in legal research on the Internet, *Law on the Net*, by Evans (Nolo Press), is a great source of URLs (addresses).

C. Accountants and Tax Advice

As you already know, organizing and operating a nonprofit corporation involves a significant amount of financial and tax work. While much of it is easy, a nit-picking attention to definitions, cross references, formulas and other elusive or downright boring details is required, particularly when preparing your federal 1023 tax exemption application. As we often suggest in the book, you may find it sensible to seek advice from an accountant or other tax advisor when organizing your nonprofit corporation. For example, you may need help preparing the income statements, balance sheets and other financial and tax information submitted with your IRS tax exemption application. Also, if your organization will handle any significant amount of money, you will need an accountant or bookkeeper to set up your double-entry accounting books (cash receipts and disbursement journals, general ledger, etc.). Double entry accounting techniques are particularly important to nonprofits that receive federal or private grant or program funds—accounting for these "restricted funds" is a special area of accounting that usually requires assistance to implement. Nonprofit corporation account books should be designed to allow for easily transferring financial data to state and federal nonprofit corporate tax returns and disclosure statements and to provide an easy way to determine, at any time, whether receipts and expenditures fall into the categories proper to maintaining your 501(c)(3) tax exemption, public charity status, and grant or program eligibility. You will also want to know whether your operations are likely to subject you to an unrelated business income tax under federal and state rules.

Once your corporation is organized and your books are set up, the ongoing work of keeping books and filing tax forms may be performed by tax publications listed at the beginning of Chapter 10. These pamphlets contain essential information on preparing and filing IRS corporation and employment tax returns.

When you select an accountant or bookkeeper, the same considerations apply as when selecting a lawyer. Choose someone you know or whom a friend or nonprofit contact recommends. Be as specific as you can regarding the services you wish performed and make sure the advisor has had experience with nonprofit taxation and tax exemption applications as well as regular payroll, tax and accounting procedures. Many nonprofit bookkeepers work part-time for several nonprofit organizations. Again, calling people in your nonprofit network is often the best way to find this type of person.

Appendix

Incorporation Checklist

Incorporation Contact Letter

Name Availability Letter

Application for Reservation of Corporate Name

Articles Filing Letter

Bylaws

Minutes

State Sheets

Incorporation Checklist

Chapter	Step	Page	Step Name	Done
6	1	6.3	Order Materials from Your Secretary of State	
6	2A	6.4	Choose a Corporate Name	
6	2D	6.12	Check Name Availability	
6	2E	6.14	Reserve Your Corporate Name	
6	2F	6.15	Perform a Name Search	
6	2G	6.18	Protect Your Name	
6	3	6.19	Prepare Articles of Incorporation	
6	4	6.35	File Articles of Incorporation	
7	5C	7.4	Prepare Bylaws	
7	5D	7.19	Prepare Membership Provisions	
8	6	8.2	Prepare and File Your Federal Tax Exemption Application	
9	7	9.2	Obtain State Corporate Income Tax Exemption	
9	8	8.3	Set Up a Corporate Records Book	
9	9	9.5	Prepare Minutes of First Board of Directors Meeting	
9	10	9.8	Place Minutes and Attachments in Corporate Records Book	
9	11	9.9	File Assumed Business Name Statement	
9	12	9.9	Apply for Federal Nonprofit Mailing Permit	
9	13	9.10	Apply for Property Tax Exemptions	
9	14	9.11	File Corporate Report Form	
9	15	9.11	Register with Attorney General	
9	16	9.12	Comply with Political Reporting Requirements	
9	17	9.12	Prepare Assignments of Leases and Deeds	
9	18	9.14	File Final Papers for Prior Organization (existing groups only)	
9	19	9.14	Notify Others of Your Incorporation (existing groups only)	

Corporate Filings Office:

I am in the process of forming a domestic nonprofit corporation. I would appreciate receiving the following forms, material and other information from your office:

- please correct the address of your corporate filings office above if it is incorrect or not completely current;

- the telephone number and contact person for inquires related to incorporating a domestic nonprofit corporation;

- Articles of Incorporation and other corporate forms (with instructions) promulgated by your office for domestic nonprofit corporations. If your office reviews nonprofit Articles of Incorporation for correctness prior to filing, please advise me of the procedure I should follow to obtain this pre-filing review;

- the name and price of a publication which may be ordered from your office or from a commercial publisher which contains the corporate statutes regulating nonprofit corporations in this state;

- the telephone number or address of the division in your office which I can call to determine if a proposed corporate name is available for my use (plus any additional information available related to checking and reserving a proposed corporate name);

- a current schedule of fees for statutory filings, forms and publications;

- All other forms, statutes, publications and other materials available from your office detailing requirements for the formation, operation and dissolution of a domestic nonprofit corporation.

If there is a fee for any of the above material (such as the nonprofit corporation statutes), please advise. I enclose a stamped, self-addressed envelope for your reply. My name, address and telephone number are listed below if you wish to contact me regarding this request.

Name:
Address:
Phone:

Thank you for your assistance.

Corporate Name Availability:

    Please advise if the following proposed corporate names, listed in order of preference, are available for corporate use:

_____

_____

    Enclosed is a stamped, self-addressed envelope for your reply. My name, address and phone number are included below if you wish to contact me regarding this request.

    Name:

    Address:

    Phone:

Thank you for your assistance.

Corporate Filings Office
Secretary of State Address

Corporate Name Reservations:

Please reserve the following corporate name for my use for
the allowable period specified under the state's corporation
statutes.

_____

I enclose the required payment of \$_____.
My name, address and phone number are included below if you wish
to contact me regarding this request.

Name:

Address:

Phone:

Thank you for your assistance,

Corporate Filings Office:

I enclose an original and _____ copies of the proposed Articles of Incorporation of _____
_____.

Please file the Articles of Incorporation and return a Certificate of Incorporation (or file-stamped copy of the original Articles) to me at the above address.

A check/money order in the amount of $_____, made payable to your office, for total filing and processing fees is enclosed.

The above corporate name was reserved for my use pursuant to reservation # _____, issued on _____.

Sincerely,

_____
                                    , Incorporator

BYLAWS

OF

_____

ARTICLE 1
OFFICES

SECTION 1. PRINCIPAL OFFICE

The principal office of the corporation is located in
_____ County, State of _____.

SECTION 2. CHANGE OF ADDRESS

The designation of the county or state of the corporation's
principal office may be changed by amendment of these Bylaws.
The Board of Directors may change the principal office from one
location to another within the named county by noting the
changed address and effective date below, and such changes of
address shall not be deemed, nor require, an amendment of these
Bylaws:

_____   Dated: _____, 19__

_____   Dated: _____, 19__

_____   Dated: _____, 19__

SECTION 3. OTHER OFFICES

The corporation may also have offices at such other places,
within or without its state of incorporation, where it is
qualified to do business, as its business and activities may
require, and as the board of directors may, from time to time,
designate.

ARTICLE 2
NONPROFIT PURPOSES

SECTION 1. IRC SECTION 501 (c) (3) PURPOSES

This corporation is organized exclusively for one or more
of the purposes as specified in Section 501(c)(3) of the
Internal Revenue Code, including, for such purposes, the making
of distributions to organizations that qualify as exempt
organizations under Section 501(c)(3) of the Internal Revenue
Code.

SECTION 2. SPECIFIC OBJECTIVES AND PURPOSES

The specific objectives and purposes of this corporation
shall be:

ARTICLE 3
DIRECTORS

SECTION 1. NUMBER

The corporation shall have _____ directors and collectively they shall be known as the Board of Directors.

SECTION 2. QUALIFICATIONS

Directors shall be of the age of majority in this state. Other qualifications for directors of this corporation shall be as follows:

SECTION 3. POWERS

Subject to the provisions of the laws of this state and any limitations in the Articles of Incorporation and these Bylaws relating to action required or permitted to be taken or approved by the members, if any, of this corporation, the activities and affairs of this corporation shall be conducted and all corporate powers shall be exercised by or under the direction of the Board of Directors.

SECTION 4. DUTIES

It shall be the duty of the directors to:

(a) Perform any and all duties imposed on them collectively or individually by law, by the Articles of Incorporation, or by these Bylaws;

(b) Appoint and remove, employ and discharge, and, except as otherwise provided in these Bylaws, prescribe the duties and fix the compensation, if any, of all officers, agents and employees of the corporation;

(c) Supervise all officers, agents and employees of the corporation to assure that their duties are performed properly;

(d) Meet at such times and places as required by these Bylaws;

(e) Register their addresses with the Secretary of the corporation, and notices of meetings mailed or telegraphed to them at such addresses shall be valid notices thereof.

SECTION 5. TERM OF OFFICE

Each director shall hold office for a period of _____ _____ and until his or her successor is elected and qualifies.

SECTION 6. COMPENSATION

Directors shall serve without compensation except that a reasonable fee may be paid to directors for attending regular and special meetings of the board. In addition, they shall be allowed reasonable advancement or reimbursement of expenses incurred in the performance of their duties.

SECTION 7. PLACE OF MEETINGS

Meetings shall be held at the principal office of the corporation unless otherwise provided by the board or at such other place as may be designated from time to time by resolution of the Board of Directors.

SECTION 8. REGULAR MEETINGS

Regular meetings of Directors shall be held on _____
_____
at _____ _M, unless such day falls on a legal holiday, in which
event the regular meeting shall be held at the same hour and place
on the next business day.

If this corporation makes no provision for members, then, at
the regular meeting of directors held on _____
_____, directors shall be elected
by the Board of Directors. Voting for the election of directors
shall be by written ballot. Each director shall cast one vote per
candidate, and may vote for as many candidates as the number of
candidates to be elected to the board. The candidates receiving
the highest number of votes up to the number of directors to be
elected shall be elected to serve on the board.

SECTION 9. SPECIAL MEETINGS

Special meetings of the Board of Directors may be called by
the Chairperson of the Board, the President, the Vice-President,
the Secretary, by any two directors, or, if different, by the
persons specifically authorized under the laws of this state to
call special meetings of the board. Such meetings shall be held
at the principal office of the corporation or, if different, at
the place designated by the person or persons calling the
special meeting.

SECTION 10. NOTICE OF MEETINGS

Unless otherwise provided by the Articles of Incorporation,
these Bylaws, or provisions of law, the following provisions
shall govern the giving of notice for meetings of the board of
directors:

(a) Regular Meetings. No notice need be given of any
regular meeting of the board of directors.

(b) Special Meetings. At least one week prior notice shall be
given by the Secretary of the corporation to each director of each
special meeting of the board. Such notice may be oral or written,
may be given personally, by first class mail, by telephone, or by
facsimile machine, and shall state the place, date and time of the
meeting and the matters proposed to be acted upon at the meeting.
In the case of facsimile notification, the director to be
contacted shall acknowledge personal receipt of the facsimile

notice by a return message or telephone call within twenty four hours of the first facsimile transmission.

   (c) <u>Waiver of Notice.</u> Whenever any notice of a meeting is required to be given to any director of this corporation under provisions of the Articles of Incorporation, these Bylaws, or the law of this state, a waiver of notice in writing signed by the director, whether before or after the time of the meeting, shall be equivalent to the giving of such notice.

SECTION 11.   QUORUM FOR MEETINGS

   A quorum shall consist of _____ of the members of the Board of Directors.

   Except as otherwise provided under the Articles of Incorporation, these Bylaws, or provisions of law, no business shall be considered by the board at any meeting at which the required quorum is not present, and the only motion which the Chair shall entertain at such meeting is a motion to adjourn.

SECTION 12.   MAJORITY ACTION AS BOARD ACTION

   Every act or decision done or made by a majority of the directors present at a meeting duly held at which a quorum is present is the act of the Board of Directors, unless the Articles of Incorporation, these Bylaws, or provisions of law require a greater percentage or different voting rules for approval of a matter by the board.

SECTION 13.   CONDUCT OF MEETINGS

   Meetings of the Board of Directors shall be presided over by the Chairperson of the Board, or, if no such person has been so designated or, in his or her absence, the President of the corporation or, in his or her absence, by the Vice President of the corporation or, in the absence of each of these persons, by a Chairperson chosen by a majority of the directors present at the meeting. The Secretary of the corporation shall act as secretary of all meetings of the board, provided that, in his or her absence, the presiding officer shall appoint another person to act as Secretary of the Meeting.

Meetings shall be governed by _____
_____, insofar
as such rules are not inconsistent with or in conflict with the
Articles of Incorporation, these Bylaws, or with provisions of
law.

SECTION 14.   VACANCIES

    Vacancies on the Board of Directors shall exist (1) on the
death, resignation or removal of any director, and (2) whenever
the number of authorized directors is increased.

    Any director may resign effective upon giving written notice
to the Chairperson of the Board, the President, the Secretary, or
the Board of Directors, unless the notice specifies a later time
for the effectiveness of such resignation. No director may resign
if the corporation would then be left without a duly elected
director or directors in charge of its affairs, except upon notice
to the Office of the Attorney General or other appropriate agency
of this state.

    Directors may be removed from office, with or without cause,
as permitted by and in accordance with the laws of this state.

    Unless otherwise prohibited by the Articles of
Incorporation, these Bylaws or provisions of law, vacancies on the
board may be filled by approval of the board of directors. If the
number of directors then in office is less than a quorum, a
vacancy on the board may be filled by approval of a majority of
the directors then in office or by a sole remaining director. A
person elected to fill a vacancy on the board shall hold office
until the next election of the Board of Directors or until his or
her death, resignation or removal from office.

SECTION 15.   NON-LIABILITY OF DIRECTORS

    The directors shall not be personally liable for the debts,
liabilities, or other obligations of the corporation.

SECTION 16. INDEMNIFICATION BY CORPORATION OF DIRECTORS
            AND OFFICERS

    The directors and officers of the corporation shall be
indemnified by the corporation to the fullest extent permissible
under the laws of this state.

SECTION 17.   INSURANCE FOR CORPORATE AGENTS

Except as may be otherwise provided under provisions of law, the Board of Directors may adopt a resolution authorizing the purchase and maintenance of insurance on behalf of any agent of the corporation (including a director, officer, employee or other agent of the corporation) against liabilities asserted against or incurred by the agent in such capacity or arising out of the agent's status as such, whether or not the corporation would have the power to indemnify the agent against such liability under the Articles of Incorporation, these Bylaws or provisions of law.

ARTICLE 4
OFFICERS

SECTION 1.   DESIGNATION OF OFFICERS

The officers of the corporation shall be a President, a Vice President, a Secretary, and a Treasurer.   The corporation may also have a Chairperson of the Board, one or more Vice Presidents, Assistant Secretaries, Assistant Treasurers, and other such officers with such titles as may be determined from time to time by the Board of Directors.

SECTION 2.   QUALIFICATIONS

Any person may serve as officer of this corporation.

SECTION 3. ELECTION AND TERM OF OFFICE

Officers shall be elected by the Board of Directors, at any time, and each officer shall hold office until he or she resigns or is removed or is otherwise disqualified to serve, or until his or her successor shall be elected and qualified, whichever occurs first.

SECTION 4.   REMOVAL AND RESIGNATION

Any officer may be removed, either with or without cause, by the Board of Directors, at any time.   Any officer may resign at any time by giving written notice to the Board of Directors or to the President or Secretary of the corporation.   Any such resignation shall take effect at the date of receipt of such notice or at any later date specified therein, and, unless otherwise specified therein, the acceptance of such resignation shall not be necessary to make it effective. The above provisions of this Section shall be superseded by any conflicting terms of a contract which has been approved or ratified by the Board of Directors relating to the employment of any officer of the corporation.

SECTION 5. VACANCIES

Any vacancy caused by the death, resignation, removal, disqualification, or otherwise, of any officer shall be filled by the Board of Directors. In the event of a vacancy in any office other than that of President, such vacancy may be filled temporarily by appointment by the President until such time as the Board shall fill the vacancy. Vacancies occurring in offices of officers appointed at the discretion of the board may or may not be filled as the board shall determine.

SECTION 6. DUTIES OF PRESIDENT

The President shall be the chief executive officer of the corporation and shall, subject to the control of the Board of Directors, supervise and control the affairs of the corporation and the activities of the officers. He or she shall perform all duties incident to his or her office and such other duties as may be required by law, by the Articles of Incorporation, or by these Bylaws, or which may be prescribed from time to time by the Board of Directors. Unless another person is specifically appointed as Chairperson of the Board of Directors, the President shall preside at all meetings of the Board of Directors and, if this corporation has members, at all meetings of the members. Except as otherwise expressly provided by law, by the Articles of Incorporation, or by these Bylaws, he or she shall, in the name of the corporation, execute such deeds, mortgages, bonds, contracts, checks, or other instruments which may from time to time be authorized by the Board of Directors.

SECTION 7. DUTIES OF VICE PRESIDENT

In the absence of the President, or in the event of his or her inability or refusal to act, the Vice President shall perform all the duties of the President, and when so acting shall have all the powers of, and be subject to all the restrictions on, the President. The Vice President shall have other powers and perform such other duties as may be prescribed by law, by the Articles of Incorporation, or by these Bylaws, or as may be prescribed by the Board of Directors.

SECTION 8. DUTIES OF SECRETARY

The Secretary shall:

Certify and keep at the principal office of the corporation the original, or a copy, of these Bylaws as amended or otherwise altered to date.

Keep at the principal office of the corporation or at such other place as the board may determine, a book of minutes of all meetings of the directors, and, if applicable, meetings of committees of directors and of members, recording therein the time and place of holding, whether regular or special, how called, how notice thereof was given, the names of those present or represented at the meeting, and the proceedings thereof.

See that all notices are duly given in accordance with the provisions of these Bylaws or as required by law.

Be custodian of the records and of the seal of the corporation and affix the seal, as authorized by law or the provisions of these Bylaws, to duly executed documents of the corporation.

Keep at the principal office of the corporation a membership book containing the name and address of each and any members, and, in the case where any membership has been terminated, he or she shall record such fact in the membership book together with the date on which such membership ceased.

Exhibit at all reasonable times to any director of the corporation, or to his or her agent or attorney, on request therefor, the Bylaws, the membership book, and the minutes of the proceedings of the directors of the corporation.

In general, perform all duties incident to the office of Secretary and such other duties as may be required by law, by the Articles of Incorporation, or by these Bylaws, or which may be assigned to him or her from time to time by the Board of Directors.

SECTION 9. DUTIES OF TREASURER

The Treasurer shall:

Have charge and custody of, and be responsible for, all funds and securities of the corporation, and deposit all such funds in the name of the corporation in such banks, trust companies, or other depositories as shall be selected by the Board of Directors.

Receive, and give receipt for, monies due and payable to the corporation from any source whatsoever.

Disburse, or cause to be disbursed, the funds of the corporation as may be directed by the Board of Directors, taking proper vouchers for such disbursements.

Keep and maintain adequate and correct accounts of the corporation's properties and business transactions, including accounts of its assets, liabilities, receipts, disbursements, gains and losses.

Exhibit at all reasonable times the books of account and financial records to any director of the corporation, or to his or her agent or attorney, on request therefor.

Render to the President and directors, whenever requested, an account of any or all of his or her transactions as Treasurer and of the financial condition of the corporation.

Prepare, or cause to be prepared, and certify, or cause to be certified, the financial statements to be included in any required reports.

In general, perform all duties incident to the office of Treasurer and such other duties as may be required by law, by the Articles of Incorporation of the corporation, or by these Bylaws, or which may be assigned to him or her from time to time by the Board of Directors.

SECTION 10. COMPENSATION

The salaries of the officers, if any, shall be fixed from time to time by resolution of the Board of Directors. In all cases, any salaries received by officers of this corporation shall be reasonable and given in return for services actually rendered to or for the corporation.

ARTICLE 5
COMMITTEES

SECTION 1. EXECUTIVE COMMITTEE

The Board of Directors may, by a majority vote of its members, designate an Executive Committee consisting of _____ board members and may delegate to such committee the powers and authority of the board in the management of the business and affairs of the corporation, to the extent permitted, and except as may otherwise be provided, by provisions of law.

By a majority vote of its members, the board may at any time revoke or modify any or all of the Executive Committee authority so delegated, increase or decrease but not below two (2) the number of the members of the Executive Committee, and fill vacancies on the Executive Committee from the members of the board. The Executive Committee shall keep regular minutes of its proceedings, cause them to be filed with the corporate records, and report the same to the board from time to time as the board may require.

SECTION 2. OTHER COMMITTEES

The corporation shall have such other committees as may from time to time be designated by resolution of the Board of Directors. These committees may consist of persons who are not also members of the board and shall act in an advisory capacity to the board.

SECTION 3. MEETINGS AND ACTION OF COMMITTEES

Meetings and action of committees shall be governed by, noticed, held and taken in accordance with the provisions of these Bylaws concerning meetings of the Board of Directors, with such changes in the context of such Bylaw provisions as are necessary to substitute the committee and its members for the Board of Directors and its members, except that the time for regular and special meetings of committees may be fixed by resolution of the Board of Directors or by the committee. The Board of Directors may also adopt rules and regulations pertaining to the conduct of meetings of committees to the extent that such rules and regulations are not inconsistent with the provisions of these Bylaws.

ARTICLE 6
EXECUTION OF INSTRUMENTS, DEPOSITS AND FUNDS

SECTION 1. EXECUTION OF INSTRUMENTS

The Board of Directors, except as otherwise provided in these Bylaws, may by resolution authorize any officer or agent of the corporation to enter into any contract or execute and deliver any instrument in the name of and on behalf of the corporation, and such authority may be general or confined to specific instances. Unless so authorized, no officer, agent, or employee shall have any power or authority to bind the corporation by any contract or engagement or to pledge its credit or to render it liable monetarily for any purpose or in any amount.

SECTION 2. CHECKS AND NOTES

Except as otherwise specifically determined by resolution of the Board of Directors, or as otherwise required by law, checks, drafts, promissory notes, orders for the payment of money, and other evidence of indebtedness of the corporation shall be signed by the Treasurer and countersigned by the President of the corporation.

SECTION 3. DEPOSITS

All funds of the corporation shall be deposited from time to time to the credit of the corporation in such banks, trust companies, or other depositories as the Board of Directors may select.

SECTION 4. GIFTS

The Board of Directors may accept on behalf of the corporation any contribution, gift, bequest, or devise for the nonprofit purposes of this corporation.

ARTICLE 7
CORPORATE RECORDS, REPORTS AND SEAL

SECTION 1. MAINTENANCE OF CORPORATE RECORDS

The corporation shall keep at its principal office:

(a) Minutes of all meetings of directors, committees of the board and, if this corporation has members, of all meetings of members, indicating the time and place of holding such meetings, whether regular or special, how called, the notice given, and the names of those present and the proceedings thereof;

(b) Adequate and correct books and records of account, including accounts of its properties and business transactions and accounts of its assets, liabilities, receipts, disbursements, gains and losses;

(c) A record of its members, if any, indicating their names and addresses and, if applicable, the class of membership held by each member and the termination date of any membership;

(d) A copy of the corporation's Articles of Incorporation and Bylaws as amended to date, which shall be open to inspection by the members, if any, of the corporation at all reasonable times during office hours.

SECTION 2. CORPORATE SEAL

The Board of Directors may adopt, use, and at will alter, a corporate seal. Such seal shall be kept at the principal office of the corporation. Failure to affix the seal to corporate instruments, however, shall not affect the validity of any such instrument.

SECTION 3. DIRECTORS' INSPECTION RIGHTS

Every director shall have the absolute right at any reasonable time to inspect and copy all books, records and documents of every kind and to inspect the physical properties of the corporation and shall have such other rights to inspect the books, records and properties of this corporation as may be required under the Articles of Incorporation, other provisions of these Bylaws, and provisions of law.

SECTION 4. MEMBERS' INSPECTION RIGHTS

If this corporation has any members, then each and every member shall have the following inspection rights, for a purpose reasonably related to such person's interest as a member:

(a) To inspect and copy the record of all members' names, addresses and voting rights, at reasonable times, upon written demand on the Secretary of the corporation, which demand shall state the purpose for which the inspection rights are requested.

(b) To obtain from the Secretary of the corporation, upon written demand on, and payment of a reasonable charge to, the Secretary of the corporation, a list of the names, addresses and voting rights of those members entitled to vote for the election of directors as of the most recent record date for which the list has been compiled or as of the date specified by the member subsequent to the date of demand. The demand shall state the purpose for which the list is requested. The membership list shall be made within a reasonable time after the demand is received by the Secretary of the corporation or after the date specified therein as of which the list is to be compiled.

(c) To inspect at any reasonable time the books, records, or minutes of proceedings of the members or of the board or committees of the board, upon written demand on the Secretary of the corporation by the member, for a purpose reasonably related to such person's interests as a member.

Members shall have such other rights to inspect the books, records and properties of this corporation as may be required under the Articles of Incorporation, other provisions of these Bylaws, and provisions of law.

SECTION 5. RIGHT TO COPY AND MAKE EXTRACTS

Any inspection under the provisions of this Article may be made in person or by agent or attorney and the right to inspection shall include the right to copy and make extracts.

SECTION 6. PERIODIC REPORT

The board shall cause any annual or periodic report required under law to be prepared and delivered to an office of this state or to the members, if any, of this corporation, to be so prepared and delivered within the time limits set by law.

ARTICLE 8
IRC 501(c)(3) TAX EXEMPTION PROVISIONS

SECTION 1. LIMITATIONS ON ACTIVITIES

No substantial part of the activities of this corporation shall be the carrying on of propaganda, or otherwise attempting to influence legislation [except as otherwise provided by Section 501(h) of the Internal Revenue Code], and this corporation shall not participate in, or intervene in (including the publishing or distribution of statements), any political campaign on behalf of, or in opposition to, any candidate for public office.

Notwithstanding any other provisions of these Bylaws, this corporation shall not carry on any activities not permitted to be carried on (a) by a corporation exempt from federal income tax under Section 501(c)(3) of the Internal Revenue Code, or (b) by a corporation, contributions to which are deductible under Section 170(c)(2) of the Internal Revenue Code.

SECTION 2. PROHIBITION AGAINST PRIVATE INUREMENT

No part of the net earnings of this corporation shall inure to the benefit of, or be distributable to, its members, directors or trustees, officers, or other private persons, except that the corporation shall be authorized·and empowered to pay reasonable compensation for services rendered and to make payments and distributions in furtherance of the purposes of this corporation.

SECTION 3. DISTRIBUTION OF ASSETS

Upon the dissolution of this corporation, its assets remaining after payment, or provision for payment, of all debts and liabilities of this corporation shall be distributed for one or more exempt purposes within the meaning of Section 501(c)(3) of the Internal Revenue Code or shall be distributed to the federal government, or to a state or local government, for a public purpose. Such distribution shall be made in accordance with all applicable provisions of the laws of this state.

SECTION 4. PRIVATE FOUNDATION REQUIREMENTS AND RESTRICTIONS

In any taxable year in which this corporation is a private foundation as described in Section 509(a) of the Internal Revenue Code, the corporation 1) shall distribute its income for said period at such time and manner as not to subject it to tax under Section 4942 of the Internal Revenue Code; 2) shall not engage in any act of self-dealing as defined in Section 4941(d) of the Internal Revenue Code; 3) shall not retain any excess business holdings as defined in Section 4943(c) of the Internal Revenue Code; 4) shall not make any investments in such manner as to subject the corporation to tax under Section 4944 of the Internal Revenue Code; and 5) shall not make any taxable expenditures as defined in Section 4945(d) of the Internal Revenue Code.

ARTICLE 9
AMENDMENT OF BYLAWS

SECTION 1. AMENDMENT

Subject to the power of the members, if any, of this corporation to adopt, amend or repeal the Bylaws of this corporation and except as may otherwise be specified under provisions of law, these Bylaws, or any of them, may be altered, amended, or repealed and new Bylaws adopted by approval of the Board of Directors.

ARTICLE 10
CONSTRUCTION AND TERMS

If there is any conflict between the provisions of these Bylaws and the Articles of Incorporation of this corporation, the provisions of the Articles of Incorporation shall govern.

Should any of the provisions or portions of these Bylaws be held unenforceable or invalid for any reason, the remaining provisions and portions of these Bylaws shall be unaffected by such holding.

All references in these Bylaws to the Articles of Incorporation shall be to the Articles of Incorporation, Articles of Organization, Certificate of Incorporation, Organizational Charter, Corporate Charter, or other founding document of this corporation filed with an office of this state and used to establish the legal existence of this corporation.

All references in these Bylaws to a section or sections of the Internal Revenue Code shall be to such sections of the Internal Revenue Code of 1986 as amended from time to time, or to corresponding provisions of any future federal tax code.

ADOPTION OF BYLAWS

We, the undersigned, are all of the initial directors or incorporators of this corporation, and we consent to, and hereby do, adopt the foregoing Bylaws, consisting of _____ preceding pages, as the Bylaws of this corporation.

Dated: _____

_____

_____

_____

_____

_____

MEMBERSHIP PROVISIONS

OF THE BYLAWS OF

_____

ARTICLE 11
MEMBERS

SECTION 1. DETERMINATION AND RIGHTS OF MEMBERS

The corporation shall have only one class of members. No member shall hold more than one membership in the corporation. Except as expressly provided in or authorized by the Articles of Incorporation, the Bylaws of this corporation, or provisions of law, all memberships shall have the same rights, privileges, restrictions and conditions.

SECTION 2. QUALIFICATIONS OF MEMBERS

The qualifications for membership in this corporation are as follows:

SECTION 3. ADMISSION OF MEMBERS

Applicants shall be admitted to membership

SECTION 4. FEES AND DUES

(a) The following fee shall be charged for making application for membership in the corporation:

(b)   The annual dues payable to the corporation by members shall be

SECTION 5.   NUMBER OF MEMBERS

There is no limit on the number of members the corporation may admit.

SECTION 6.   MEMBERSHIP BOOK

The corporation shall keep a membership book containing the name and address of each member. Termination of the membership of any member shall be recorded in the book, together with the date of termination of such membership. Such book shall be kept at the corporation's principal office.

SECTION 7.   NONLIABILITY OF MEMBERS

A member of this corporation is not, as such, personally liable for the debts, liabilities, or obligations of the corporation.

SECTION 8.   NONTRANSFERABILITY OF MEMBERSHIPS

No member may transfer a membership or any right arising therefrom. All rights of membership cease upon the member's death.

SECTION 9.   TERMINATION OF MEMBERSHIP

The membership of a member shall terminate upon the occurrence of any of the following events:

(1)   Upon his or her notice of such termination delivered to the President or Secretary of the corporation personally or by mail, such membership to terminate upon the date of delivery of the notice or date of deposit in the mail.

(2)   If this corporation has provided for the payment of dues by members, upon a failure to renew his or her membership by paying dues on or before their due date, such termination to be effective thirty (30) days after a written notification of

delinquency is given personally or mailed to such member by the Secretary of the corporation. A member may avoid such termination by paying the amount of delinquent dues within a thirty (30) day period following the member's receipt of the written notification of delinquency.

(3) After providing the member with reasonable written notice and an opportunity to be heard either orally or in writing, upon a determination by the Board of Directors that the member has engaged in conduct materially and seriously prejudicial to the interests or purposes of the corporation. Any person expelled from the corporation shall receive a refund of dues already paid for the current dues period.

All rights of a member in the corporation shall cease on termination of membership as herein provided.

ARTICLE 12
MEETINGS OF MEMBERS

SECTION 1. PLACE OF MEETINGS

Meetings of members shall be held at the principal office of the corporation or at such other place or places as may be designated from time to time by resolution of the Board of Directors.

SECTION 2. REGULAR MEETINGS

A regular meeting of members shall be held on _____ _____, at _____ M., for the purpose of electing directors and transacting other business as may come before the meeting. The candidates receiving the highest number of votes up to the number of directors to be elected shall be elected. Each voting member shall cast one vote, with voting being by ballot only. The annual meeting of members for the purpose of electing directors shall be deemed a regular meeting.

Other regular meetings of the members shall be held on _____, at _____ M.

If the day fixed for a regular meeting falls on a legal holiday, such meeting shall be held at the same hour and place on the next business day.

SECTION 3. SPECIAL MEETINGS OF MEMBERS

Special meetings of the members shall be called by the Board of Directors, the Chairperson of the Board, or the President of the corporation, or, if different, by the persons specifically authorized under the laws of this state to call special meetings of the members.

SECTION 4. NOTICE OF MEETINGS

Unless otherwise provided by the Articles of Incorporation, these Bylaws, or provisions of law, notice stating the place, day and hour of the meeting and, in the case of a special meeting, the purpose or purposes for which the meeting is called, shall be delivered not less than ten (10) nor more than fifty (50) days before the date of the meeting, either personally or by mail, by or at the direction of the President, or the Secretary, or the persons calling the meeting, to each member entitled to vote at such meeting. If mailed, such notice shall be deemed to be delivered when deposited in the United States mail addressed to the member at his or her address as it appears on the records of the corporation, with postage prepaid. Personal notification includes notification by telephone or by facsimile machine, provided however, in the case of facsimile notification, the member to be contacted shall acknowledge personal receipt of the facsimile notice by a return message or telephone call within twenty four hours of the first fascimile transmission.

The notice of any meeting of members at which directors are to be elected shall also state the names of all those who are nominees or candidates for election to the board at the time notice is given.

Whenever any notice of a meeting is required to be given to any member of this corporation under provisions of the Articles of Incorporation, these Bylaws, or the law of this state, a waiver of notice in writing signed by the member, whether before or after the time of the meeting, shall be equivalent to the giving of such notice.

SECTION 5. QUORUM FOR MEETINGS

A quorum shall consist of _____ of the voting members of the corporation.

Except as otherwise provided under the Articles of Incorporation, these Bylaws, or provisions of law, no business shall be considered by the members at any meeting at which the required quorum is not present, and the only motion which the Chair shall entertain at such meeting is a motion to adjourn.

SECTION 6.   MAJORITY ACTION AS MEMBERSHIP ACTION

Every act or decision done or made by a majority of voting members present in person or by proxy at a duly held meeting at which a quorum is present is the act of the members, unless the Articles of Incorporation, these Bylaws, or provisions of law require a greater number.

SECTION 7.   VOTING RIGHTS

Each member is entitled to one vote on each matter submitted to a vote by the members. Voting at duly held meetings shall be by voice vote. Election of Directors, however, shall be by written ballot.

SECTION 8.   ACTION BY WRITTEN BALLOT

Except as otherwise provided under the Articles of Incorporation, these Bylaws, or provisions of law, any action which may be taken at any regular or special meeting of members may be taken without a meeting if the corporation distributes a written ballot to each member entitled to vote on the matter. The ballot shall:

1.   set forth the proposed action;

2.   provide an opportunity to specify approval or disapproval of each proposal;

3.   indicate the number of responses needed to meet the quorum requirement and, except for ballots soliciting votes for the election of directors, state the percentage of approvals necessary to pass the measure submitted; and

4.   shall specify the date by which the ballot must be received by the corporation in order to be counted. The date set shall afford members a reasonable time within which to return the ballots to the corporation.

Ballots shall be mailed or delivered in the manner required for giving notice of membership meetings as specified in these bylaws.

Approval of action by written ballot shall be valid only when the number of votes cast by ballot within the time period specified equals or exceeds the quorum required to be present at a meeting authorizing the action, and the number of approvals equals or exceeds the number of votes that would be required to approve the action at a meeting at which the total number of votes cast was the same as the number of votes cast by ballot.

Directors may be elected by written ballot. Such ballots for the election of directors shall list the persons nominated at the time the ballots are mailed or delivered.

SECTION 9. CONDUCT OF MEETINGS

Meetings of members shall be presided over by the Chairperson of the Board, or, if there is no Chairperson or, in his or her absence, by the President of the corporation or, in his or her absence, by the Vice President of the corporation or, in the absence of all of these persons, by a Chairperson chosen by a majority of the voting members, present at the meeting. The Secretary of the corporation shall act as Secretary of all meetings of members, provided that, in his or her absence, the presiding officer shall appoint another person to act as Secretary of the Meeting.

Meetings shall be governed by _____ _____, as such rules may be revised from time to time, insofar as such rules are not inconsistent with or in conflict with the Articles of Incorporation, these Bylaws, or with provisions of law.

WAIVER OF NOTICE AND CONSENT TO HOLDING
OF FIRST MEETING OF BOARD OF DIRECTORS

OF

_____

We, the undersigned, being all the directors of
_____, hereby waive
notice of the first meeting of the Board of Directors of the
corporation and consent to the holding of said meeting at

_____,
on _____, 19__, at _____ M., and
consent to the transaction of any and all business by the
directors at the meeting, including, without limitation, the
adoption of Bylaws, the election of officers and the selection of
the place where the corporation's bank accounts will be
maintained.

Dated: _____

_____
, Director

_____
, Director

_____
, Director

_____
, Director

_____
, Director

MINUTES OF FIRST MEETING OF BOARD OF DIRECTORS

OF

_____

The Board of Directors of_____
_____ held its first meeting on
_____, 19___
at _____
_____.

    The following directors, constituting a quorum of the full
board, were present at the meeting:

        _____

        _____

        _____

        _____

    The following directors were absent:

        _____

        _____

        _____

        _____

    On motion and by unanimous vote,_____
was elected temporary Chairperson and then presided over the
meeting. _____ was elected
temporary Secretary of the meeting.

    The Chairperson announced that the meeting was held pursuant
to written waiver of notice signed by each of the directors. Upon
a motion duly made, seconded and unanimously carried, the waiver
was made a part of the records of the meeting. It now precedes the
minutes of this meeting in the corporate records book.

ARTICLES OF INCORPORATION

The Chairperson announced that the Articles of Incorporation or similar organizing instrument of this corporation was filed with the office of _____

_____ on _____.

RESOLVED, that the Secretary of this corporation is directed to see that a copy of the Articles of Incorporation or similar organizing instrument of this corporation, file-stamped or certified by the Secretary of State or other appropriate state office or official, is kept at the corporation's principal office.

BYLAWS

There was then presented to the meeting for adoption a proposed set of Bylaws of the corporation. The Bylaws were considered and discussed and, on motion duly made and seconded, it was unanimously

RESOLVED, that the Bylaws presented to this meeting be and hereby are adopted as the Bylaws of the corporation;

RESOLVED FURTHER, that the Secretary of this corporation is directed to see that a copy of the Bylaws is kept at the corporation's principal office.

CORPORATE TAX EXEMPTIONS

The Chairperson announced that, upon application previously submitted to the Internal Revenue Service, the corporation was determined to be exempt from payment of federal corporate income taxes under Section 501(c)(3) of the Internal Revenue Code per Internal Revenue Service determination letter dated _____, 19__. The Chairperson then presented the federal tax exemption determination letter and the Secretary was instructed to insert this letter in the corporate records book.

The Chairperson announced that the corporation was exempt from applicable state corporate income, franchise or similar taxes. The Chairperson instructed the Secretary to place a copy of any correspondence related to the corporation's state corporate tax exemption in the corporate records book.

ELECTION OF OFFICERS

The Chairperson then announced that the next item of business was the election of officers. Upon motion, the following persons were unanimously elected to the offices shown after their names:

_____ President

_____ Vice President

_____ Secretary

_____ Treasurer

Each officer who was present accepted his or her office. Thereafter, the President presided at the meeting as Chairperson of the meeting, and the Secretary of the corporation acted as secretary of the meeting.

PRINCIPAL OFFICE

After discussion as to the exact location of the corporation's principal office for the transaction of business in the county named in the Bylaws, upon motion duly made and seconded, it was

RESOLVED, that the principal office of this corporation shall be located at _____ _____.

BANK ACCOUNT

Upon motion duly made and seconded, it was

RESOLVED, that the funds of this corporation shall be deposited with _____.

RESOLVED FURTHER, that the Treasurer of this corporation be and hereby is authorized and directed to establish an account with said bank and to deposit the funds of this corporation therein.

RESOLVED FURTHER, that any officer, employee or agent of this corporation be and is authorized to endorse checks, drafts or other evidences of indebtedness made payable to this corporation, but only for the purpose of deposit.

RESOLVED FURTHER, that all checks, drafts and other instruments obligating this corporation to pay money shall be signed on behalf of this corporation by any _____ of the following persons:

_____

_____

_____

RESOLVED FURTHER, that said bank be and hereby is authorized to honor and pay all checks and drafts of this corporation signed as provided herein.

RESOLVED FURTHER, that the authority hereby conferred shall remain in force until revoked by the Board of Directors of this corporation and until written notice of such revocation shall have been received by said bank.

RESOLVED FURTHER, that the Secretary of this corporation be and hereby is authorized to certify as to the continuing authority of these resolutions, the persons authorized to sign on behalf of this corporation and the adoption of said bank's standard form of resolution, provided that said form does not vary materially from the terms of the foregoing resolutions.

COMPENSATION OF OFFICERS

There followed a discussion concerning the compensation to be paid by the corporation to its officers. Upon motion duly made and seconded, it was unanimously

RESOLVED, that the following annual salaries be paid to the officers of this corporation:

President $_____

Vice President $_____

Secretary $_____

Treasurer $_____

CORPORATE SEAL

The Secretary presented to the meeting for adoption a proposed form of seal of the corporation. Upon motion duly made and seconded, it was:

RESOLVED, that the form of corporate seal presented to this meeting be and hereby is adopted as the seal of this corporation, and the Secretary of the corporation is directed to place an impression thereof in the space next to this resolution.

(Impress seal here)

CORPORATE CERTIFICATES

The Secretary then presented to the meeting proposed director, sponsor, membership or other forms of corporate certificates for approval by the board. Upon motion duly made and seconded, it was

RESOLVED, that the form of certificates presented to this meeting are hereby adopted for use by this corporation and the Secretary is directed to attach a copy of each form of certificate to the minutes of this meeting.

Since there was no further business to come before the meeting, on motion duly made and seconded, the meeting was adjourned.

Dated: _____

_____, Secretary

How to Use the State Sheets

The State Sheets that follow are intended to provide users of this book in all states with the essential, state-specific information necessary to prepare Articles of Incorporation, Bylaws and other state incorporation forms. Locate the State Sheet pages for the state in which you plan to incorporate, then tear out and refer to these pages as you follow your incorporation steps (starting with Chapter 6, Step 1, "Choose a Corporate Name").

Be aware that this information changes frequently and may not always be current on all points in every state. For this reason—and so you'll be able to obtain forms, statutes and other assistance—we've included the addresses and phone numbers (also subject to change) of the corporate filing and tax agencies that deal with nonprofit corporations. What you receive from them should be current and correct, although you may still find that they cannot supply you with certain forms or statutes which have changed and haven't yet been reprinted. Persevere—phone calls often work better than letters—and eventually you'll get what you need.

Each State Sheet is divided into five main sections:

Secretary of State Information

Corporate Name Requirements

Articles of Incorporation

Bylaws

State Corporate Tax Exemption

The following is a summary of the information contained in each State Sheet section.

Secretary of State Information

This sections shows you where to write for incorporation information and forms. The name and address of the secretary of state or other corporate filings office is shown, along with a phone number for the corporate filing office or for general corporate information. In this edition, we have also included the Internet address for the secretary of state or other corporate filing office. (Some states have excellent web sites, with corporate forms, filing instructions and corporate name databases, while others are still creating sites.) Next we indicate whether your secretary of state provides a sample or ready-to-use Articles of Incorporation form or publishes guidelines for preparing this form. In the few states where neither forms nor published guidelines are available, incorporators should consult their Articles statute to determine the specific requirements for preparing Articles in their state (see the discussion under the Articles of Incorporation subsection below). The last item here indicates whether your secretary of state or a commercial publisher provides a copy of your state's nonprofit corporation statutes. If so, we give the ordering information. If you cannot acquire your statutes in this way, we indicate in what type of library you should look for them. Also, be sure to check your state government's web site—often the relevant statutes can be found online for free. For a further discussion of obtaining secretary of state materials, see Chapter 6, Step 1.

Corporate Name Requirements

First we indicate if you are required to include a corporate designator, such as "Corporation," "Incorporated," "Corp.," "Inc.," etc., in your corporate name. Then, if appropriate, we list specific corporate name restrictions and requirements under your state's nonprofit statutes. For further information on selecting a corporate name, see Chapter 6, Step 2.

Articles of Incorporation

Chapter 6, Step 3 explains how to fill in standard nonprofit Articles of Incorporation. The State Sheets provide additional information you'll need to complete the Articles in your state.

Articles of Incorporation Statute This section gives the citation for the section of your state's nonprofit corporation law that states what you need to put in your Articles of Incorporation. As we've said, in most cases your secretary of state provides either a standard form for filling in the information required in the Articles or guidelines for creating your own Articles. If not, you'll be able to look up your state's requirements for preparing Articles of Incorporation by referring to this citation (see Chapter 11 for information on doing your own research).

The following information, generally required to be included in the Articles, is also covered:

Registered Agent Requirements If the registered agent and/or registered office are specified in the Articles, we note any special requirements here. We also indicate if a separate registered agent form must be filed with the secretary of state. For a discussion of the general requirements applicable to registered agents and registered offices, see Chapter 6, Step 3.

Director Qualifications We show the number of directors required in your state and other applicable qualifications, such as age and residency.

Incorporator Qualifications If your state requires more than one incorporator, the number necessary will be indicated here. We also tell you whether there are age, residency or other requirements for incorporators.

Special Requirements This section contains information on any special notice, filing or other requirements for preparing and filing Articles in your state.

Bylaws

This section contains state-specific information necessary to prepare the tear-out Bylaws (and, if appropriate, the tear-out membership provisions), found in the Appendix. For detailed directions on creating Bylaws, see Chapter 7. This information includes:

Quorum Requirements for Directors' and Members' Meetings We give the state rule on how many directors or members must be present to hold a valid meeting under state law. In many instances, the state quorum rules only go into effect if the corporation does not specify its own quorum rules in its Bylaws.

Executive Committee If the directors can delegate management authority to an executive committee of directors, we indicate how many directors must serve on the committee and other rules and restrictions that apply.

Directors' Term of Office We give the state rule for how long a director may serve on the board.

Officers We indicate the officer positions that must be filled in each state and any special officer qualifications or other requirements under state law.

Corporate Report Requirements Most states require a nonprofit corporation to file a periodic report with the secretary of state (or occasionally with another agency, such as the department of revenue). We indicate the type of information that must be supplied and when this report must be filed.

State Corporate Tax Exemption

Finally, each State Sheet includes information on obtaining a state exemption from corporate income tax. The information presented here answers the following questions:

Does your state have a corporate income or franchise tax?

What are the address and phone number of the state agency concerned with corporate income tax?

What do you have to do to be exempt from your state corporate tax (if any)?

There are four common scenarios here, labeled in the State Sheets as follows:

Automatic upon filing Articles You are automatically eligible for the state exemption upon filing nonprofit Articles of Incorporation with your secretary of state.

Automatic with federal 501(c)(3) exemption You are automatically eligible for a state exemption when you receive your federal 501(c)(3) exemption—no separate state notification or registration is required.

Separate state notification required but determination follows federal You are eligible for the state exemption once you notify the state of your federal 501(c)(3) tax exemption. Copies of your Articles and Bylaws, as well as financial and program information, may need to be submitted to the state tax department.

Separate state determination You must apply and qualify for a separate state corporate tax exemption.

Any additional state tax information is listed at the end of this State Sheet section. Keep in mind that we are mostly interested in state corporate or franchise tax requirements and exemptions. As discussed in Chapter 5, Section E, there may be other state and local taxes you'll either be eligible to apply for exemption from, or liable to pay, including sales and use taxes, property tax, excise tax and hotel and meal taxes. You may also be subject to state and local license fees. Check with your state and local tax agencies to find out about these additional nonprofit taxes and exemptions.

ALABAMA

SECRETARY OF STATE INFORMATION

Secretary of State
Corporations Division
P.O. Box 5616
Montgomery, AL 36103-5616
http://alalinc.net/alsecst/corporat.htm
e-mail: alabiz@alalinc.net
Phone number of Corporations Division: (334) 242-5324
Provides Articles of Incorporation: yes
Provides statutes: provides pamphlet, "Alabama Nonprofit Corporation Law," Title 10-3A, no charge

CORPORATE NAME REQUIREMENTS

Corporate Designator: not required

Corporate name may not contain language that indicates the corporation is organized for a purpose other than that stated in its Articles; may not be deceptively similar to the name of profit or nonprofit domestic or qualified foreign corporation or reserved or registered name; must be written in English or transliterated into English alphabet

ARTICLES OF INCORPORATION

Articles Statute: Alabama Code, Nonprofit Corporation Law, Title 10-3A-61

Registered Agent Requirements:

Director Qualifications:
　Number: 3 or more
　Residency: no
　Age: no

Incorporator Qualifications:
　Residency: no
　Age: no

Special Requirements:

Articles (plus two copies) must be filed with the probate judge in the county of incorporation; within ten days of filing, the probate judge must send a copy of the certificate of incorporation and the Articles to the secretary of state

BYLAWS

Directors' Quorum: majority of the directors in office unless a percentage is specified in the Articles or Bylaws, which may not be less than 1/3 of the number in office

Members' Quorum: as stated in Bylaws, or else 10% of the number of voting members, in person or represented by proxy

Executive Committee: as provided in Bylaws, the board of directors may designate a committee of two or more directors to exercise the authority of the entire board, except to amend Articles or Bylaws, approve or disapprove new committee members, appoint or remove directors or officers, plan for merger or consolidation of the corporation or dispose of all or most of its assets and property. The full board remains responsible for the actions of the committee

Directors' Term of Office: as specified in Bylaws; if not specified, then one year

Required Officers: president, one or more vice presidents, secretary and treasurer. One person may hold any two offices except president and secretary

Special Officer Requirements: no age or residency requirements; officers' term may not exceed three years

Corporate Report Requirements: must be filed annually between January 1 and March 15 on a form provided by the secretary of state. Includes the following:

1. Corporate name and jurisdiction of incorporation
2. Name and address of registered agent
3. Brief statement of character of business
4. Name and address of president and secretary

STATE CORPORATE TAX EXEMPTION

Corporate Income or Franchise Tax: yes

Name and address of state agency to contact:

Alabama Department of Revenue
Income Tax Division
Corporate Income Tax Section
P.O. Box 900
Montgomery, AL 36132
(334) 242-9800

State Tax Exemption Requirements:

Separate state notification required but determination follows federal

Send a copy of your federal determination letter to the Department of Revenue to receive your state corporate income tax exemption

In addition to corporate income tax, there is a corporate permit fee. The permit fee ranges from $10 to $100, and only religious, benevolent and educational corporations are exempt; other types of nonprofits must file Form FT2-1N in their first year of existence and Form FT2-1 thereafter. Exempt organizations must report unrelated business income on Form 20

ALASKA

SECRETARY OF STATE INFORMATION

Alaska Dept. of Commerce & Economic Development
Corporations Section
P.O. Box 110808
Juneau, AK 99811-0808
http://www.commerce.state.ak.us/dced/bsc/corps.htm
Phone number of Corporations Section: (907) 465-2530;
    Fax: (907) 465-3257
Provides Articles of Incorporation: yes
Provides statutes: provides AK Nonprofit Corporation Act, Ch.
    10.20; also on web site

CORPORATE NAME REQUIREMENTS

Corporate Designator: not required
Corporate name may not contain language that implies the
    corporation is organized for a purpose other than that stated
    in its Articles; may not be deceptively similar to the name of
    a domestic or authorized foreign corporation, or registered or
    reserved name, except with written consent of name holder
    or court judgment authorizing use of name

ARTICLES OF INCORPORATION

Articles Statute: AK Statutes, Sec. 10.20.151
Registered Agent Requirements:
Director Qualifications:
    Number: 3 or more
    Residency: no
    Age: no
Incorporator Qualifications:
    Number: 3 or more
    Residency: no
    Age: 19 or older
Special Requirements:
Two notarized originals of Articles must be submitted to the
    Dept. of Commerce and Economic Development

BYLAWS

Directors' Quorum: majority of directors in office, or else a
    greater percentage as stated in Articles or Bylaws
Members' Quorum: as stated in Bylaws, but no lower than 10%
    of voting membership, or else 10% of the voting membership
Executive Committee: majority of the board of directors may
    designate two or more directors to exercise the authority of
    the full board in management of the corporation
Directors' Term of Office: as specified in the Bylaws; if not
    specified, then one year between annual meetings
Required Officers: president, one or more vice presidents,
    secretary and treasurer. Any offices may be held simulta-
    neously by the same person, except president and secretary

Special Officer Requirements: no age or residency requirements
Corporate Report Requirements: must be filed every other year
    by July 2. Contains the following information:
1. Corporate name and jurisdiction of incorporation
2. Name and address of registered agent
3. Brief statement of character of business
4. Names and addresses of directors and officers
5. Real and personal property assets

STATE CORPORATE TAX EXEMPTION

Corporate Income or Franchise Tax: yes
Name and address of state agency to contact:
Alaska Department of Revenue
State Office Bldg.
P.O. Box 110420
Juneau, AK 99811-0420
(907) 465-2372
Fax (907) 465-2389
State Tax Exemption Requirements:
Automatic with federal 501(c)(3) exemption
Alaska adopts by reference those portions of the IRC that
    concern nonprofit corporations (including exemption
    requirements, unrelated business income tax filings, etc.)

ARIZONA

SECRETARY OF STATE INFORMATION

Arizona Corporation Commission
1300 W. Washington St.
P.O. Box 6019
Phoenix, AZ 85005

http://www.cc.state.az.us/corp/index.html

Phone number of corporate filing section: (602) 542-3135; AZ toll-free (800) 345-5819; Fax: (602) 542-4111

Note: Corporate filings and phone calls are also handled by Tucson office (800) 345-5819

Provides Articles of Incorporation: sample form to be used as guideline

Provides statutes: no; ARS Title 10, Corporations and Associations (includes nonprofit sections 10-2301—2577), available from libraries or from West Publishing, (800) 328-9352 (order Volume 3 for $60)

CORPORATE NAME REQUIREMENTS

Corporate Designator: not required

Corporate name may not be misleading or contrary to purpose stated in Articles; may not be deceptively similar to the name of a domestic or authorized foreign corporation, or registered or reserved name, except with written consent of name holder or court judgment authorizing use of name

ARTICLES OF INCORPORATION

Articles Statute: ARS Title 10, Corporations and Associations 10-2342

Registered Agent Requirements:

Director Qualifications:
    Number: yes; 3 or more
    Residency: no
    Age: no

Incorporator Qualifications:
    Residency: no
    Age: capable of contracting

Special Requirements:

Certificate of Disclosure must be submitted with the Articles; this contains information about officers, directors, incorporators: whether any felony convictions for securities violations, consumer fraud, antitrust, theft, restraint of trade during seven previous years; whether subject to any federal injunction, judgment during the same period.

Publication of Articles is required within 60 days of filing, in three consecutive issues in newspaper of general circulation in the county of incorporation; affidavit of proof of publication must be filed with the Arizona Corporations Commission within 90 days of filing Articles

BYLAWS

Directors' Quorum: majority of the directors in office unless a percentage is specified in Bylaws or Articles, which may not be less than 1/3 of the number in office

Members' Quorum: as stated in Bylaws, or else 10% of voting members represented in person or by proxy

Executive Committee: majority of the board may designate an unspecified number of directors to exercise the authority of the full board, except the authority to submit matters to the membership for a vote, fill a vacancy on the board or on a committee, alter the Bylaws or fix director compensation. The board may dissolve the committee or remove a director at any time

Directors' Term of Office: as specified in Bylaws; if not specified, then one year

Required Officers: president, secretary and treasurer. One person may hold any two offices except president and secretary

Special Officer Requirements: no age or residency requirements

Corporate Report Requirements: must be filed by the 15th day of the 4th month of the corporation's fiscal year (or by April 15 if no different fiscal year has been adopted). Contains the following information:

1. Corporate name; address and jurisdiction of incorporation
2. Name and address of registered agent
3. Brief statement of character of affairs conducted within the state
4. Officers' and directors' names and addresses, and dates of election
5. Statement that all tax returns have been filed and a statement of financial condition
6. Certificate of disclosure regarding conduct of officers, directors. (This is the same certificate that must be filed with the Articles of Incorporation.)

STATE CORPORATE TAX EXEMPTION

Corporate Income or Franchise Tax: yes

Name and address of state agency to contact:

Department of Revenue
Corporate Section
1200 W. Washington St.
Phoenix, AZ 85007
(602) 542-3935; Fax (602) 542-4111

State Tax Exemption Requirements:

Separate state notification required but determination follows federal

To apply for the state exemption, submit a copy of your federal determination letter and a copy of Articles and Bylaws to the Corporations Commission.

ARKANSAS

SECRETARY OF STATE INFORMATION

Secretary of State

Corporations Division

Arkansas State Capitol, Rm. 058

Little Rock, AR 72201-1094

http://sos.state.ar.us/corp/corp.html

Phone number of corporations section: (501) 682-3409; toll-free (888) 233-0325; Fax: (501) 682-1284

Provides Articles of Incorporation: yes

Provides statutes: relevant sections of Arkansas Nonprofit Corporation Act, Title 4, Chapter 28, available on request from Elections Division at (501) 682-5070

CORPORATE NAME REQUIREMENTS

Corporate Designator: name shall contain "corporation," "company," "limited," "incorporated" or an abbreviation; name may not end in "company" if preceded by "and."

Corporate name may not contain language that implies the corporation is organized for a purpose other than that specified in its Articles; may not be the same or similar to name of corporation authorized to transact business in the state or to a reserved or registered name

ARTICLES OF INCORPORATION

Articles Statute: Arkansas Code Annotated, Title 4, Sec. 28-206

Registered Agent Requirements:

Director Qualifications:

Number: 3 or more

Residency: no

Age: no

Incorporator Qualifications:

Residency: no

Age: 21 or older

Special Requirements:

Articles must be approved by Circuit Court of county in which principal place of business is located; if the court approves it will submit a copy of its approval along with two copies of the Articles to the secretary of state, who will then file the Articles when the fee is paid

BYLAWS

Directors' Quorum: a majority of the directors in office, or a greater percentage specified in Articles or Bylaws, which may not be less than 1/3 of the number in office

Members' Quorum: majority of voting members represented in person or by proxy, unless specified in Bylaws, but not less than 1/3 of voting members

Executive Committee: majority of the board may create a committee of three directors to exercise the authority of the full board, except to elect officers, fill board vacancies or appoint executive committee members; or change Articles or Bylaws. The full board remains responsible for the actions of the committee

Directors' Term of Office: as specified in Articles, but it may not be less than one year or more than six years

Required Officers: president, vice president, secretary, treasurer

Special Officer Requirements: no age or residency requirements; term of office is limited to 3 years

Corporate Report Requirements: not required, but charitable organizations that receive more than $10,000 in a year must file forms provided by Attorney General by March 31 of the following year

STATE CORPORATE TAX EXEMPTION:

Corporate Income or Franchise Tax: yes

Name and address of state agency to contact:

Department of Finance and Administration

7th & Wolfe Streets

P.O. Box 919

Little Rock, AR 72203-0919

(501) 682-4779

Fax (501) 682-7900

State Tax Exemption Requirements:

Separate state notification required but determination follows federal

To apply for state exemption, submit copies of the federal determination letter and federal Form 1023 or 1024 to the Income Tax Director

Exempt organizations must report unrelated business income on Form 1100CT

CALIFORNIA

SECRETARY OF STATE INFORMATION

Office of the Secretary of State
Corporate Division
1500 11th St., 3rd Floor
Sacramento, CA 95814

http://www.ss.ca.us

Phone number of corporate filing section: (916)657-5448;
Fax: (916) 324-4573

Note: corporate filings and phone calls are also handled by Los
Angeles, San Diego and San Francisco branch offices of the
secretary of state

Provides Articles of Incorporation: no forms, but provides
sample Articles for public benefit, mutual benefit and
religious corporations

Provides statutes: no; order Corporations Code, 1997 Compact
Edition (includes nonprofit sections 5000–12000); from
West Publishing, (800) 328-9352, for $27; secretary of state
provides a "Guide to Corporate Filing," for $15, from the
above address

Note: the following information applies to California public
benefit corporations (formed for public or charitable
purposes), since most corporations applying for a 501(c)(3)
tax exemption will be classified as public benefit corporations
under California law. Requirements for religious corporations
are the same in most cases, but religious corporations have
more flexibility in tailoring certain provisions. Requirements
for mutual benefit corporations also differ slightly

CORPORATE NAME REQUIREMENTS

Corporate Designator: not required

Corporate name may not be likely to mislead the public as to
the purposes of the corporation; may not resemble closely the
name of other domestic or authorized foreign corporations, or
reserved or registered corporate names, except with written
consent of name holder and the secretary of state finds that
the public won't be misled; may not contain the words
"bank," "trust" or "trustee" without the approval of the
Superintendent of Banks

ARTICLES OF INCORPORATION

Articles Statute: Cal. Code, Nonprofit Corporation Law: Public
Benefit corporations, Section 5130

Registered Agent Requirements:

Director Qualifications:
  Number: 1 or more
  Residency: no
  Age: no

Incorporator Qualifications:
  Residency: no
  Age: no

Special Requirements:

Articles require a statement specifying whether the corporation
being formed is a public benefit, mutual benefit or religious
corporation, using specific terms that can be found in the
statute (sec. 5130)

An additional copy of the Articles must be provided to the
secretary of state at the time of filing for forwarding to the
attorney general

BYLAWS

Directors' Quorum: majority of the number of directors in
office, or else the percentage stated in the Articles or Bylaws,
which may not be less than 1/5 of the number in office. A
quorum may not however, be less than two directors, unless
there is only one director

Members' Quorum: as stated in Bylaws, or else a majority of the
members entitled to vote, represented in person or by proxy

Executive Committee: majority of the board of directors may
delegate authority to two or more directors as an executive
committee, which may exercise full powers of the board to
the extent of the resolution authorizing the committee,
except that it may not approve any action that requires
approval by the membership, fill vacancies on the board or
other committees, fix directors' compensation, alter Bylaws,
appoint committees, or use corporate funds to support a
nominee to the board after more people have already been
nominated than can be elected

Directors' Term of Office: as specified in Articles or Bylaws; if
not specified, then one year. The maximum term for a
director of a membership corporation is three years; of a
nonmembership corporation, six years

Required Officers: president or chairman of the board, secretary
and chief financial officer. One person may hold any two
positions, except that neither the secretary nor the chief
financial officer may serve concurrently as the president or
chairman of the board

Special Officer Requirements: no age or residency requirement.
The length of an officer's term is as specified in the Bylaws or
one year if not otherwise specified, but may not be more than
three years

Corporate Report Requirements: must be filed within 90 days of
incorporation and each year thereafter, before the anniversary date of incorporation. It must include following
information:

1. Corporate name and address
2. Name and address of registered agent
3. Officers' names and addresses
4. Brief description of character of business

STATE CORPORATE TAX EXEMPTION

Corporate Income or Franchise Tax: yes

Name and address of state agency to contact:

Franchise Tax Board
9645 Butterfield Way
Sacramento, CA 95827
(800) 852-5711
Fax (916) 369-4505

State Tax Exemption Requirements:

Separate state determination

The California franchise tax exemption application (Form FTB 3500) requires the following:

1. Current financial statements itemized to show income and expenses, or a proposed budget from a new organization

2. Articles of Incorporation and Bylaws or constitution; or trust instrument if organized as a trust

3. Supporting documents including a detailed description of activities, Articles and publications (if any)

4. The corporation's elected accounting period

5. $25 fee

If you file your Articles and exemption application at the same time, you are not required to pay California's $800 franchise tax, but your Articles will not be filed until your exemption is processed (about 3 months). If you file your Articles alone, you must pay the fee, which will be held until your exemption application is processed (about 3 months). If the exemption is granted, the money will be returned

Starting January 1, 1997, certain "qualified new corporations" are entitled to a reduced prepaid minimum tax of $600. Read the handout entitled "Prepaid Minimum Franchise Tax," in the secretary of state materials to find out if your corporation qualifies (if you estimate that your corporation will have a tax liability under $800)

Nonprofit corporations must also file a state annual informational tax return

For complete forms and instructions on how to form a California nonprofit corporation, see *The California Nonprofit Corporation Handbook* by Mancuso, published by Nolo Press. Nolo offers the California book at a discount to purchasers of *How to Form a Nonprofit Corporation*

COLORADO

SECRETARY OF STATE INFORMATION

Secretary of State
Corporations Office
1560 Broadway, Suite 200
Denver, CO 80202

http://www.state.co.us/gov_dir/sos/nonprof.html

Phone number of corporate filing section: (303) 894-2251; Fax: (303) 894-2242

Provides Articles of Incorporation: yes

Provides statutes: provides "Nonprofit Corporation Guide" online or in print; you can also order the 1996 Colorado Secretary of State Revised Filing Manual, including instructions and forms, from the above address. (Hard copy is $30; software on disk is $10.)

CORPORATE NAME REQUIREMENTS

Corporate Designator: not required

Corporate name may not contain language that indicates corporation is organized for any purpose other than that stated in its Articles; may not be the same or similar to the name of a domestic or authorized foreign corporation, or registered or reserved name; must be written in English or transliterated into the English alphabet; if the name is comprised of initials, they must be separated by one typewriter space or by a period.

ARTICLES OF INCORPORATION

Articles Statute: CRS, Nonprofit Corporations Act, Title 7, Articles Title 7-21-102

Registered Agent Requirements:

Director Qualifications:
Number: one or more
Residency: not required
Age: no

Incorporator Qualifications:
Residency: no
Age: 18 or older

Special Requirements:

BYLAWS

Directors' Quorum: majority of the number in office, unless a percentage is specified in the Articles or Bylaws, which may not be less than 1/3 of the number in office

Members' Quorum: as specified in Bylaws, or else 10% of the voting membership represented in person or by proxy

Executive Committee: if the Articles or Bylaws provide, a majority of directors may delegate the authority of the full board to a committee of two or more directors, which may exercise the authority of the full board to the extent of the resolution authorizing the committee, except that it may not alter the Articles or Bylaws; appoint or remove committee members, directors or officers; adopt a plan of merger or consolidation; authorize any financial transaction involving all or most of the corporate assets; authorize voluntary dissolution; or repeal any resolution of the full board. Designation of a committee does not relieve the full board of responsibility for its actions

Directors' Term of Office: as specified in the Articles or Bylaws; if not specified, then one year

Required Officers: president, one or more vice presidents, secretary and treasurer. One person may hold more than one office at a time, except offices of president and secretary

Special Officer Requirements: no age requirement and nonresident may serve. Officers' terms may be set in the Bylaws, but may not be more than three years

Corporate Report Requirements: file with secretary of state between January 1 and May 1 every two years; corporations incorporated in even-number years file in next even-number year; odd-number year corporations file in the next odd-number year. The report includes the following information:

1. Corporate name and jurisdiction of incorporation
2. Name and address of registered agent; address of registered office if different
3. Names and addresses of directors and officers
4. Brief statement of nature of business

STATE CORPORATE TAX EXEMPTION:

Corporate Income or Franchise Tax: yes

Name and address of state agency to contact:

Department of Revenue
Taxpayer Service Division
1375 Sherman St.
Denver, CO 80261
(303) 534-1208

State Tax Exemption Requirements:

Automatic with federal 501(c)(3) exemption

CONNECTICUT

SECRETARY OF STATE INFORMATION

Office of the Secretary of State
104 State Capitol
210 Capitol Ave.
Hartford, CT 06106

http://www.state.ct.us/sots

Phone number of Secretary of State's Office: (860) 509-6200
Fax: (860) 509-6209

Provides Articles of Incorporation: yes

Provides statutes: . Connecticut Revised Nonstock Corporation Act, Sections 33-1000—1290, from above address, for $25.85

CORPORATE NAME REQUIREMENTS

Corporate Designator: name must contain "corporation," "company," "incorporated" or an abbreviation

Corporate name shall not describe powers, purposes or authority the corporation does not possess; must be distinguishable from the names of other domestic or authorized foreign corporations or companies and from any reserved or registered name, except with written consent of name holder or court judgment authorizing use of name; must be written in English letters and Arabic or Roman numerals

ARTICLES (CERTIFICATE) OF INCORPORATION

Articles Statute: Conn. General Statutes, Nonstock Corporations, Sec. 33-1026

Registered Agent Requirements:

Director Qualifications:
Number: 3 or more
Residency: no
Age: no

Incorporator Qualifications:
Residency: no
Age: no

Special Requirements:

A nonwaivable $30 franchise fee must be paid at the time Articles of Incorporation are filed

Special provisions, both general and by denomination, concern the formation and operation of religious corporations. If you are planning to form a religious nonprofit corporation, check Conn. General Statutes Sec. 33-264a-281

A person or organization planning to grant college credit or call itself a college or university must comply with Sec. 10a-34 of Conn. General Statutes

BYLAWS

Directors' Quorum: majority of number of directors in office, unless a percentage is specified in the Bylaws, which may not be less than 1/3 of the directors in office or at least two directors

Members' Quorum: unless otherwise stated in Bylaws, the number of members present at a meeting who are entitled to vote, represented in person or by proxy, constitutes a quorum

Executive Committee: majority of the board may designate two or more directors to exercise authority as stipulated in the Bylaws or by resolution of the board, except to plan for distribution of corporate assets or corporate dissolution, approve or recommend acts to members required to be approved by the board, fill vacancies on the board or on committees, adopt a plan of merger or consolidation, dispose of assets or do anything inconsistent with the resolution authorizing the committee

Directors' Term of Office: until next annual meeting unless terms are staggered

Required Officers: as specified in Articles or Bylaws. One person may hold any two offices

Special Officer Requirements: no age or residency requirements

Corporate Report Requirements: the first such report must be filed within 30 days of first organizational meeting incorporation, afterwards every two years; on a form provided by secretary of state. Contains the following information:

1. Name and address of the principal office of the corporation and jurisdiction of incorporation

2. Directors' and officers' names and business and residence addresses

3. Name and address of registered agent

STATE CORPORATE TAX EXEMPTION

Corporate Income or Franchise Tax: yes

Name and address of state agency to contact:

Department of Revenue Services
92 Farmington Ave.
Hartford, CT 06105
(203) 566-8520
Fax (203) 297-5714

State Tax Exemption Requirements:

Automatic with federal 501(c)(3) exemption

DELAWARE

SECRETARY OF STATE INFORMATION

Department of State

Division of Corporations

P.O. Box 898

Dover, DE 19903

http://www.state.de.us/govern/agencies/corp/corp.htm

Phone number for general information: (302) 736-3073; Fax: (302) 739-3811

Provides Articles of Incorporation: yes

Provides statutes: order the General Corporation Law of the State of Delaware, from Michie Co., (800) 446-3410 for $22 (nonprofit statutes are interspersed with regular for-profit corporation law)

CORPORATE NAME REQUIREMENTS

Corporate Designator: name must include one of following: "Association," "Company," " Corporation," "Club," "Foundation," "Fund," "Incorporated," "Institute," "Society," "Union," "Syndicate," "Limited;" or "Co.," "Corp.," "Inc.," "Ltd."

Corporate name must be distinguishable from the names of other domestic or authorized foreign corporations or limited partnerships, and from reserved or registered corporate names, except with written consent of name holder, filed with secretary of state; name must be written in English or transliterated into the English alphabet

ARTICLES (CERTIFICATE) OF INCORPORATION

Articles Statute: DCA Title 8 (General Corporation Law), Sec. 102 (called Certificate of Incorporation)

Registered Agent Requirements:

Director Qualifications:

    Number: one or more

    Residency: no

    Age: no

Incorporator Qualifications:

    Residency: no

    Age: no

Special Requirements:

 A certified copy of the Certificate of Incorporation endorsed by the secretary of state must be recorded in the recorder's office of the county where the corporation's registered office is located within 20 days of the filing date

BYLAWS

Directors' Quorum: majority or greater of the directors in office, unless a percentage is specified in the Bylaws, which may not be less than 1/3 of the number in office. If a one-director board is authorized, then one director constitutes a quorum. Note, however, under GCL §141(j), the Certificate of Incorporation of a non-stock corporation may provide for a quorum of less than 1/3 of the board

Members' Quorum: if not specified in the Certificate of Incorporation or Bylaws, 1/3 of the voting members constitute a quorum

Executive Committee: majority of the board of directors may designate one or more directors to exercise the authority of the full board, except to amend corporate Articles or Bylaws; recommend any transaction involving most or all corporate assets; recommend dissolution or merger

Directors' Term of Office: as specified in the Articles or Bylaws

Required Officers: as specified in Bylaws or by resolution of board, so long as there are as many as are needed to sign legal documents. Any number of offices can be held by one person

Special Officer Requirements: no age or residency requirements

Corporate Report Requirements: must be filed by June 30 and must contain the following information:

1. Corporate name and address
2. Name and address of registered agent
3. Directors' and officers' names and addresses
4. Date of next annual meeting
5. Amount invested in real and personal property in the state
6. Reasons for tax exemption

STATE CORPORATE TAX EXEMPTION

Corporate Income or Franchise Tax: yes

Name and address of state agency to contact:

Department of Finance

Division of Revenue

Carvel Office Bldg.

820 French St.

Wilmington, DE 19801

(302) 577-3315

Fax (302) 577-3106

State Tax Exemption Requirements:

Separate state notification required but determination follows federal

Send a copy of your federal determination letter to the Division of Revenue to receive your state corporate income tax exemption

DISTRICT OF COLUMBIA

SECRETARY OF STATE INFORMATION

Dept. of Consumer and Regulatory Affairs
Corporations Division
614 H St., NW
Washington, DC 20001
http://www.ci.washington.dc.us/DCRA/dcrahome.htm

Phone number for general information: (202) 727-7283; Fax: (202) 727-7842

Provides Articles of Incorporation: no; but provides guideline for creating form

Provides statutes: Nonprofit Corporations—DC Code, Title 29, Chapter 5; available in all branches of the DC Public Library, and the James Madison Bldg. of the Library of Congress

CORPORATE NAME REQUIREMENTS

Corporate Designator: not required

Corporate name may not contain language that implies the corporation is organized for purposes other than those stated in its Articles; may not be the same or deceptively similar to the name of a profit or nonprofit domestic or qualified foreign corporation, or registered or reserved name; must be in English or transliterated into English alphabet; shall not indicate that corporation is organized under an act of Congress

ARTICLES OF INCORPORATION

Articles Statute: DC Code, Title 29, Sec. 530

Registered Agent Requirements:

Director Qualifications:
Number: 3 or more
Residency: no
Age: no

Incorporator Qualifications:
Number: 3 or more
Residency: no
Age: 18 or older

Special Requirements:

BYLAWS

Directors' Quorum: majority of directors in office, unless a percentage is specified in Bylaws, but not less than 1/3 of the number in office

Members' Quorum: as specified in Bylaws or else 10% of voting membership

Executive Committee: majority of board may designate two or more directors to exercise the authority of the full board. The board is not relieved of its responsibility for the actions of the committee

Directors' Term of Office: as specified in Bylaws, but not to exceed 3 years; if not specified, then one year

Required Officers: president, secretary and treasurer. One person may hold two offices simultaneously, except offices of president and secretary

Special Officer Requirements: no age or residency requirements

Corporate Report Requirements: must be filed every two years by January 15, on forms provided by mayor. Includes the following information:

1. Name of corporation and jurisdiction of incorporation
2. Name and address of registered agent
3. Brief statement of affairs conducted in DC
4. Directors' and officers' names and addresses

STATE CORPORATE TAX EXEMPTION

Corporate Income or Franchise Tax: yes

Name and address of state agency to contact:

Department of Finance and Revenue
300 Indiana Ave. NW
Washington, DC 20001
(202) 727-6083
Fax (202) 727-6083

State Tax Exemption Requirements:

Separate state notification required but determination follows federal

DC has single exemption application for Income and franchise tax, sales and use tax, and personal property tax, which must be filed with the following:

1. Copy of federal tax determination letter
2. Statement of activities engaged in during the past year, or planned to be engaged in during the coming year
3. Copy of Articles and Bylaws
4. Complete statement of assets and liabilities, receipts and expenditures, at the end of the most recent accounting period
5. Sample copies of organization's publications and literature, if any

FLORIDA

SECRETARY OF STATE INFORMATION

Department of State
Division of Corporations
P.O. Box 6327
Tallahassee, FL 32314
http://dos.state.fl.us/doc/index.html
Phone number of Division of Corporations: (904) 488-9000;
  Fax: (904) 487-2214
Provides Articles of Incorporation: yes
Provides statutes: Not For Profit Corporations Act, FS Ch. 617;
  no charge, from above address

CORPORATE NAME REQUIREMENTS

Corporate Designator: name must contain one of the following:
  "corporation," "incorporated," or their abbreviations. It may
  not contain the word "company" or its abbreviation
Corporate name may not contain language that implies
  corporation is organized for a purpose other than that
  permitted in its Articles; may not contain language implying
  that corporation is connected with a state or federal
  government agency; must be distinguishable from other
  names on file, registered or reserved with the Division of
  Corporations

ARTICLES OF INCORPORATION

Articles Statute: Not For Profit Corporations Act, FS 617.0202
Registered Agent Requirements:
A separate Certificate of Designation of Registered Agent/
  Registered Office must be filed with Articles
Director Qualifications:
  Number: 3 or more
  Residency: no
  Age: 18 or older
Incorporator Qualifications:
  Number: 3 or more
  Residency: no
  Age: no
Special Requirements:

BYLAWS

Directors' Quorum: majority of the directors in office, or else as
  specified in the Articles or Bylaws, but no fewer than 1/3 of
  the number in office
Members' Quorum: as stated in the Articles or Bylaws
Executive Committee: a majority of the board may designate an
  executive committee, comprised of any number of directors,
  to exercise the authority of the full board, except to approve
  or recommend actions the membership must vote on, fill
vacancies on the board or any committee, or amend the
  Articles or Bylaws
Directors' Term of Office: as specified in Articles or Bylaws; if
  not specified, then one year
Required Officers: as specified in Articles or Bylaws. One
  person may hold more than one office simultaneously
Special Officer Requirements: no age or residency requirements
Corporate Report Requirements: must be filed by May 1.
  Includes the following information:
1. Corporate name and address and jurisdiction of incorporation
2. Date of incorporation
3. Federal employer identification number
4. Directors' and officers' names and addresses
5. Name and address of registered agent

STATE CORPORATE TAX EXEMPTION

Corporate Income or Franchise Tax: yes
Name and address of state agency to contact:
Dept. of Revenue
The Carlton Bldg., #104
Tallahassee, FL 32399-0100
(904) 488-6800
State Tax Exemption Requirements:
Separate state notification required but determination follows
  federal
For state income tax exemption, federal determination letter,
  attached to Form FL1120 (Florida Corporation Income Tax),
  must be filed with Florida Dept. of Revenue. No further state
  filings necessary, except to report and pay any unrelated
  business income taxes owed

GEORGIA

SECRETARY OF STATE INFORMATION

Secretary of State
Corporations Division
Suite 315, West Tower
2 Martin Luther King Jr. Dr.
Atlanta, GA 30334
http://www.SOS.State.Ga.US/corporations/default.htm
Phone number of corporate filing section: (404) 656-2817; Fax: (404) 651-9059

Provides Articles of Incorporation: not a form, but provides "Procedure for Incorporation," which includes a sample format to use as a guide in creating your own form

Provides statutes: order Georgia Code Annotated, Nonprofit Corporations, Title 14 (nonprofit sections 14-3-101—1703) from Michie Co., (800) 446-3410, for $22

CORPORATE NAME REQUIREMENTS

Corporate Designator: name shall contain "corporation," "company," "incorporation," "limited," or an abbreviation

Corporate name may not contain language that implies the corporation is organized for a purpose other than that permitted in its Articles; may not contain an obscenity; may not be the same as the name of an existing nonprofit or for-profit, domestic or authorized company, or a reserved or registered name, unless with written consent of the name holder and an agreement by the consenting corporation to change its name slightly; may not contain more than 80 characters, including spaces and punctuation

ARTICLES OF INCORPORATION

Articles Statute: GCA, Title 14-3-202

Registered Agent Requirements:

Director Qualifications:
  Number: 1 or more
  Residency: no
  Age: 18 or older

Incorporator Qualifications:
  Residency: no
  Age: no

Special Requirements:

Publication is required (once a week for two consecutive weeks) of notice of filing of Articles in newspaper in the county of principal place of business

BYLAWS

Directors' Quorum: majority of the directors in office, unless a percentage is specified in the Articles or Bylaws, which may not be less than 1/3 of the directors in office

Members' Quorum: as specified in Bylaws, or else 10% of the voting members

Executive Committee: majority of board may designate two or more directors and any number of former board members to exercise the authority of the board, except to approve or recommend to members dissolution, merger, sale or transfer of all or most of the assets; appoint or remove directors or fill vacancies on board or any committee; or amend Articles or Bylaws. Designation of the committee does not relieve the board of responsibility for the actions of the committee

Directors' Term of Office: as specified in the Articles or Bylaws; if not specified, then one year

Required Officers: as specified in the Articles or Bylaws. One person may hold more than one office simultaneously

Special Officer Requirements: no age or residency requirements

Corporate Report (Registration) Requirements: must be filed between January 1 and April 1. It must contain the following information:

1. Corporate name and jurisdiction of incorporation
2. Name and address of registered agent
3. Mailing address of principal office
4. Names and addresses of CEO, CFO and secretary, or the individuals holding similar positions
5. Federal employer identification number

STATE CORPORATE TAX EXEMPTION

Corporate Income or Franchise Tax: yes

Name and address of state agency to contact:

Georgia Dept. of Revenue
Tax Exemption
P.O. Box 38467
Atlanta, GA 30334
(404) 656-7043

State Tax Exemption Requirements:

Separate state notification required but determination follows federal

State exemption application (Form 3605) asks principally for copies of Articles, Bylaws, federal determination letter, certificate of Georgia corporate registration and description of organization's activities. Exempt organizations that file federal Form 990-T must also file Georgia Form 660-T to report unrelated business income

HAWAII

SECRETARY OF STATE INFORMATION

Dept. of Commerce and Consumer Affairs
Business Registration Division
Kamamalu Bldg.
1010 Richards St.
Honolulu, HI 96813

http://www.hawaii.gov/dcca/dcca.html

Phone number of Business Registration Division: (808) 586-2727; Fax: (808) 586-2733

Provides Articles of Incorporation: yes

Provides statutes: no; Hawaii Nonprofit Corporation Act (Chapter 415B, Sections 1–159) available at public libraries, state library

CORPORATE NAME REQUIREMENTS

Corporate Designator: not required

Corporate name may not be the same or deceptively similar to the name of another domestic or foreign corporation or partnership, or a registered or reserved name or trade name, unless with written consent of the name holder and you add or delete one or two words to change the name slightly, or else with a court judgment authorizing use of the name

ARTICLES OF INCORPORATION

Articles Statute: HRS Title 23, Ch. 415B, Sec. 34 (415B-34)

Registered Agent Requirements:

Director Qualifications:
Number: 3 or more
Residency: 1 of the directors must be a resident of the state
Age: no

Incorporator Qualifications:
Residency: no
Age: no

Special Requirements:

BYLAWS

Directors' Quorum: majority of the directors in office, or else as specified in the Articles or Bylaws

Members' Quorum: must be specified in Bylaws

Executive Committee: a majority of the board may designate any number to exercise the authority of the full board, except to alter Articles or Bylaws or board resolutions; appoint or remove directors, officers or committee members; authorize the sale or transfer of all or most of the assets; initiate or revoke dissolution proceedings; or adopt a plan of merger, consolidation or distribution of corporate assets

Directors' Term of Office: as specified in the Articles or Bylaws; if not specified, then one year

Required Officers: president, vice president, secretary and treasurer. One person may hold any two or more offices simultaneously, so long as the corporation has at least two officers

Special Officer Requirements: no age or residency requirements

Corporate Report Requirements: must be filed between January 1 and March 31. Contains the following information:

1. Corporate name and jurisdiction of incorporation
2. Address of principal office
3. Name and address of registered office
4. Brief statement of character of affairs
5. Directors' and officers' names and residence addresses

STATE CORPORATE TAX EXEMPTION

Corporate Income or Franchise Tax: yes

Name and address of state agency to contact:

Department of Taxation
Keelikalani Bldg.
830 Punchbowl St.
P.O. Box 259
Honolulu, HI 96809
(808) 587-1510
Fax (808) 587-1633

State Tax Exemption Requirements:

Automatic with federal 501(c)(3) exemption

IDAHO

SECRETARY OF STATE INFORMATION

Secretary of State
700 W. Jefferson St., Basement West
P.O. Box 83720
Boise, ID 83720-0080
http://www.idsos.state.id.us/corp/corindex.htm

Phone number of Secretary of State's office: (208) 334-2300; Fax: (208) 334-2282

Provides Articles of Incorporation: no forms; use statutes as guidelines

Provides statutes: Nonprofit Corporation Act, Sections 30-1-1—30-3-145; no charge, from above address

CORPORATE NAME REQUIREMENTS

Corporate Designator: name shall contain "Corporation," "Company," "Incorporated," "Limited" or an abbreviation; "Company" shall not be preceded immediately by "and"

Corporate name may not indicate that the corporation is organized for purposes other than those stated in its Articles; may not be deceptively similar to the name of any domestic or authorized foreign corporation, or registered or reserved name, unless with the consent of name holder

ARTICLES OF INCORPORATION

Articles Statute: Idaho Code, Sec. 30-3-17

Registered Agent Requirements:

Director Qualifications:
    Number: 3 or more; for a religious corporation, 1 or more
    Residency: no
    Age: no

Incorporator Qualifications:
    Residency: no
    Age: no

Special Requirements:

BYLAWS

Directors' Quorum: majority of the number of directors unless specified in the Bylaws or Articles, but no fewer than 1/3 of the number in office (but if there are less than 6 directors, no fewer than 2 directors for quorum)

Members' Quorum: as specified in Bylaws, or else 10% of the voting members present or represented by proxy

Executive Committee: majority of the board of directors may designate two or more directors to exercise the authority of the full board, except to recommend dissolution, fill vacancies on board or any committee, remove directors or amend the Articles or Bylaws. The full board remains responsible for the actions of the committee

Directors' Term of Office: as specified in the Articles or Bylaws, but not to exceed 5 years; if not specified, then one year

Required Officers: president, secretary and treasurer. (Religious corporations are not required to have officers.) One person may hold more than one office simultaneously, except offices of president and secretary

Special Officer Requirements: no age or residency requirements

Corporate Report Requirements: must be filed between July 1 and November 1 (no fee) on forms furnished by the secretary of state and includes the following information:

1. Name of corporation and jurisdiction of incorporation
2. Name and address of registered agent
3. Brief statement of character of business engaged in
4. Directors' and officers' names and addresses

STATE CORPORATE TAX EXEMPTION

Corporate Income or Franchise Tax: yes

Name and address of state agency to contact:

State Tax Commission
Dept. of Revenue and Taxation
800 Park Blvd.
Boise, ID 83722
(208) 334-7660

State Tax Exemption Requirements:

Automatic with federal exemption

Note that federal 501(c)(3) income tax exemption also qualifies corporation for state property tax exemption

ILLINOIS

SECRETARY OF STATE INFORMATION

Secretary of State
Department of Business Services
501 South Second St.
Howlett Building
Springfield, IL 62756
http://www.sos.state.il.us

Phone numbers for corporate information: (217) 782-7880; Fax: (217) 785-0358

Note: Corporate filings and phone calls are also handled by the Chicago office (312) 793-3380

Provides Articles of Incorporation: yes

Provides statutes: provides General Not For Profit Corporation Act, Chapter 805,105, 101.01 et seq., no charge, from above address; also provides "Guide for Organizing Not-for-Profit Corporations," no charge, from above address

CORPORATE NAME REQUIREMENTS

Corporate Designator: although not required, corporate name may contain "corporation," "incorporated," "company," "limited," or an abbreviation

Corporate name may not contain language that implies the corporation is organized for a purpose other than that specified in its Articles; must be distinguishable from the name of a profit or nonprofit domestic or authorized foreign corporation, or registered or reserved name; shall not contain the words, "regular democrat," "regular democratic," "regular republican," "democrat," "republican," or the name of any other established political party, unless consent is given by the state central committee of the affected political party; must be written in English letters and Arabic or Roman numerals

ARTICLES OF INCORPORATION

Articles Statute: Ill. Annotated Statutes 805 ILCS 105/102.10

Registered Agent Requirements:

Director Qualifications:
  Number: 3 or more
  Residency: no
  Age: no

Incorporator Qualifications:
  Residency: no
  Age: 18 or older

Special Requirements:

Within 15 days of the secretary of state filing your Articles and returning other documents to you, they must be filed with the Recorder of Deeds in the county in which the corporation's registered office is located

BYLAWS

Directors' Quorum: majority of the directors in office, unless a percentage is specified in the Articles or Bylaws, which may not be less than 1/3 of the directors in office

Members' Quorum: as specified in Bylaws, or else 10% of the voting membership, in person or represented by proxy

Executive Committee: majority of directors may create a committee of two or more directors and other natural persons (the majority of the committee must be directors) to exercise the authority of the full board, except to plan for distribution of corporate assets or corporate dissolution, approve or recommend acts to members required to be approved by the members, fill vacancies on the board or on committees, appoint or remove directors, officers or committee members, adopt a plan of merger or consolidation, dispose of assets or do anything inconsistent with the resolution authorizing the committee

Directors' Term of Office: until next meeting for election of directors, unless terms are staggered

Required Officers: as specified in Bylaws. One person may hold any two or more offices

Special Officer Requirements: no age or residency requirements

Corporate Report Requirements: must be filed before first day of the anniversary month of incorporation on forms provided by the secretary of state. Contains the following information:

1. Name of corporation
2. Name and address of registered agent
3. Address of principal office
4. Officers' and directors' names and addresses
5. Brief statement of the character of affairs the corporation is conducting

STATE CORPORATE TAX EXEMPTION

Corporate Income or Franchise Tax: yes

Name and address of state agency to contact:

Illinois Dept. of Revenue
Income Tax Division
101 W. Jefferson St.
Springfield, IL 92794
(217) 782-9922
or
100 West Randolph
Concourse 300
Chicago, IL 60601
(312) 917-3222

State Tax Exemption Requirements:

Automatic with federal 501(c)(3) exemption

INDIANA

SECRETARY OF STATE INFORMATION

Secretary of State
Corporations Division
302 W. Washington St., Rm. E018
Indianapolis, IN 46204

http://www.ai.org/state.html

Phone number of Corporations Division: (317) 232-6576;
Fax: (317) 233-3283

Provides Articles of Incorporation: yes

Provides statutes: no; Indiana Not-For-Profit Corporation Act,
Title 23, Art. 17, available from libraries; provides "Starting
a Business in Indiana," no charge, from the above address

CORPORATE NAME REQUIREMENTS

Corporate Designator: name must include "corporation,"
"incorporated," "limited," "company" or an abbreviation

Corporate name must be distinguishable from the name of an
Indiana domestic or authorized foreign corporation, or
reserved name; name may not indicate the corporation is
organized for a purpose other than that stated in its Articles

ARTICLES OF INCORPORATION

Articles Statute: Indiana Statutes Annotated, Sec. 23-17-3-2

Registered Agent Requirements:

Director Qualifications:
    Number: 3 or more
    Residency: no
    Age: no

Incorporator Qualifications:
    Residency: no
    Age: no

Special Requirements:

BYLAWS

Directors' Quorum: majority of the directors in office, or else
the percentage specified in the Articles or Bylaws, which
may not be less than 1/3 of the number in office (but if there
are less than 6 directors, no fewer than 2 directors for
quorum)

Members' Quorum: as specified in Bylaws, or 10% of members
qualified to vote

Executive Committee: majority of directors may designate two
or more directors to exercise the authority of the full board
except to approve or recommend to members dissolution,
merger or sale; appoint or remove directors or fill vacancies
on board or any committee; or amend Articles or Bylaws.
Designation of the committee does not relieve the board of
responsibility for the actions of the committee

Directors' Term of Office: as specified in the Articles or Bylaws
but not more than three years

Required Officers: as specified in Bylaws. One person may hold
any two or more offices, except president and secretary (or
their equivalents, by whatever titles)

Special Officer Requirements: no age or residency requirements

Corporate Report Requirements: must be filed during the
anniversary month in which the corporation was incorporated, on forms sent by the secretary of state at least 30 days
before the report is due. Includes the following information:

1. Corporate name and address of principal office
2. Name and address of registered agent
3. Date of incorporation
4. Jurisdiction of incorporation
5. Officers' and directors' names and addresses

STATE CORPORATE TAX EXEMPTION

Corporate Income or Franchise Tax: yes

Name and address of state agency to contact:

Dept. of Revenue
N 248 Indiana Government Center N
100 Senate Ave.
Indianapolis, IN 46204-2253
(317) 232-2188

State Tax Exemption Requirements:

Separate state notification required but determination follows
federal

For state tax exemption, a nonprofit corporation must file Form
IT-35A (state tax exemption application), along with a copy
of Articles and Bylaws and a copy of the federal determination letter, within 120 days of incorporation. Exempt
organizations must report unrelated business income and
must also file an annual informational report (Form IT-
35AR) by the 15th day of the 5th month following the close
of the taxable year

IOWA

SECRETARY OF STATE INFORMATION

Secretary of State
Corporations Division
Hoover Bldg.
Des Moines, IA 50319
http://www.sos.state.ia.us

Phone number of Corporations Division: (515) 281-5204;
Fax: (515) 242-5953

Provides Articles of Incorporation: no, but provides "suggested form to be used as guideline"

Provides statutes: Selected Provisions of the Iowa Code on Nonprofit Corporations, IA Code Annotated, Chapter 504A, no charge, from above address

CORPORATE NAME REQUIREMENTS

Corporate Designator: not required

Corporate name may not imply purposes contrary to those contained in the Articles; may not be the same or similar to the name of a domestic or authorized foreign corporation or limited partnership, or to a reserved or registered name, unless with written consent of the name holder and an agreement by the consenting corporation to change its name slightly, or else with a court judgment authorizing use of the name; must be transliterated into letters of the English alphabet

ARTICLES OF INCORPORATION

Articles Statute: Iowa code Annotated, Nonprofit Corporations, 504A.29

Registered Agent Requirements:

Director Qualifications:
  Number: 1 or more
  Residency: not required
  Age: no

Incorporator Qualifications:
  Residency: no
  Age: capacity to contract (of legal age)

Special Requirements:

 The secretary of state will send a duplicate executed copy of the certificate of incorporation to the recorder of the county where the corporation's registered office is located; the recorder will file the document upon payment of the filing fee by the incorporator

Articles must state "incorporated under Chapter 504A of the Iowa Code"

BYLAWS

Directors' Quorum: majority of the directors in office, or else the percentage specified in the Bylaws, which may not be less than 1/3 of the number in office

Members' Quorum: as stated in Bylaws, but no lower than 10% of voting membership, or else 10% of the voting membership

Executive Committee: majority of directors may designate directors to exercise the authority of the full board, except to amend Articles or Bylaws, plan for merger or consolidation, recommend to members any transaction that deals with all or most of the corporation's property and assets or voluntarily dissolve the corporation

Directors' Term of Office: as specified in the Articles or Bylaws; if not specified, then one year

Required Officers: president, vice president, secretary, treasurer. One person may hold any two or more offices simultaneously

Special Officer Requirements: no age or residency requirements

Corporate Report Requirements: must be filed every two years between January 1 and March 31 (the first annual report must be filed between those dates in the first odd-numbered year following incorporation), on forms provided by the secretary of state, and must contain the following information:

1. Corporate name and jurisdiction of incorporation
2. Name and address of registered agent
3. Brief statement of character of affairs
4. Names and addresses of principal officers and one director

STATE CORPORATE TAX EXEMPTION

Corporate Income or Franchise Tax: yes

Name and address of state agency to contact:

Iowa Dept. of Revenue
Business Section
Hoover Office Bldg.
Des Moines, IA 50319
(515) 281-3114
Fax (515) 242-6040

State Tax Exemption Requirements:

Separate state notification required but determination follows federal

State income tax exemption application must be submitted (with date of incorporation, purpose for which incorporated, actual activities, source of income, declaration of noninurement of funds to private persons) with a copy of federal determination letter. Exempt organizations report unrelated business income on Form IA 1120

KANSAS

SECRETARY OF STATE INFORMATION

Secretary of State
Corporation Division
2nd Floor, State Capitol
300 S.W. 10th Ave.
Topeka, KS 66612-1594
http:/www.ink.org/public/sos
e-mail: kssos@ssmail.wpo.state.ks.us

Phone number of Corporation Division: (785) 296-2236; Fax: (785) 296-4570

Provides Articles of Incorporation: yes

Provides statutes: Kansas Statutes Annotated, Vol. 2, may be ordered from above address for $36; General Corporations Code, Sections 17-6001—7515 available in libraries

CORPORATE NAME REQUIREMENTS

Corporate Designator: name must include "incorporated," "association," "church," "college," "club," "company," "corporation," "foundation," "fund," "institute," "limited," "society," "syndicate," "union," or an abbreviation such as "co.," "corp.," "inc.," "ltd."

Corporate name may not be the same as or similar to a name already in use by a KS corporation, or reserved or registered name, unless with that corporation's written, signed and acknowledged consent; must be written in Roman characters or letters

ARTICLES OF INCORPORATION

Articles Statute: KSA, Corporations, 17-6002

Registered Agent Requirements:

Director Qualifications:
    Number: 1 or more
    Residency: no
    Age: no

Incorporator Qualifications:
    Residency: no
    Age: no

Special Requirements:

Certified copy of Articles returned by the secretary of state after filing must be recorded with register of deeds in county where corporation's registered office is located, within 20 days of filing

BYLAWS

Directors' Quorum: unless otherwise specified, a majority of the directors in office, but the Bylaws may specify as few as 1/3 of that number, or one if there is only one director

Members' Quorum: as specified in the Articles or Bylaws, or 1/3 of members

Executive Committee: majority of directors may designate one or more directors to exercise the authority of the full board, except to amend Articles or Bylaws, issue shares or distribute corporate assets, dissolve the corporation or revoke its dissolution, adopt merger or consolidation plan, or recommend sale or exchange of all or most of the assets

Directors' Term of Office: as specified in Bylaws

Required Officers: the Bylaws or a resolution of the board of directors may specify offices to be filled and whether or not one person may hold more than one office

Special Officer Requirements: one officer must be designated to record the proceedings of meetings; no age or residency requirements

Corporate Report Requirements: if the corporation is required to file an income tax return, the annual report must be filed by April 15 (otherwise, by the 15th day of the 6th month following close of the corporation's fiscal year). Includes the following information:

1. Corporate name and address
2. Officers' and directors' names and addresses
3. Stock information if applicable
4. Number of memberships
5. Information required for agricultural assets if there are any

STATE CORPORATE TAX EXEMPTION

Corporate Income or Franchise Tax: yes

Name and address of state agency to contact:

Kansas Dept. of Revenue
Docking State Office Bldg.
915 S.W. Harrison St.
Topeka, KS 66612-1588
(913) 296-6661
Fax (913) 296-7928

State Tax Exemption Requirements:

Automatic with federal 501(c)(3) exemption

KENTUCKY

SECRETARY OF STATE INFORMATION

Secretary of State
State Capitol
700 Capitol Ave.
P.O. Box 718
Frankfort, KY 40602
http://www.sos.state.ky.us/busser/GENINFO.HTM

Phone number of corporate filing section: (502) 564-2848; Fax: (502) 564-4075

Provides Articles of Incorporation: no form or sample; use statutes as guidelines

Provides statutes: no, order Kentucky Business Organizations Laws (includes nonprofit sections 273.010-400) from Michie Co., (800) 562-1197, for $32.50; secretary of state does provide a pamphlet, "Guide to Incorporating in Kentucky," no charge, from above address.

CORPORATE NAME REQUIREMENTS

Corporate Designator: name shall include "corporation," "incorporated" "company," "inc.," or "co."; but if "company" or "co." is used, it may not be immediately preceded by "and" or "&"

Corporate name may not contain language that implies the corporation is organized for a purpose other than that stated in its Articles; must be distinguishable from the name of a domestic or authorized foreign profit or nonprofit corporation, or registered, reserved, or fictitious name, unless the name holder consents in writing or consent is given by a court judgment

ARTICLES OF INCORPORATION

Articles Statute: Kentucky Revised Statutes, Nonstock, Nonprofit Corporations, Chapter 273.247

Registered Agent Requirements:

Director Qualifications:
Number: 3 or more
Residency: not required
Age: no

Incorporator Qualifications:
Residency: no
Age: no

Special Requirements:

Copy of documents filed with secretary of state must also be filed with county clerk of the county where the registered office is located

BYLAWS

Directors' Quorum: majority of the directors in office, or else as stated in Articles or Bylaws

Members' Quorum: as specified in the Bylaws, or else 10% of the voting membership present or represented by proxy

Executive Committee: majority of directors may designate two or more directors to exercise powers to the extent of board authorization, but the committee may not alter Articles or Bylaws, appoint or remove directors or committee members, plan for merger or consolidation, conduct any transaction involving all or most of the corporation's assets, dissolve or revoke dissolution of the corporation, or alter board resolutions

Directors' Term of Office: as specified in the Bylaws; if not specified, then one year

Required Officers: as specified in the Bylaws. One person may hold more than one office at a time

Special Officer Requirements: no age requirement or residency requirement. Officers' term is limited to three years

Corporate Report Requirements: must be filed by June 30th of each year. It must include:

1. Corporate name and address of principal office
2. Jurisdiction of incorporation
3. Officers' and directors' names and addresses
4. Name and address of registered agent

STATE CORPORATE TAX EXEMPTION

Corporate Income or Franchise Tax: yes

Name and address of state agency to contact:

Commonwealth of Kentucky
Revenue Cabinet
Corporation Income Tax Section
Capitol Annex Bldg.
Frankfort, KY 40620
(502) 564-3658

State Tax Exemption Requirements:

Separate state notification required but determination follows federal

To apply for exemption, send a letter requesting one to the Revenue Cabinet, along with a copy of your federal exemption application and federal determination letter. Once exemption is granted no further filings are necessary, except for unrelated business income tax returns if applicable

LOUISIANA

SECRETARY OF STATE INFORMATION

Secretary of State
Corporations Division
P.O. Box 94125
Baton Rouge, LA 70804-9125
http://www.sec.state.la.us/comm-1a.htm

Phone number of corporate filing section: (502) 925-4704; Fax: (502) 925-4726

Provides Articles of Incorporation: yes

Provides statutes: Corporation Laws Booklet (including Nonprofit Laws 12:201—269) from above address for $10; also "Doing Business in Louisiana," with forms, available from above address for $4

CORPORATE NAME REQUIREMENTS

Corporate Designator: not required

Corporate name may be in any language, but must be expressed in English characters; may not imply the corporation is an administrative agency of any parish, or of the state or US government; shall not contain any of the following words—"bank," "banking," "banker," "savings," "trust," "deposit," "insurance," "mutual," "assurance," "indemnity," "casualty," "fiduciary," "homestead," "building and loan," "surety," "security," "guarantee," "cooperative," "state," "parish," "redevelopment corporation," "electric cooperative," or "credit union"

Corporate name may not be the same or deceptively similar to the name of another Louisiana corporation or registered trade name, unless the other corporation is about to change its status or name and gives written consent; or the other corporation has failed to do business in the state for 2 years, failed to pay franchise or other taxes for 5 years, or is a foreign corporation not authorized to do business in the state

ARTICLES OF INCORPORATION

Articles Statute: Louisiana Statutes Annotated, Nonprofit Corporation Law, Section 12:203

Registered Agent Requirements:

Director Qualifications:
Number: 3 or more; in a membership corporation, if there are less than 3 members, then the same number of directors as there are members.
Residency: no
Age: no

Incorporator Qualifications:
Residency: no
Age: capable of contracting (legal age)

Special Requirements:

A multiple original or certified copy of the Articles, along with a copy of the certificate of incorporation, must be filed with recorder of mortgages of the parish in which the registered office of the corporation is located, within 30 days of filing

BYLAWS

Directors' Quorum: majority of the directors in office

Members' Quorum: majority of voting members, in person or represented by proxy

Executive Committee: majority of directors may designate two or more directors to exercise the authority granted to them by the board. This delegation of authority does not relieve the board of responsibilities imposed by law

Directors' Term of Office: as specified in the Bylaws, but may not exceed five years; if not specified, then one year

Required Officers: president, secretary and treasurer. One person may hold two offices; but if 2 signatures required on form, must be 2 persons

Special Officer Requirements: no age or residency requirement

Corporate Report Requirements: must be filed by May 15. It must include:

1. Corporate name and address
2. Name and address of the registered agent
3. Names and addresses of all directors and officers and when their terms expire

STATE CORPORATE TAX EXEMPTION

Corporate Income or Franchise Tax: yes

Name and address of state agency to contact:

Dept. of Revenue and Taxation
330 Ardenwood Drive
P.O. Box 201
Baton Rouge, LA 70821
(504) 925-4611

State Tax Exemption Requirements:

Automatic with federal 501(c)(3) exemption

MAINE

SECRETARY OF STATE INFORMATION

Secretary of State

Bureau of Corporations, Elections and Commissions

101 State House Station

Augusta, ME 04333-0101

http://www.state.me.us/sos/cec/cel.htm

Phone number of Bureau of Corporations: (207) 287-4195; Fax: (207) 287-8598

Provides Articles of Incorporation: yes

Provides statutes: yes, Maine Revised Statutes Annotated, Nonprofit Corporations, Title 13-B, from above address for $5; also provides pamphlet, "Rules for Nonprofit Corporations," no charge, from above address;

CORPORATE NAME REQUIREMENTS

Corporate Designator: not required

Corporate name may not contain language that implies the corporation is organized for purposes contrary to the Maine Nonprofit Corporation Act. The name may not be the same or similar to the name of any business or corporation existing or incorporated under Maine law; nor to any registered mark; nor to the name of any state agency, bureau or department

ARTICLES OF INCORPORATION

Articles Statute: MRSA Nonprofit Corporations, 13B, Section 403

Registered Agent Requirements:

Director Qualifications:

Number: 3 or more

Residency: no

Age: no

Incorporator Qualifications:

Residency: no

Age: no

Special Requirements:

BYLAWS

Directors' Quorum: majority of directors in office, unless a percentage is specified in the Articles or Bylaws, which may not be less than 1/5 of the number in office

Members' Quorum: as specified in Bylaws or else 10% of the voting membership, represented in person or by proxy

Executive Committee: majority of directors may designate two or more directors to exercise the authority of the full board, except to amend Articles or Bylaws, plan for merger or consolidation, recommend to members the sale or other disposition of all or most of the assets or recommend or revoke corporate dissolution

Directors' Term of Office: as specified in the Bylaws; if not specified, then one year

Required Officers: president, secretary or clerk and treasurer. One person may hold two or more offices

Special Officer Requirements: no age or residency requirements

Corporate Report Requirements: must be filed by June 1, on form provided by the secretary of state. It include the following information:

1. Corporate name and jurisdiction of incorporation
2. Name and address of registered agent (address of registered office, if different)
3. Officers' names and addresses

STATE CORPORATE TAX EXEMPTION

Corporate Income or Franchise Tax: yes

Name and address of state agency to contact:

Bureau of Taxation

Dept. of Finance and Administration

State House Station 24

Augusta, ME 04333

(207) 287-2086

Fax (207) 287-4028

State Tax Exemption Requirements:

Separate state notification required but determination follows federal

To provide this notification, mail a copy of the federal determination letter to the Bureau of Taxation

MARYLAND

SECRETARY OF STATE INFORMATION

State Department of Assessments & Taxation
Corporate Charter Division
301 W. Preston St.
Baltimore, MD 21201
http://www.dat.state.md.us/charter.html
Phone number for corporate inquiries: (410) 767-1350;
   Fax: (410) 333-7097
Provides Articles of Incorporation: yes
Provides statutes: no; Corporations and Associations, Title 2,
   Sec. 101—612, available in law libraries; provides "Informa-
   tion Guide for Forming a Corporation in Maryland," no
   charge, from above address

CORPORATE NAME REQUIREMENTS

Corporate Designator: name must include "corporation,"
   "limited," "incorporated" or an abbreviation, unless it is the
   name of a religious corporation
Corporate name may not contain language that implies the
   corporation is organized for a purpose other than that stated
   in its charter; may not be the same or similar to name of
   domestic or qualified foreign corporation or limited partnership or limited liability company authorized to do business in
   state, or to a reserved or registered name

ARTICLES (CHARTER) OF INCORPORATION

Articles Statute: Annotated Code of Maryland, Corporations
   and Associations, Section 2-104
Registered Agent Requirements:
Director Qualifications:
   Number: 3 or more; if the corporation is nonstock, 1 or more
   Residency: no
   Age: no
Incorporator Qualifications:
   Residency: not required, but in a religious corporation, must
   be member of the church
   Age: 18 or older; in a religious corporation, an adult member
   of the church
Special Requirements:

BYLAWS

Directors' Quorum: majority of the directors in office, unless a
   percentage is specified in the Bylaws, but not less than 1/3 of
   the board (but if 2 or 3 directors, at least 2 directors for
   quorum)
Members' Quorum: majority of the voting members represented
   in person or by proxy, or else as specified in the charter or
   Bylaws

Executive Committee: majority of board may appoint two or
   more directors to exercise the authority of the full board,
   except to change Bylaws or approve a merger. Appointment
   of a committee does not constitute compliance with duty of
   care by any director
Directors' Term of Office: as specified in the Bylaws, but not to
   exceed 5 years; if not specified, then one year between
   annual meetings
Required Officers: president, secretary and treasurer; one person
   may hold any two offices except president and vice president
   (if there is one); but if 2 signatures required on form, must be
   2 persons
Special Officer Requirements: no age or residency requirements
Corporate Report Requirements: an annual report in the form
   of a personal property return is due April 15; the form will
   automatically be sent to the corporation's principal office.
   Failure to file may result in forfeiture of the corporate charter
Nonprofits that intend to solicit contributions may be required
   to register with the secretary of state. Contact the secretary's
   office in Annapolis, (410) 974-5534, for further information.

STATE CORPORATE TAX EXEMPTION

Corporate Income or Franchise Tax: yes
Name and address of state agency to contact:
Comptroller of the Treasury
301 W. Preston St.
Baltimore, MD 21201
(410) 767-1313
State Tax Exemption Requirements:
Separate state notification required but determination follows
   federal
To obtain state income tax exemption, send a copy of your
   federal determination letter to the Comptroller's office. Note
   that there is a single Combined Registration Application for
   exemption from all state taxes other than income tax

MASSACHUSETTS

SECRETARY OF STATE INFORMATION

Office of the Secretary of the Commonwealth
Corporations Division
Rm. 1717
One Ashburton Pl.
Boston, MA 02108
http://www.state.ma.us/sec/cor/coridx.htm

Phone number of corporate filing section: (617) 727-9640;
Fax: (617) 742-4722

Provides Articles of Incorporation: yes

Provides statutes: no; order Corporation Laws (includes
nonprofit sections 180-1—11C & 180-1-26A) from State
Bookstore, Rm. 116, State House, Boston, MA 02133, (617)
727-2834

CORPORATE NAME REQUIREMENTS

Corporate Designator: name must include "Limited," "Incorporated," "Corporation," or an abbreviation. A church,
religious society or religious corporation may use a name that
doesn't indicate it's a corporation

Corporate name may not contain language that implies the
corporation is organized for purposes other than those stated
in its Articles; may not be the same or similar to the name of
another domestic or authorized foreign corporation, or to a
registered or reserved name

ARTICLES OF INCORPORATION (ORGANIZATION)

Articles Statute: Massachusetts General Laws, Chapter 180,
Section 3

Registered Agent Requirements:
not necessary if clerk is a resident of state

Director Qualifications:
Number: 3 or more; in a membership corporation with fewer
than three members, the number of directors should equal
the number of members.
Residency: no
Age: no

Incorporator Qualifications:
Residency: no
Age: 18 or older

Special Requirements:

BYLAWS

Directors' Quorum: majority of the directors in office, or else as
specified in the Bylaws

Members' Quorum: majority of the voting members or else as
specified in Articles or Bylaws

Executive Committee: to the extent authorized by the Articles
or Bylaws, a corporation may provide for an executive
committee elected from board, and the board may delegate
all powers to the committee, except the power to change the
principal corporate office, amend the Bylaws, elect officers or
fill vacancies on the board of directors, remove officers or
directors, or authorize a merger

Director's Term: one year between annual meetings unless the
directors are divided into classes with staggered terms

Required Officers: president, treasurer and clerk. The statutes
do not specify whether or not one person may hold more
than one office at a time

Special Officer Requirements: clerk must be Massachusetts
resident if there is no resident agent

Corporate Report Requirements: must be filed by November 1
each year, and must contain the following information:

1. Corporate name and address of principal office

2. Directors' and officers' names and addresses and date of
expiration of each term in office

3. Date of latest annual meeting

Tax-exempt nonprofits (except certain churches, schools, fire
fighter and police organizations) must also file Form PC with
the Division of Public Charities. To obtain this form,
contact:

Division of Public Charities
Office of the Attorney General
21st Fl.
One Ashburton Pl.
Boston, MA 02108
(617) 727-2235

STATE CORPORATE TAX EXEMPTION

Corporate Income or Franchise Tax: yes

Name and address of state agency to contact:

Department of Revenue
Determinations Bureau
100 Cambridge St., 3rd Fl.
Boston, MA
(617) 727-0135
Fax (617) 727-0379

State Tax Exemption Requirements:

Separate state notification required but determination follows
federal

For state income tax exemption, file Form TA1 and a copy of
your federal determination letter with the Determinations
Bureau

MICHIGAN

SECRETARY OF STATE INFORMATION

Consumer and Industry Services

Corporation, Securities and Land Development Bureau

Corporation Division

P.O. Box 30022

Lansing, MI 48909

http://www.cis.state.mi.us/corp/corpinfo.htm

Phone number of Corporation & Securities Bureau: (517) 334-6206; Fax: (517) 334-8329

Provides Articles of Incorporation: yes

Provides statutes: may provide Nonprofit Corporation Act (Sections 450.2101—3192) & related statutes, for a small fee, from above address; also provides "Entrepreneur's Guide" with instructions, no charge

CORPORATE NAME REQUIREMENTS

Corporate Designator: not required

Corporate name may not contain language that implies the corporation is organized for purposes other than those stated in its Articles or that implies it is a banking, surety, insurance or trust company; may not be the same or similar to the name of a domestic or authorized foreign corporation, or reserved or registered name, unless with the name holder's written consent or by a court judgment that permits use of the name

ARTICLES OF INCORPORATION

Articles Statute: MI Compiled Laws, MSA §21.197/202

Registered Agent Requirements:

Director Qualifications:

Number: one or more

Residency: no

Age: no

Incorporator Qualifications:

Residency: no

Age: 18 or older

Special Requirements:

If there are three or more incorporators they may, by resolution, designate one to sign the Articles; if so, a certified copy of that resolution must be filed along with the Articles

A nonstock corporation's Articles must include the value of its assets, classified as personal and real property, along with the general financing terms of the corporation

BYLAWS

Directors' Quorum: majority of the directors in office, or else a greater percentage specified in the Bylaws or Articles (but if there are more than 7 directors, the Articles or Bylaws may specify a percentage less than a majority, but not less than 1/3 of the number in office)

Members' Quorum: as specified in Articles or Bylaws, or else a majority of the voting members

Executive Committee: majority of the board may choose one or more directors to exercise the authority of the full board, except to alter the Bylaws or Articles, recommend disposal of property or assets, recommend dissolution or revocation of dissolution; fill board vacancies, adopt a merger or consolidation plan, fix director compensation or terminate membership

Directors' Term of Office: as specified in the Articles or Bylaws, or else one year between annual meetings

Required Officers: president, secretary and treasurer. One person may hold more than one office at a time, but alone may not execute a document required to be signed by two people

Special Officer Requirements: no age or residency requirements

Corporate Report Requirements: an "Updated Corporate Information Report" must be filed by October 1, and includes the following:

1. Corporate name
2. Name and address of registered agent
3. Officers' and directors' names and addresses
4. Purposes of the corporation
5. Nature of business in which the corporation has engaged during the year

STATE CORPORATE TAX EXEMPTION

Corporate Income or Franchise Tax: yes

Name and address of state agency to contact:

Dept. of Treasury

Bureau of Collections

Treasury Bldg.

Lansing, MI 48922

(517) 373-8030

State Tax Exemption Requirements:

Automatic with federal 501(c)(3) exemption

Note that Michigan has a single business tax, which is a value-added tax (VAT) replacing corporate income and various franchise taxes. Although not required, we suggest you notify the Dept. of Treasury of your federal 501(c)(3) tax-exempt status with Form C8030, or by letter to the Single Business Tax Administration

MINNESOTA

SECRETARY OF STATE INFORMATION

Secretary of State
Business Services Division
100 Constitution Ave.
180 State Office Bldg.
St. Paul, MN 55115-1299

http://www.sos.state.mn.us/bus.html

Phone number for corporate information: (612) 296-2803;
Fax: (612) 296-9073

Provides Articles of Incorporation: yes

Provides statutes: no; order Nonprofit Corporation Act,
Chapter 317A from state bookstore, (612) 297-3000

CORPORATE NAME REQUIREMENTS

Corporate Designator: not required

Corporate name must be in English characters or letters; must
be distinguishable from the name of a domestic or authorized
foreign profit or nonprofit corporation, limited partnership or
limited liability company, or a registered, reserved or trade
name, except with written consent of name holder, an
affidavit of non-use by the other company or court judgment
authorizing use of name

ARTICLES OF INCORPORATION

Articles Statute: MN Nonprofit Corporation Act, Section
317A.111

Registered Agent Requirements:
registered office only required

Director Qualifications:
Number: 3 or more; if there are less than 3 members, then
equal to that number
Residency: no
Age: no

Incorporator Qualifications:
Residency: no
Age: "adult"

Special Requirements:

Religious corporations authorized by Ch. 315 of MN statutes
may be organized under that Chapter or Chapter 317A

Religious corporations may benefit members as follows: support
and payment of ministers, teachers, employees and payment
of benefits to their survivors; may create, maintain and
disburse an endowment that funds a "church Plan" as defined
in IRC Sec. 414(e). Property of religious corporations is
exempt from taxation. The board of directors may appoint its
own peace officers to keep order on its own grounds

BYLAWS

Directors' Quorum: majority of the directors in office, unless a
percentage is specified in the Articles or Bylaws, which may
not be less than 1/3 of the number in office

Members' Quorum: as specified in the Bylaws or else 10% of the
voting membership present or represented by proxy

Executive Committee: board of directors may designate one or
more persons to exercise the authority delegated by the
board, in the intervals between board meetings and subject
to board approval; subject to direction and control of board
at all times

Directors' Term of Office: as specified in Bylaws, but not to
exceed 10 years; if not specified, then one year

Required Officers: president and treasurer. One person may
hold any two or more offices simultaneously

Special Officer Requirements: officers need not be directors
unless this is required in Bylaws; no age or residency
requirements

Corporate Report (Registration) Requirements: the secretary of
state will send registration form by February 1 each year,
which must be filed before December 31. It includes the
following information:

1. Corporate name and address
2. Name and address of registered agent
3. Name of president

STATE CORPORATE TAX EXEMPTION

Corporate Income or Franchise Tax: yes

Name and address of state agency to contact:

Minnesota Dept. of Revenue
10 River Park Plaza
St. Paul, MN 55146
(612) 296-0555 in Twin Cities; (800) 652-9747 elsewhere in
MN

State Tax Exemption Requirements:

Separate state notification required but determination follows
federal

To obtain your state income tax exemption, send Form M-120
(which requires only the corporate name and address, with
an officer's signature) along with a copy of the federal
exemption application and federal determination letter.
Exempt organizations must also file a copy of federal Form
990 (Return of Organization Exempt from Federal Income
Tax)

MISSISSIPPI

SECRETARY OF STATE INFORMATION

Secretary of State
Corporate Division
P.O. Box 136
Jackson, MS 39205

http://www.sos.state.ms.us

Phone number of Corporate Division: (601) 359-1350;
Fax: (601) 354-6243

Provides Articles of Incorporation: yes

Provides statutes: no; MS Nonprofit Corporation Act, Sections 79-11-101–403, available at state library in Jackson, or at law school libraries

CORPORATE NAME REQUIREMENTS

Corporate Designator: none required, but secretary of state "prefers" that the name include "corporation," "incorporated," "company," or "limited"

Corporate name may not contain language that implies the corporation was formed for a purpose other than that stated in its Articles; must be distinguishable from the name of a nonprofit or for-profit, domestic or authorized foreign corporation and from reserved or registered name, unless with written consent of the name holder and an agreement by the consenting corporation to change its name slightly, or else with a court judgment authorizing use of the name

ARTICLES OF INCORPORATION

Articles Statute: MS Nonprofit Corporation Act, Sec. 79-11-137

Registered Agent Requirements:

Director Qualifications:
   Number: not specified in the statutes; may be fixed by Articles or Bylaws.
   Residency: no
   Age: no

Incorporator Qualifications:
   Residency: no
   Age: no

Special Requirements:

Some of the nonprofit corporation requirements do not apply to religious corporations (see 79-11-403)

BYLAWS

Directors' Quorum: majority of the directors in office, unless a percentage is specified in the Articles or Bylaws

Members' Quorum: 10% of the voting membership or else as specified in the Articles or Bylaws

Executive Committee: majority of the board of directors may designate two or more directors to exercise the authority of the full board, except to approve or recommend a merger, dissolution or sale of all or most of the assets; appoint or remove directors, or fill vacancies on the board or any committee; or alter Articles or Bylaws

Directors' Term of Office: as specified in the Articles or Bylaws but not more than five years (except for religious corporations); if not specified, then one year

Required Officers: as specified in the Bylaws. One person may hold more than one office at a time

Special Officer Requirements: no age or residency requirements

Corporate (Status) Report Requirements: submission is not automatically required, but rather is requested by the secretary of state, not more often than every five years. You must reply within 90 days of a request with the following information:

1. Corporate name and address and jurisdiction of incorporation
2. Name and address of registered agent
3. Officers' and directors' names and addresses
4. Brief description of nature of activities in the state
5. Whether or not there are members

STATE CORPORATE TAX EXEMPTION

Corporate Income or Franchise Tax: yes

Name and address of state agency to contact:

Miss. State Tax Commission
Income and Franchise Tax Division
P.O. Box 1033
Jackson, MS 39125
(601) 359-1141

State Tax Exemption Requirements:

Automatic with federal 501(c)(3) exemption

MISSOURI

SECRETARY OF STATE INFORMATION

Secretary of State
Corporations Division
P.O. Box 778
Jefferson City, MO 65102
http://mosl.sos.state.mo.us

Phone numbers for general corporate information: (573) 751-2127

Provides Articles of Incorporation: yes

Provides statutes: Missouri Not-for-Profit Corporation Laws (Sections 355.001—881), no charge, from the above address; included with statutes in the same handbook are general information, procedures, phone numbers, etc., necessary to form a business or nonprofit corporation, and complete sample corporate forms

CORPORATE NAME REQUIREMENTS

Corporate Designator: not required

Corporate name must be in English; may not be the same as the name of domestic or authorized foreign profit or nonprofit corporation or limited partnership, or a reserved name; may not contain language that implies the corporation is organized for any purposes other than those stated in its Articles

ARTICLES OF INCORPORATION

Articles Statute: RSM, Chap. 355.096

Registered Agent Requirements:

Director Qualifications:
    Number: 3 or more
    Residency: no
    Age: no

Incorporator Qualifications:
    Residency: US citizen
    Age: 18 or older

Special Requirements:

Articles must specify whether the corporation being formed is a public benefit or mutual benefit corporation

BYLAWS

Directors' Quorum: majority of the directors in office unless a percentage is specified in the Articles or Bylaws, which may not be less than 1/3 of the number in office

Members' Quorum: as specified in the Bylaws or else 10% of the voting membership present or represented by proxy

Executive Committee: majority of directors may designate two or more directors to exercise the authority of the full board, except to approve or recommend to members a merger, dissolution, sale of all or most of assets (unless okay in Bylaws or Articles); appoint or remove directors or fill vacancies on the board or any committee; or alter Bylaws or Articles

Directors' Term of Office: as specified in the Articles or Bylaws, but not to exceed three years; if not specified, then one year

Required Officers: president, secretary and treasurer. One person may hold any two offices simultaneously, except for president and secretary

Special Officer Requirements: no age or residency requirements

Corporate Report Requirements: must be filed by August 31 each year, on form supplied by the secretary of state. Contains the following information:

1. Corporate name and jurisdiction of incorporation
2. Name and address of registered agent and office
3. Directors' and officers' names and addresses
4. Brief description of nature of activities
5. Whether public benefit or mutual benefit corporation

STATE CORPORATE TAX EXEMPTION

Corporate Income or Franchise Tax: yes

Name and address of state agency to contact:

Missouri Dept. of Revenue
Income Taxes Bureau
P.O. Box 700
Jefferson City, MO 65105-0700
(314) 751-4541

State Tax Exemption Requirements:

Automatic with federal 501(c)(3) exemption

If the corporation files federal Form 990 (Return of Organization Exempt from Income Tax) there is no need for further filing in Missouri. Exempt organizations must file Form MO-1120 for unrelated business income tax

MONTANA

SECRETARY OF STATE INFORMATION

Secretary of State
Corporation Bureau
Montana State Capitol
P.O. Box 202801
Helena, MT 59620
http://www.mt.gov/sos/biz.htm

Phone number of Business Services Bureau: (406) 444-3665; Fax: (406) 444-3976

Provides Articles of Incorporation: no; use statutes as guidelines

Provides statutes: MT Code, Title 35, Corporations, Partnerships, and Associations, $10, from above address; may also be found at all county clerks' and recorders' offices (nonprofit sections 35-2-113—1402)

CORPORATE NAME REQUIREMENTS

Corporate Designator: not required

Corporate name may not contain language that implies the corporation is organized for purposes other than those stated in its Articles; may not be the same or deceptively similar to the name of a domestic or authorized foreign profit or nonprofit corporation, reserved, registered or fictitious name, limited partnership or trademark name, unless with written consent of the name holder and an agreement by the consenting corporation to change its name slightly, or else with a court judgment authorizing use of the name

ARTICLES OF INCORPORATION

Articles Statute: Revised Code of Montana 35-2-213

Registered Agent Requirements:

Director Qualifications:
Number: 3 or more
Residency: no
Age: no

Incorporator Qualifications:
Residency: no
Age: no

Special Requirements:

Articles must specify whether the corporation being formed is a public benefit, mutual benefit or religious corporation

BYLAWS

Directors' Quorum: majority of the directors in office, unless a percentage is specified in the Articles or Bylaws, which may not be less than 1/3 of the number in office (but if there are less than 6 directors, no fewer than 2 directors for quorum)

Members' Quorum: as specified in the Bylaws or else 10% of the voting members represented in person or by proxy

Executive Committee: majority of the board of directors may designate two or more directors to exercise the authority of the full board, except to alter Articles or Bylaws; appoint or remove directors or committee members; or recommend to members the merger, dissolution, sale or transfer of all or most of the assets of the corporation. The full board remains legally responsible for the actions of the committee

Directors' Term of Office: as specified in Bylaws, but not to exceed 5 years; if not specified, then one year

Required Officers: president, secretary and treasurer. One person may hold more than one office at the same time

Special Officer Requirements: no age or residency requirements; officer's term may not exceed three years

Corporate Report Requirements: must be filed each year between January 1 and April 15 on a form provided by the secretary of state. Includes the following information:

1. Corporate name and address and jurisdiction of incorporation
2. Name and address of registered agent
3. Brief statement of character of affairs
4. Directors' and officers' names and addresses
5. Whether or not there are members

STATE CORPORATE TAX EXEMPTION

Corporate Income or Franchise Tax: yes

Name and address of state agency to contact:

State Dept. of Revenue
Natural Resource Incorporation Tax Division
P.O. Box 5835
Helena, MT 59620
(406) 444-2441

State Tax Exemption Requirements:

Separate state determination

After filing Articles with the scretary of state, you should receive a welcome letter, which will include a form for the state income tax exemption. To apply for state tax exemption, you must send the following information to the Dept. of Revenue:

1. Character of the organization, the purpose for which it was organized and its actual activities
2. Sources and disposition of its income and whether or not the income may inure to the benefit of any private shareholder or individual.
3. In addition the applicant must supply a copy of the corporate Articles and Bylaws; and the latest financial statement showing assets, liabilities, receipts and disbursements
4. A copy of the federal exemption letter
5. Copies of Articles and Bylaws

NEBRASKA

SECRETARY OF STATE INFORMATION

Secretary of State
Corporate Office
Suite 2304
State Capitol Bldg.
Lincoln, NE 68509
http://www.nol.org/home/SOS

Phone number of Corporate Office: (402) 471-4079; Fax: (402) 471-3666

Provides Articles of Incorporation: yes

Provides statutes: no; NE Nonprofit Corporation Act (sections 21-1901—19,177), available at law libraries or from county clerk offices

CORPORATE NAME REQUIREMENTS

Corporate Designator: not required

Corporate name may not contain language that indicates the corporation is organized for purposes other than those stated in its Articles; may not be the same or deceptively similar to the name of another domestic or qualified foreign, profit or nonprofit corporation, trade name or registered or reserved name; if the name is written in foreign characters it must be transliterated into English

ARTICLES OF INCORPORATION

Articles Statute: RSN, Ch. 21-1928

Registered Agent Requirements:

Director Qualifications:

  Number: 3 or more
  Residency: no
  Age: no

Incorporator Qualifications:

  Number: 2 or more
  Residency: no
  Age: no

Special Requirements:

A duplicate copy of the filed Articles must be recorded in the office of the clerk of the county where the registered office is located

BYLAWS

Directors' Quorum: majority of the directors in office, unless a percentage is specified in the Articles or Bylaws, which may not be less than 1/3 of the directors in office

Members' Quorum: as specified in the Bylaws or else 10% of the voting membership

Executive Committee: majority of the board may designate two or more directors to exercise the authority of the full board to the extent granted by a resolution of the board, except to alter Articles, Bylaws or board resolutions; appoint committee or board members; adopt a plan for merger or consolidation; conduct any transaction involving all or most of the corporation's assets; authorize voluntary dissolution or revocation of dissolution; plan for the distribution of corporate assets. The full board remains responsible for the actions of the committee

Required Officers: president, vice president, secretary and treasurer. One person may hold more than one office at a time, but may not simultaneously be both president and secretary or president and vice president

Special Officer Requirements: no age or residency requirements

Corporate Report Requirements: the secretary of state provides forms for the report, which is due every other January 1, depending on year of incorporation, and is delinquent on June 2. It contains the following information:

1. Corporate name
2. Directors' and officers' names and addresses
3. Name and address of registered agent
4. Brief statement of character of affairs of organization

STATE CORPORATE TAX EXEMPTION

Corporate Income or Franchise Tax: yes

Name and address of state agency to contact:

Nebraska Dept. of Revenue
P.O. Box 94818
Lincoln, NE 68509-4818
(402) 471-2971
Fax (402) 471-5608

State Tax Exemption Requirements:

Automatic with federal 501(c)(3) exemption

NEVADA

SECRETARY OF STATE INFORMATION

Office of the Secretary of State

Capitol Complex

Carson City, NV 89710-0003

http://jvm.com/sos

Phone number of Secretary of State's office: (702) 687-5203;
Fax: (702) 687-3471

Provides Articles of Incorporation: yes

Provides statutes: Nevada Revised Statutes, Nonprofit
Corporations, Chapter 82; available upon request from the
above address

CORPORATE NAME REQUIREMENTS

Corporate Designator: not required; unless a natural person's
name used (e.g., Peterson & Sons). Then must add "incorporated," "corporations," "limited," "company," or an abbreviation.

Corporate name may not be the same or deceptively similar to
the name of a domestic or authorized foreign corporation,
partnership or company, or a reserved name, except with
written consent of name holder; may not contain any form of
the words "trust" or "engineer"

ARTICLES OF INCORPORATION

Articles Statute: NRSA 82.086

Registered Agent Requirements:

Separate form is supplied by secretary of state, "Certificate of
Acceptance of Registered Agent," which must be filed with
the Articles

Director (or Trustee) Qualifications:

Number: 1 or more

Residency: no

Age: 18 or older

Incorporator Qualifications:

Residency: no

Age: no

Special Requirements:

BYLAWS

Directors' Quorum: a majority of the directors in office or else
as specified in Articles or Bylaws

Members' Quorum: as specified in the Bylaws or else 10% of the
voting membership

Executive Committee: a majority of the board may designate
one or more directors and other natural persons to exercise
the authority of the full board to the extent of the board
resolution authorizing the committee, except that it may not
alter the Articles or Bylaws; appoint or remove committee
members, directors or officers; adopt a plan of merger or
consolidation; authorize any financial transaction involving
all or most of the corporate assets; authorize voluntary
dissolution; or repeal any resolution of the full board.
Designation of a committee does not relieve the full board of
responsibility for its actions

Directors (Trustees) Term of Office: as stated in the Articles or
Bylaws

Required Officers: president, secretary, treasurer. Officers who
are natural persons may hold two or more offices, without
restrictions

Special Officer Requirements: no age or residency requirements

Corporate Report Requirements: report must be filed each year
on forms provided by the secretary of state by the last day of
the anniversary month of incorporation. It includes the
following:

1. Names and address of all officers and directors/trustees
2. Name and address of registered agent

STATE CORPORATE TAX EXEMPTION

Corporate Income or Franchise Tax: no state corporate income
tax or franchise tax

Name and address of state agency to contact for information
about other taxes:

Dept. of Taxation

Capitol Complex

Carson City, NV 89710-0003

(702) 687-4892

(800) 992-0900

Fax (702) 687-5981

State Tax Exemption Requirements: none

NEW HAMPSHIRE

SECRETARY OF STATE INFORMATION

Secretary of State

Corporation Division

Rm. 204 State House

Concord, NH 03301

http://www.state.nh.us

Phone number for general corporate information: (603) 271-3244; Fax: (603) 271-6316

Provides Articles of Incorporation: yes

Provides statutes: secretary of state does provide pamphlet of selected statutes and instructions; for full text of law, order For-Profit and Nonprofit Business Laws (includes nonprofit sections 292-1—30) from Michie Co., (800) 562-1197

CORPORATE NAME REQUIREMENTS

Corporate Designator: not required

Corporate name may not be the same or deceptively similar to the name of an existing corporation, reserved or registered name, partnership or trade name, unless with written consent of the name holder

ARTICLES OF INCORPORATION
(Articles of Agreement):

Articles Statute: NHRSA, 292:2

Registered Agent Requirements:

Person who is registered agent must also be the secretary of the corporation

Director Qualifications:

Number: one or more

Residency: no

Age: no

Incorporator Qualifications:

Number: 5 or more

Residency: no

Age: lawful age (capable of contracting)

Special Requirements:

Articles of Agreement must be recorded in the office of the clerk of the town in which the principal office of the corporation is located, *prior* to filing with secretary of state

Religious Corporations Note: in its statement of purpose in the Articles, the corporation must declare that its purpose is to maintain, propagate, practice and forever perpetuate religious worship, services, sacraments, and teachings in accordance with the doctrine, law and traditions of the church. See NH statutes, Voluntary Corporations and Associations, 292:17

There are additional limitations for charitable corporations; see 292:2a

BYLAWS

Directors' Quorum: majority of the directors in office, or else as specified in Articles or Bylaws

Members' Quorum: as specified in the Articles; if not specified, a majority of members

Executive Committee: a majority of the board may designate two or more directors to exercise the authority of the full board, except to change directors or committee members or amend Bylaws

Directors' Term of Office: one year between annual meetings, unless directors terms' are staggered

Required Officers: as in Articles or Bylaws

Special Officer Requirements: no age or residency requirements

Corporate Report Requirements: New Hampshire nonprofits must file a report every five years, on forms provided by the secretary of state. The only required information is officers' and directors' names and addresses

STATE CORPORATE TAX EXEMPTION

Corporate Income or Franchise Tax: no

Name and address of state agency to contact for other tax information:

Dept. of Revenue Administration

61 S. Spring St.

P.O. Box 457

Concord, NH 03302-0637

(603) 271-2186

Fax (603) 271-2355

State Tax Exemption Requirements:

New Hampshire has no corporate income tax (nor sales tax).

Federally tax-exempt organizations are also exempt from the New Hampshire Business Profits Tax

For information on financial reporting requirements for charitable corporations, contact the Charitable Trusts Division of the Attorney General's Office

NEW JERSEY

SECRETARY OF STATE INFORMATION

Department of State
Division of Commercial Recording
CN-308
Trenton, NJ 08625

http://www.state.nj.us/state/dcr/dcrpg1.html

Phone number for general corporate information: (609) 530-6400; Fax: (609) 292-7665

Provides Articles of Incorporation: yes (certificate of incorporation)

Provides statutes: no; NJSA, Title 15A available from legal supply store or in libraries. Materials from the Center for Nonprofit Corporations; provided by secretary of state; include summaries of most statutes relevant to writing Articles and Bylaws (see sections 15A:1-1—16-2)

CORPORATE NAME REQUIREMENTS

Corporate Designator: the name shall contain "a New Jersey nonprofit corporation," "incorporated," "corporation," "corp.," or "inc.", unless it is a religious corporation

Corporate name may not be the same as or deceptively similar to the name of a domestic or qualified foreign corporation, or to a reserved or registered name, except with written consent of name holder or court judgment authorizing use of name; may not contain language that implies the corporation is organized for purposes contrary to those stated in its Articles

ARTICLES (CERTIFICATE) OF INCORPORATION

Articles Statute: NJSA 15A:2-8

Registered Agent Requirements:

The registered agent must be at least 18 years of age

Director (Trustee) Qualifications:
  Number: 3 or more
  Residency: no
  Age: 18 or older

Incorporator Qualifications:
  Residency: no
  Age: 18 or older

Special Requirements:

The secretary of state sends a copy of the certificate of incorporation to the attorney general

BYLAWS

Directors' (Trustees') Quorum: majority of the directors in office, or else as specified in Bylaws, but no less than 1/3 of the number in office (but if less than 6 directors, no fewer than 2 directors for quorum)

Members' Quorum: a majority of the number of voting members present or represented by proxy, or else as specified in Articles or Bylaws

Executive Committee: majority of the board may appoint one or more trustees to exercise the authority of the full board to the extent delegated by resolution of the board; except that the committee may not alter the certificate or Bylaws, appoint or remove officers or trustees, submit anything to the membership for approval, or change a previous board resolution. The committee must report its actions at the next board meeting; the full board is responsible for the actions of the committee

Directors' (Trustees') Term of Office: one or two years, between annual or biennial meetings

Required Officers: president, secretary and treasurer. One person may hold any two or more offices at the same time; but if 2 signatures required on form, must be 2 persons

Special Officer Requirements: no age or residency requirements

Corporate Report Requirements: must be filed annually (whether or not the corporation is actively engaged in pursuit of its exempt purpose) on a form provided by the secretary of state, sent 90 days before due. The following information is included:

1. Corporate name and jurisdiction of incorporation
2. Name and address of registered agent
3. Directors' and officers' names and addresses

STATE CORPORATE TAX EXEMPTION

Corporate Income or Franchise Tax: yes

Name and address of state agency to contact:

Dept. of Treasury
Division of Taxation
50 Barrack St.
CN-269
Trenton, NJ 08646
(609) 292-5994

State Tax Exemption Requirements:

Separate state notification required but determination follows federal

To obtain state income tax exemption, send to the Division of Taxation:

1. An affidavit signed by a corporate officer that the corporation is not operated for profit, that it is organized without capital stock and is incorporated under provisions of RSNJ Titles 15, 15A, 16 or 17
2. Copy of Certificate of Incorporation and Bylaws
3. Copy of federal determination letter

No further filings are necessary, except for Form CIT-1 to report any unrelated business income

NEW MEXICO

SECRETARY OF STATE INFORMATION

State Corporation Commission
Corporation Dept.
P.O. Box 1269
Santa Fe, NM 87504-1269

http://www.state.nm.us/scc

Phone number of Corporation Commission: (505) 827-4511; Fax: (505) 827-4387

Provides Articles of Incorporation: yes

Provides statutes: no; NMSA Nonprofit Corporations, Sections 53-8-1—99, available in libraries

CORPORATE NAME REQUIREMENTS

Corporate Designator: not required

Corporate name may not contain language that implies it is organized for purposes other than those stated in its Articles; may not be the same or confusingly similar to the name of a domestic or qualified foreign profit or nonprofit corporation, reserved or registered name

ARTICLES OF INCORPORATION

Articles Statute: NMSA, Section 53-8-31

Registered Agent Requirements:

There is a separate form of affidavit of acceptance by registered agent, to be filed with the Articles

Director Qualifications:
Number: 3 or more
Residency: no
Age: no

Incorporator Qualifications:
Residency: no
Age: no

Special Requirements:

Duplicate originals of the Articles must be filed with the Corporation Commission

BYLAWS

Directors' Quorum: majority of the number of directors in office, unless a percentage is specified in the Articles or Bylaws, which may not be less than 1/3 of the number in office

Members' Quorum: as specified in Bylaws, or else 10% of the voting membership

Executive Committee: a majority of the board may designate two or more directors to exercise the authority of the full board, except to alter Articles or Bylaws; appoint or remove directors, officers or committee members; plan a merger or consolidation; transfer all or most of the property or assets; voluntarily dissolve or revoke a dissolution of the corpora-tion; or alter a board resolution. The full board remains responsible for the actions of the committee

Directors' Term of Office: as specified in the Articles or Bylaws, or else one year

Required Officers: as stated in Bylaws or by board resolution. One person may hold two offices at the same time

Special Officer Requirements: no age or residency requirements

Corporate Report Requirements: the annual report is due by the 15th day of the 5th month following the end of the corporation's tax year (except that the first annual report must be filed within 30 days of incorporation); the secretary of state provides forms 30 days before the report is due. Information required includes:

1. Corporate name, address of principal office and jurisdiction of incorporation
2. Name and address of registered agent
3. Brief statement of character of affairs
4. Directors' and officers' names and addresses

STATE CORPORATE TAX EXEMPTION

Corporate Income or Franchise Tax: yes

Name and address of state agency to contact:

NM Taxation and Revenue Dept.
P.O. Box 630
Santa Fe, NM 85709-0630
(505) 827-0700
Fax (505) 827-0469

State Tax Exemption Requirements:

Automatic with federal 501(c)(3) exemption

Federally exempt nonprofits are also automatically exempt from $50 franchise tax. The only further filing necessary is Form CIT-1 for unrelated business income taxes

NEW YORK

SECRETARY OF STATE INFORMATION

Department of State
Bureau of Corporations
162 Washington Ave.
Albany, NY 12231-0001

http://www.dos.state.ny.us/corp/corpwww.html

Phone number of Corporations Division: (518) 473-2492;
Fax: (518) 474-4765

Provides Articles of incorporation: no. One supplier of corporate forms is Blumberg's Law Products, Albany, NY, whose forms can be obtained at legal stationery stores throughout the state

Provides statutes: provides excerpts from the Not-for-Profit Corporation Law, which defines the four types (A, B, C and D) of nonprofit corporations in NY State; Corporation Law Handbook (includes nonprofit sections 201, et seq.) available from Gould Publications, 199-300 State St., Binghamton, NY 13901-2782, (607) 724-3000, for $24.95 plus $4 handling

CORPORATE NAME REQUIREMENTS

Corporate Designator: unless the corporation is formed for charitable or religious purposes, name shall contain "corporation," "incorporated," "limited" or an abbreviation

Corporate name must be distinguishable from the name of a domestic or authorized foreign corporation, and from reserved or fictitious names; it may not contain language that implies the corporation is organized for purposes other than those stated in its Articles

Corporate name may not contain any words prohibited by NY statutes, including the following: "acceptance," "annuity," "assurance," "bank," "bond," "casualty," "doctor," "endowment," "fidelity," "finance," "guaranty," "indemnity," "insurance," "investment," "lawyer," "loan," "mortgage," "savings," "state police," "state trooper," "surety," "title," "trust," "underwriter." [See §301 of NY Not-For-Profit Corporation Law]

ARTICLES (CERTIFICATE) OF INCORPORATION

Articles Statute: NY Not-For-Profit Corporation Law, Sec. 402

Registered Agent Requirements:

The corporation may designate the secretary of state as its agent for service of process, along with a P.O. address inside or outside the state to which the secretary of state shall mail a copy of any notice or process served. If the corporation appoints its own registered agent, he or she must be a resident or have an in-state business address

Director Qualifications:
Number: 3 or more

Residency: no
Age: Generally, 18 or older

Incorporator Qualifications:
Residency: no
Age: 18 or older

Special Requirements:

There are four types of not-for-profit corporations in NY; 501(c)(3) nonprofits formed for charitable, educational, religious, scientific, or literary purposes are classified as Type B nonprofit corporations under NY law. Your Articles must state that you are forming a Type B corporation—see Blumberg's Nonprofit Certificate of Incorporation form

Certificate of Incorporation for Type B corporations must be approved by a justice of the supreme court (a lower-level state court) of the judicial district of the corporation's office. Bring proposed Certificate of Incorporation to clerk of administrative justice of supreme court in district of corporation's principal office—approval in most cases should take just a few minutes (no fee for approval)

Additional approvals by various departments, agencies and functionaries of state government are needed for nonprofit corporations that will engage in certain activities (for example, you must get approval from the SPCA to incorporate an animal shelter) or approval of Education Dept. for a school; check Sec. 404 of the NY Not-For-Profit Corporation Law to see if your group's purposes will require further approval

Articles must state incorporated "under section 402 of the Not-for-Profit Corporation Law"

BYLAWS

Directors' Quorum: majority of the directors in office, or else the percentage stated in the Certificate of Incorporation, but in the case of a board with fifteen or fewer members, no less than 1/3 of directors. If there are more than 15 members, the quorum must be at least 5, plus one additional person for every 10 members (or fraction of) in excess of 15

Members' Quorum: majority of voting members, or else as specified in Bylaws, but in no case less than 10% of the voting members, or 100 votes, whichever is less

Executive Committee: majority of board may designate 3 or more directors and delegate authority by resolution of the full board, but a committee may not: submit any action for membership approval, fill a vacancy on the board or on a committee, fix directors' compensation, alter the Bylaws or change a board resolution

Directors' Term of Office: as specified in Bylaws, but not more than five years; if not specified, then one year

Required Officers: as specified in Articles or Bylaws. One person may hold two offices simultaneously, except for offices of president and secretary, or similar offices

Special Officer Requirements: no age or residency requirements; unless otherwise stated in Articles or Bylaws, an officer's term shall be one year

Corporate Report Requirements: as required from time to time by secretary of state [see sec. 520]

STATE CORPORATE TAX EXEMPTION

Corporate Income or Franchise Tax: yes

Name and address of state agency to contact:

NY State Dept. of Taxation and Finance
Technical Services Bureau
Bldg. 9, Rm. 104
State Campus
Albany, NY 12227
(518) 457-6139
Fax (518) 457-2486

State Tax Exemption Requirements:

Separate state notification required but determination follows federal

For exemption from state corporate franchise tax, file Form CT-247 with the following information:

1. Corporate name, address, principal activity, date of incorporation

2. What federal return the organization files (i.e., 990, 990-T, 1120 or other)

3. Certify that corporation is organized and operated as a nonprofit, whether it is authorized to issue capital stock, whether its income goes to the benefit of anyone associated with the corporation or a private individual

4. State whether exempt from federal income tax and enclose a copy of federal determination letter. If not federally exempt, state why not

5. If any unrelated business activities, list

6. List officers and agents and their duties

7. List real property in NY

Unrelated business income is reported on state Form CT-13

NORTH CAROLINA

SECRETARY OF STATE INFORMATION

Department of the Secretary of State
Corporations Division
300 North Salisbury St.
Raleigh, NC 27603-5909

http://www.state.nc.us/secstate

Phone number of Corporations Division: (919) 733-4201;
 Fax: (919) 733-1837

Provides Articles of Incorporation: yes

Provides statutes: no; order General Statutes of North Carolina,
 Corporations, Partnerships and Securities Laws (nonprofit
 sections 55A-1-01—55A-17-05), from Michie Co., 1-800-
 446-3410; Corporations Division does provide "Nonprofit
 Corporation Guidelines," no charge, from above address

CORPORATE NAME REQUIREMENTS

Corporate Designator: not required

Corporate name may not contain language that implies the
 corporation is organized for purposes other than those stated
 in its Articles; may not be the same or deceptively similar to
 the name of domestic or qualified foreign profit or nonprofit
 corporation, partnership or limited liability company, or to a
 reserved or registered name, unless with written consent of
 the name holder and an agreement by the consenting
 corporation to change its name slightly, or else with a court
 judgment authorizing use of the name

ARTICLES OF INCORPORATION

Articles Statute: GSNC Nonprofit Corporation Act,
 Ch. 55A-2-02

Registered Agent Requirements:

Director Qualifications:
 Number: 1 or more
 Residency: no
 Age: no

Incorporator Qualifications:
 Residency: no
 Age: no

Special Requirements:

BYLAWS

Directors' Quorum: majority of directors in office, but if the
 Articles or Bylaws specify another percentage, it may not be
 less than 1/3 of the directors in office

Members' Quorum: as specified in Bylaws or else 10% of the
 voting membership, present or represented by proxy

Executive Committee: a majority of the board may designate
 two or more directors to exercise the authority of the full
 board to the extent specified by the board, except to dissolve
the corporation or plan its merger or consolidation; change
the Articles or Bylaws; approve or recommend any transaction involving all or most of the corporate assets or property;
appoint or remove directors or fill board or committee
vacancies. The full board remains responsible for the actions
of the committee

Directors' Term of Office: as specified in Bylaws; if not
 specified, then one year

Required Officers: as specified in Bylaws. One person may hold
 two or more offices, but if 2 signatures required on form, must
 be 2 persons

Special Officer Requirements: no age or residency requirements

Corporate Report Requirements: the annual report is due
 within 60 days of the last day of the anniversary month of
 incorporation, on a form provided by the secretary of state.
 Information required includes:

1. Corporate name, address of principal office and jurisdiction
 of incorporation
2. Name and address of registered agent
3. Brief statement of nature of affairs
4. Directors' and officers' names and addresses
5. Whether or not there are members

STATE CORPORATE TAX EXEMPTION

Corporate Income or Franchise Tax: yes

Name and address of state agency to contact:

NC Dept. of Revenue
P.O. Box 25000
Raleigh, NC 27640
(919) 733-3166

State Tax Exemption Requirements:

Separate state determination

After the corporation is incorporated, the Department of
 Revenue will request a copy of its Articles of Incorporation
 and Bylaws in order to determine its tax status. The
 department will then issue a letter to the corporation
 showing its tax status and filing requirements. Most
 501(c)(3) organizations except hospitals have no further
 filing requirements, other than Form CD-404 to report any
 unrelated business income

NORTH DAKOTA

SECRETARY OF STATE INFORMATION

Secretary of State
Corporations Division
Main Capitol Bldg.
600 East Boulevard Ave.
Bismarck, ND 58505-0500

http:// www.state.nd.us

Phone number of Corporations Division: (701) 328-4284;
Fax: (701) 328-2292

Provides Articles of Incorporation: yes

Provides statutes: yes, ND Nonprofit Corporation Act, Chapter 10-24, Sections 10-24-01—41, no charge, from above address

CORPORATE NAME REQUIREMENTS

Corporate Designator: not required

Corporate name may not contain language that implies the corporation is organized for purposes other than those stated in its Articles; may not be the same or deceptively similar to the name of a domestic or qualified foreign profit or nonprofit corporation, reserved, registered or fictitious name or name of limited partnership, unless with written consent from the name holder; must be written in English or transliterated into letters of the English alphabet

ARTICLES OF INCORPORATION

Articles Statute: ND Nonprofit Corporation Act,
Ch. 10-24-29

Registered Agent Requirements:

A separate Consent to Serve as Registered Agent form must be filed with the Articles

Director Qualifications:
Number: 3 or more
Residency: no
Age: no

Incorporator Qualifications:
Residency: no
Age: no

Special Requirements:

BYLAWS

Directors' Quorum: majority of the directors in office, unless a percentage is specified in the Articles or Bylaws, which may not be less than 1/3 of the number in office

Members' Quorum: as specified in the Bylaws, or else 10% of the voting membership

Executive Committee: majority of the board may designate two or more directors to exercise the authority of the full board to the extent provided in the resolution, except to alter the Articles or Bylaws; appoint or remove committee members, officers or directors; plan for merger or consolidation; authorize the sale or transfer of all or most of the property or assets; voluntarily dissolve or revoke dissolution of corporation; alter board resolutions. The full board remains responsible for the actions of the committee

Directors' Term of Office: as specified in Bylaws; if not specified, then one year

Required Officers: president, vice president, secretary and treasurer. One person may hold two or more offices, except for president and secretary

Special Officer Requirements: no age or residency requirements; officers' term is limited to three years; if not specified, officers' term is one year

Corporate Report Requirements: must be filed each year by February 1, on forms provided by the secretary of state. Includes the following information:

1. Corporate name and address and jurisdiction of incorporation
2. Name and address of registered agent
3. Name and address of officers and directors
4. Federal tax code by which exemption is recognized
5. Brief description of purpose actually pursuing in the state

STATE CORPORATE TAX EXEMPTION

Corporate Income or Franchise Tax: yes

Name and address of state agency to contact:

Corporate Income Tax Supervisor
ND State Tax Dept.
600 E. Boulevard Ave.
Bismarck, ND 58505
(701) 224-2045
(800) 472-2110 x3470

State Tax Exemption Requirements:

Automatic with federal 501(c)(3) exemption

Exempt organizations must file Form 99 (Information from Organization Exempt from Income Tax) annually with the Office of State Tax Commissioner, along with a copy of federal Form 990 (Return of Organization Exempt from Income Tax). Form 99 simply identifies a nonprofit's claim of exemption according to its IRC Section 501 classification. Exempt organizations report unrelated business income on Form 40

OHIO

SECRETARY OF STATE INFORMATION

Secretary of State
Corporations Section
30 East Broad St., 14th Floor
Columbus, OH 43266-0418

http://www.state.oh.us/sos/buispage.html

Phone number of corporate filing section: (614) 466-8438;
Fax: (614) 466-2892

Note: Corporate filings and phone calls are also handled by the
Cleveland office (216) 622-3260

Provides Articles of Incorporation: yes

Provides statutes: no; Ohio Revised Code Annotated, Nonprofit Corporation Law, Section 1702.01—99, available in
law libraries and large public libraries

CORPORATE NAME REQUIREMENTS

Corporate Designator: not required

Corporate name may not contain language that implies the
corporation is organized for purposes other than those stated
in its Articles; corporate name may not be misleadingly
similar to the name of an Ohio domestic or qualified foreign
profit or nonprofit corporation, or a registered trade name,
unless by written consent of the name holder, filed with
secretary of state

ARTICLES OF INCORPORATION

Articles Statute: ORC, Nonprofit Corporation Law, Ch.
1702.04

Registered Agent Requirements:

A separate form is included with secretary of state materials for
appointment of statutory (registered) agent, to be signed by
incorporators and agent, to be filed with Articles

Director (Trustee) Qualifications:
Number: 3 or more; if not specified in Articles or Bylaws, 3
Residency: no
Age: no

Incorporator Qualifications:
Residency: no
Age: no

Special Requirements:

BYLAWS (REGULATIONS)

Directors' (Trustees') Quorum: a majority of the number
authorized in the Articles or regulations, or else as specified
in Articles or regulations

Members' Quorum: the number of voting members present
constitutes a quorum, but Articles or regulations may require
a higher percentage to be present for certain actions

Executive Committee: no fewer than three trustees may serve as
an executive committee, subject to the control and direction
of the full board, and shall act only in intervals between
trustee meetings

Required Officers: president, secretary and treasurer. One
person may hold any number of offices simultaneously
without restrictions

Special Officer Requirements: no age or residency requirement;
officers' term is one year unless otherwise stated

Corporate Report Requirements: no annual report as such, but a
statement of continued existence, must be filed each five
years from the date of incorporation or from the last
corporate filing. The statement must contain:

1. Corporate name and address of its principal office
2. Fact that the corporation is still active
3. Name and address of its statutory (registered) agent
4. Date of incorporation

STATE CORPORATE TAX EXEMPTION

Corporate Income or Franchise Tax: yes

Name and address of state agency to contact:
Secretary of State
Corporate Income Tax Division
30 E. Broad St., 14th Fl.
Columbus, OH 43266-0418
(614) 846-6712

State Tax Exemption Requirements:

Automatic upon filing Articles

Certification by the secretary of state as a nonprofit corporation
is sufficient for state corporate income tax exemption. Tax
liability is incurred, however, if the federal exemption
application is denied

OKLAHOMA

SECRETARY OF STATE INFORMATION

Secretary of State
Corporate Filing Division
2300 N Lincoln Blvd., Rm. 101
Oklahoma City, OK 73105
http://www.state.ok.us
Phone number of Secretary of State's office: (405) 522-4560;
Fax: (405) 521-3771
Provides Articles of Incorporation: yes
Provides statutes: OK Statutes, Title 18, General Corporations
Act, $21.50, from above address

CORPORATE NAME REQUIREMENTS

Corporate Designator: name must contain one of following:
"association," "company," "corporation," "club," "foundation," "fund," "incorporated," "institute," "society," "union,"
"syndicate," or "limited," or one of the abbreviations "co.,"
"corp.," "inc.," "ltd.," or words or abbreviations of like import
in other languages so long as they are written in Roman
characters or letters
Corporate name must be distinguishable from those of
corporations or partnerships authorized to do business in the
state, from trade names and from reserved or fictitious names

ARTICLES (CERTIFICATE) OF INCORPORATION

Articles Statute: OK Statutes, Corporations, Title 18, Sec. 1006
Registered Agent Requirements:
Director Qualifications:
   Number: 1 or more
   Residency:
   Age: no
Incorporator Qualifications:
   Residency: no
   Age: no
Special Requirements:

BYLAWS

Directors' Quorum: majority of the directors in office, unless
   the certificate or Bylaws require a greater percentage. A
   nonstock corporation, however, can specify a percentage less
   than a majority, but it may not be less than 1/3 of the
   number in office. (If there is 1 director, at least 1 director for
   quorum)
Members' Quorum: as specified in Bylaws, or else a majority of
   the voting members present or represented by proxy
Executive Committee: majority of the board may designate one
   or more directors to exercise the authority of the full board,
   except to alter Bylaws or certificate of incorporation,

recommend transfer of all or most of the property and assets,
   recommend corporate dissolution or revocation of dissolution
Directors' Term of Office: as specified in the Articles or Bylaws
Required Officers: as specified in the Bylaws or by resolution of
   the board. One person may hold two or more offices
   simultaneously without restrictions
Special Officer Requirements: no age or residency requirements
Corporate Report Requirements: all religious, charitable and
   educational corporations subject to the Oklahoma Solicitation of Charitable Contributions Act [includes all 501(c)(3)
   organizations] that solicit funds from the general public,
   which have received contributions from the general public
   during the year, must file a report with the Oklahoma State
   Tax Commission by March 31. The report must contain the
   following information:

1. Gross amount of contributions pledged or collected
2. How much of that amount has been or will be given to the
   group's charitable purpose
3. The aggregate cost of soliciting the amount collected
4. The aggregate amount paid to professional fund raisers and
   solicitors

STATE CORPORATE TAX EXEMPTION

Corporate Income or Franchise Tax: yes
Name and address of state agency to contact:
Oklahoma Tax Commission
2501 Lincoln Blvd.
Oklahoma City, OK 73194
(405) 521-1350
State Tax Exemption Requirements:
Automatic with federal 501(c)(3) exemption
Exempt organizations must file Form 512-E (informational
   return) annually

OREGON

SECRETARY OF STATE INFORMATION

Secretary of State
Corporation Division
Public Services Building, Suite 151
255 Capitol St. NE
Salem, OR 97310-1327

http://www.sos.state.or.us/corporation/corphp.htm

Phone number of Corporation Division: (503) 986-2200; Fax: (503) 378-6520

Provides Articles of Incorporation: yes

Provides statutes: ORS, Nonprofit Corporations, Title 7, Ch. 65, from above address for a small fee; also provides "Oregon Business Guide," no charge, from above address

CORPORATE NAME REQUIREMENTS

Corporate Designator: the name must contain one of the following: "corporation" "incorporated," "company," "limited" or an abbreviation of one or more of those words, but shall not contain "cooperative."

Corporate name may not contain language that implies the corporation is organized for purposes other than those stated in its Articles; corporate name shall be written in Roman letters and may include Arabic and Roman numerals and incidental punctuation; the name must be distinguishable from the names of corporations, limited partnerships, cooperatives or business trusts and from reserved, registered or fictitious names

ARTICLES OF INCORPORATION

Articles Statute: ORS Nonprofit Corporations, Ch. 65.047

Registered Agent Requirements:

Director Qualifications:
    Number: 1 or more
    Residency: no
    Age: no

Incorporator Qualifications:
    Residency: no
    Age: 18 or older

Special Requirements:

Articles must specify whether the corporation being formed is a public benefit, mutual benefit or religious corporation

BYLAWS

Directors' Quorum: majority of the directors in office, unless a percentage is specified in the Articles or Bylaws, which may not be less than 1/3 of the number in office

Members' Quorum: the voting members actually present or represented by proxy, or else a greater number specified in the Articles or Bylaws

Executive Committee: majority of the board may designate two or more directors, who are empowered by resolution to exercise the authority of the full board, except to change the Articles or Bylaws; appoint or remove officers, directors or committee members; or approve or recommend merger, consolidation, or transfer of all or most of the property or assets. The full board remains responsible for the actions of the committee

Directors' Term of Office: as specified in Bylaws, but not to exceed 5 years; if not specified, then one year

Required Officers: president and secretary. One person may hold two or more offices simultaneously without restriction

Special Officer Requirements: no age or residency requirements

Corporate Report Requirements: must be filed each year by the anniversary date of incorporation on forms provided by the secretary of state. Includes the following information:

1. Corporate name and address and jurisdiction of incorporation

2. Name and address of registered agent (address of registered office if different)

3. Name and address of president and secretary

4. Secretary of state classification code most closely designating group's principal activity (this information is included with the annual report form supplied by the secretary of state); federal employer identification number

5. Brief description of nature of activities

6. Whether or not there are members

7. Whether the corporation being formed is a public benefit, mutual benefit or religious corporation

STATE CORPORATE TAX EXEMPTION

Corporate Income or Franchise Tax: yes

Name and address of state agency to contact:

Oregon Dept. of Revenue
955 Center St. NE
Salem, OR 97310
(503) 378-3725

State Tax Exemption Requirements:

Automatic with federal 501(c)(3) exemption

No need for further filing, except OR Form 20 and a copy of federal Form 990-T for any unrelated business income; but the Dept. of Revenue has the right to ask for further information regarding the activities of an exempt organization

PENNSYLVANIA

SECRETARY OF STATE INFORMATION

Department of State
Corporation Bureau
Rm. 308 North Office Bldg.
Harrisburg, PA 17120

http://www.state.pa.us/PA_Exec/State

Phone numbers for general corporate information: (717) 787-1057

Provides Articles of Incorporation: yes

Provides statutes: no; Nonprofit Corporations Sections 15 PA 5101—6162 can be found at law libraries; secretary of state does provide "Corporation Laws Guide" (no statutes) from above address, no charge

CORPORATE NAME REQUIREMENTS

Corporate Designator: the name must include "incorporated," "corporation," "company," "limited," or an abbreviation, or "association," "fund" or "syndicate." If "company "or "co." is immediately preceded by "and" or "&," "corporation," "incorporated," or "limited" or an abbreviation must immediately follow.

Corporate name must be expressed in English language or Roman letters and Arabic or Roman numerals; may not contain a blasphemy or swear word; may not contain language that implies the corporation is organized for purposes other than those stated in its Articles or that it is a government agency of Pennsylvania or the US or that it is a bank, insurance company, public utility or credit union; may not be the same or similar to the name of another corporation or partnership operating in PA, or to a reserved or registered name, unless with written consent of name holder and an affidavit of non-use by the other company or agreement by consenting company to change name slightly, or with a court judgment authorizing use of name

ARTICLES OF INCORPORATION

Articles Statute: Laws of PA, Corporations and Unincorporated Associations, Sec. 5306

Registered Agent Requirements:

Director Qualifications:
    Number: 1 or more if specified in Bylaws; if not specified, 3
    Residency: no
    Age: "of full age" (capable of contracting)

Incorporator Qualifications:
    Residency: no
    Age: "of full age" (capable of contracting)

Special Requirements:

Publication of either filing or intent to file must be made in two newspapers on one day

A "Docketing Statement" must be filed in triplicate with the Secretary of State, at the same time Articles are filed. This includes information on the type of corporation, corporate name, address of registered office, federal identification number, a brief description of activities and names and addresses of officers

An educational nonprofit that wishes to confer degrees must have the following information in its Articles: 1) Amount of assets incorporators have for establishing the institution; 2) Minimum number of regular faculty; 3) Brief statement of admissions requirements and courses. The clerk of the Court of Common Pleas in the county where the registered office of the corporation is located must send the Articles to the Superintendent of Public Instruction for approval

BYLAWS

Directors' Quorum: majority of the directors in office, unless a percentage is specified in Bylaws

Members' Quorum: as specified in the Bylaws, or a majority of members present at meeting who are entitled to vote

Executive Committee: majority of board may designate one or more directors to exercise the authority of the full board, except to submit anything to the membership for a vote, fill vacancies, change Bylaws or resolutions of the board, encroach on another committee's responsibilities authorized in Bylaws or by board resolution

Required Officers: president, secretary and treasurer (or similar officers by different titles). One person may hold all offices

Special Officer Requirements: president and secretary must be of full age; treasurer may be a corporation or a person of full age

Corporate Report Requirements: if there is any change in officers, a statement must be filed by April 30 of that year. It must include the following:

1. Corporate name and address
2. Names and titles of principal officers

STATE CORPORATE TAX EXEMPTION

Corporate Income or Franchise Tax: yes

Name and address of state agency to contact:

Dept. of Revenue
Bureau of Corporation Taxes
P.O. Box 8911
Harrisburg, PA 17127
(717) 783-6035

State Tax Exemption Requirements:

Separate state determination

To obtain state tax exemption, complete initial Docketing Statement and file with Department of State. Generally, nonprofit corporations without authority to issue capital stock are exempt from state corporate income and capital stock taxes. Exempt organizations must file Form RCT-101 to report any unrelated business income

Nonprofits that solicit funds from PA citizens must register with:

Department of State
Bureau of Charitable Organizations
124 Pine St., Suite 300
Harrisburg, PA 17101
(717) 783-1720

RHODE ISLAND

SECRETARY OF STATE INFORMATION

Secretary of State
Corporations Division
100 N. Main St.
Providence, RI 02903
http://www.state.ri.us
Phone number of Corporations Division: (401) 277-3040; Fax: (401) 277-1356
Provides Articles of Incorporation: yes
Provides statutes: Laws of RI Relating to Corporations, Associations and Partnerships, from above address, no charge (nonprofit sections 7-6-1—108)

CORPORATE NAME REQUIREMENTS

Corporate Designator: not required
Corporate name may not contain language that implies the corporation was organized for purposes other than those stated in its Articles; may not be the same or deceptively similar to the name of domestic or qualified foreign profit or nonprofit corporation in state, or reserved, registered or fictitious name; must be written in English or transliterated into letters of English alphabet

ARTICLES OF INCORPORATION

Articles Statute: General Laws of RI, Non-Profit Corporation Act, Sec 7-6-34
Registered Agent Requirements:
Director Qualifications:
Number: no less than 3
Residency: no
Age: no
Incorporator Qualifications:
Residency: no
Age: no
Special Requirements:
Duplicate originals of the Articles must be filed with the secretary of state

BYLAWS

Directors' Quorum: majority of the number in office, unless a percentage is specified in the Articles or Bylaws, which may not be less than 1/4 of the number in office
Members' Quorum: as specified in Bylaws, or else 10% of voting members represented in person or by proxy
Executive Committee: majority of the board may designate two or more directors to exercise the authority of the full board to the extent provided in resolution, except to change the Articles or Bylaws; appoint or remove officers, directors or committee members; plan a merger or consolidation; authorize the sale or transfer or distribution of all or most of the assets or property; voluntarily dissolve or revoke the dissolution of the corporation; or alter a resolution of the full board. The full board remains responsible for the actions of the committee
Directors' Term of Office: as specified in the Bylaws; if not specified, then one year
Required Officers: president, vice president, secretary and treasurer. One person may hold any two offices simultaneously, except for the offices of president and secretary
Special Officer Requirements: no age or residency requirements; an officer's term may not exceed three years and if not specified in the Articles or Bylaws it shall be one year
Corporate Report Requirements: must be filed each year during the month of June and includes the following information:
1. Corporate name and jurisdiction of incorporation
2. Name and address of registered agent
3. Brief statement of character of affairs actually conducting
4. Directors' and officers' names and addresses

STATE CORPORATE TAX EXEMPTION

Corporate Income or Franchise Tax: yes
Name and address of state agency to contact:
Dept. of Administration
Division of Taxation
289 Promenade St.
Providence, RI 02908
(401) 277-2905
Fax (401) 277-6006
State Tax Exemption Requirements:
Generally, automatic upon filing Articles
Note that certain exempt organizations may have further filing requirements and, if so, may have to pay a minimum $100 filing fee; check with the Division of Taxation about your filing obligations

SOUTH CAROLINA

SECRETARY OF STATE INFORMATION

Secretary of State
Corporation Dept.
P.O. Box 11350
Columbia, SC 29211
http://www.state.sc.us

Phone number of Corporation Department: (803) 734-2158;
Fax (803) 734-2164

Provides Articles of Incorporation: yes

Provides statutes: no; Nonprofit Corporation Act, Sections 33-31-101—1701, may be found in libraries

CORPORATE NAME REQUIREMENTS

Corporate Designator: name must include "corporation," "incorporated," "company," "limited," or an abbreviation

Corporate name may not contain language that implies the corporation was organized for purposes other than those stated in its Articles; must be distinguishable from the name of a domestic or authorized foreign profit or nonprofit corporation or limited partnership, or a reserved or registered name, unless with written consent of the name holder and an agreement by the consenting corporation to change its name slightly, or else with a court judgment authorizing use of the name

ARTICLES OF INCORPORATION

Articles Statute: Code of Laws of SC, Title 33-31-202

Registered Agent Requirements:

Director Qualifications:
 Number: 3 or more
 Residency: no
 Age: no

Incorporator (Petitioner) Qualifications:
 Residency: no
 Age: no

Special Requirements:

Articles must specify whether the corporation being formed is a public benefit, mutual benefit or religious corporation

BYLAWS

Directors' Quorum: majority of the directors in office, or else as specified in Bylaws, but no less than 1/3 of the number in office (but if less than 6 directors, no fewer than 2 directors for quorum)

Members' Quorum: as specified in Bylaws, or else 10% of voting members represented in person or by proxy

Executive Committee: a majority of the board may designate two or more directors to exercise the authority of the full board to extent specified by board, except to approve or propose to the membership dissolution or merger, appoint or remove directors, fill vacancies on the board or any committee, or amend Articles or Bylaws. Creation of the committee alone doesn't constitute director compliance with its actions

Directors' Term of Office: as specified in Bylaws, but not to exceed 5 years; if not specified, then one year

Required Officers: president, secretary and treasurer

Special Officer Requirements: no age or residency requirements

Corporate Report Requirements: no report is required for secretary of state; nonprofits that have received a federal tax exemption no longer have to file an annual report with the Department of Revenue

STATE CORPORATE TAX EXEMPTION

Corporate Income or Franchise Tax: yes

Name and address of state agency to contact:

South Carolina Department of Revenue
P.O. Box 125
Columbia, SC 29214
(803) 737-5000
Fax (803) 737-9881

State Tax Exemption Requirements:

Automatic with federal 501(c)(3) exemption

Exempt organizations must file Form SC 990, along with copies of Federal Forms 990 (Return of Organization Exempt from Income Tax) and 990-T (Exempt Organization Business Income Tax Return) for any unrelated business income

SOUTH DAKOTA

SECRETARY OF STATE INFORMATION

Secretary of State
State Capitol
500 E. Capitol
Pierre, SD 57501

http://www.state.sd.us/state/executive/sos/sos.htm

Phone number of Secretary of State's office: (605) 773-4845;
Fax: (605) 773-4550

Provides Articles of Incorporation: yes

Provides statutes: no; Nonprofit Corporations, Sections 22-1—28-17, available at libraries; secretary of state does provide brief guide, "Domestic Nonprofit Corporations," no charge, from above address

CORPORATE NAME REQUIREMENTS

Corporate Designator: not required

Corporate name may not contain language that implies the corporation was organized for purposes other than those specified in its Articles; must be distinguishable from the name of any domestic or qualified foreign profit or nonprofit corporation or limited partnership, or a reserved or registered name, unless with written consent of the name holder and an agreement by the consenting corporation to change its name slightly, or else with a court judgment authorizing use of the name; a name written in characters other than those of the English alphabet must be transliterated into English

ARTICLES OF INCORPORATION

Articles Statute: SD Codified Laws, Nonprofit Corporations, Sec. 47-22-6

Registered Agent Requirements: note that there is a separate section on the official Articles form for Consent of Appointment by the Registered Agent

Director Qualifications:
　Number: 3 or more
　Residency: no
　Age: no

Incorporator Qualifications:
　Number: 3 or more
　Residency:
　Age: 18 or older

Special Requirements:

BYLAWS

Directors' Quorum: majority of number in office, unless a percentage is specified in the Articles or Bylaws, which may not be less than 1/3 of the number in office

Members' Quorum: as specified in Bylaws, or else 10% of voting members represented in person or by proxy

Executive Committee: majority of board may designate two or more directors, who are empowered to act to the extent of the resolution authorizing them. The full board remains responsible for the actions of the committee

Directors' Term of Office: as specified in the Bylaws, or else one year

Required Officers: president, vice president, secretary and treasurer. Two or more offices may be held by the same person, except the offices of president and secretary

Special Officer Requirements: no age or residency requirements; an officer's term may not exceed three years

Corporate Report Requirements: must be filed on forms provided by secretary of state, every three years, by the first day of second month following the anniversary of incorporation, and contains the following information:

1. Corporate name and address and jurisdiction of incorporation
2. Name and address of registered agent at registered office
3. Brief statement of nature of affairs the corporation is conducting
4. Amount of property the corporation holds
5. Directors' and officers' names and addresses

STATE CORPORATE TAX EXEMPTION

Corporate Income or Franchise Tax: no

Name and address of state agency to contact for other tax information:
SD Dept. of Revenue
700 Governors Dr.
Pierre, SD 57501-2276
605) 773-5141
Fax (605) 773-5129

State Tax Exemption Requirements: no corporate income tax

No further filings necessary, but exempt organizations must apply for sales tax exemption

TENNESSEE

SECRETARY OF STATE INFORMATION

Secretary of State
Division of Business Services
18th Fl., James K. Polk Bldg.
Nashville, TN 37243-0306
http://www.state.tn.us/sos/soshmpg.htm
e-mail: rgrunow@mail.state.tn.us

Phone number for general corporate information: (615) 741-0537; Fax: (615) 741-7310

Provides Articles of Incorporation: yes

Provides statutes: no; Corporations, Partnerships, Associations Law (nonprofit sections 48-51-101—48-68-105) is available from Michie Co., (800) 562-1197, for $35; secretary of state does provide "Filing Guide for Nonprofit Corporations," no charge, from the above address

CORPORATE NAME REQUIREMENTS

Corporate Designator: not required

Corporate name may not imply that the corporation does any of the following unless it has authorization in writing: that the corporation can do anything that requires state authorization, that it is affiliated with a charitable, religious, fraternal, veterans' or professional organization, or that the corporation is an agency of or is affiliated with any office or agency of state or federal government; may not contain language that implies the corporation is organized for purposes other than those stated in its charter; the name must be distinguishable from the names of other domestic or qualified foreign profit or nonprofit companies, or a reserved or registered name, except with written consent of name holder and the consenting company agrees to change its name slightly, or with a court judgment authorizing use of name

ARTICLES (CHARTER) OF INCORPORATION

Articles Statute: TN Nonprofit Corporation Act, Sec. 48-52-102

Registered Agent Requirements:
Director Qualifications:
  Number: 3 or more
  Residency: no
  Age: no
Incorporator Qualifications:
  Residency: no
  Age: (capable of contracting)
Special Requirements:
The Charter must be filed with the Register of Deeds in the county of incorporation

The corporation must be identified in the Charter as a public benefit or mutual benefit corporation. If the corporation is a religious corporation, it must say so in the Charter

BYLAWS

Directors' Quorum: majority of the directors in office, or else as specified in Bylaws, but no less than 1/3 of the number in office (but if less than 6 directors, no fewer than 2 directors for quorum)

Members' Quorum: as specified in the Bylaws or else 10% of the voting membership

Executive Committee: majority of the board may designate one or more directors or natural persons who are not directors to exercise the authority of the full board, except to approve or recommend dissolution, merger or the transfer or sale of all or most of the assets; appoint or remove directors or fill vacancies on the board or any committee; or alter Charter or Bylaws

Directors' Term of Office: As specified in the charter or Bylaws, but may not be more than five years; if not specified, then one year

Required Officers: president and secretary. One person may hold more than one office simultaneously, except for the offices of president and secretary

Special Officer Requirements: no age or residency requirements

Corporate Report Requirements: must be filed by the first day of the 4th month following the close of the corporation's fiscal year, on a form provided by the secretary of state. It contains the following:

1. Corporation control number (this may be the Federal Employee Identification Number obtained by filing federal Form SS-4 with the IRS)
2. Corporate name and mailing address, address of principal office, jurisdiction of incorporation
3. Name and address of registered agent
4. Whether the corporation is a public benefit, mutual benefit or religious corporation

STATE CORPORATE TAX EXEMPTION

Corporate Income or Franchise Tax: yes

Name and address of state agency to contact:
Tennessee Dept. of Revenue
Andrew Jackson Office Bldg.
500 Deaderick St.
Nashville, TN 37242-1099
(615) 741-4105
Fax (615) 741-0682

State Tax Exemption Requirements:
Automatic upon filing Articles

TEXAS

SECRETARY OF STATE INFORMATION

Secretary of State
Corporations Section
P.O. Box 13697
Austin, TX 78711-3697
http://www.sos.state.tx.us

Phone number for general corporate information: (512) 463-5555, toll-free (800) 735-2989; Fax: (512) 463-5709

Provides Articles of Incorporation: no; provides guidelines for creating Articles. Provides statutes: Texas Corporation and Partnership Laws pamphlet (includes nonprofit sections 1396-1.01 et seq.) available from West Publishing, 1-800-328-9352, for $24.50; secretary of state does provide "Filing Guide," for $15, from above address

CORPORATE NAME REQUIREMENTS

Corporate Designator: not required

Corporate name may not contain language that indicates the corporation is organized for purposes other than those stated in its Articles; may not contain the word "lottery"; may not be the same or deceptively similar to the name of a domestic or authorized foreign profit or nonprofit corporation or reserved or registered name, unless with written consent of the name holder

ARTICLES OF INCORPORATION

Articles Statute: Texas Nonprofit Corporation Act, Article 1396-3.02

Registered Agent Requirements:

Director Qualifications:
  Number: 3 or more
  Residency: no
  Age: no

Incorporator Qualifications:
  Residency: no
  Age: 18 or older

Special Requirements:

BYLAWS

Directors' Quorum: majority of the number in office, or else as specified in the Articles or Bylaws, but a quorum may never be less than 3. Note that directors represented by proxy may not be counted towards a quorum

Members' Quorum: as specified in Bylaws or else 10% of the voting membership represented in person or by proxy

Executive Committee: majority of board may designate two or more persons, the majority of whom are directors, to exercise the authority of the full board, but the board is not relieved of responsibility for the actions of the committee

Directors' Term of Office: as specified in the Bylaws; if not specified, then one year

Required Officers: president, secretary and treasurer. One person may hold two or more offices simultaneously without restrictions

Special Officer Requirements: no age or residency requirements; officers' term is limited to three years

Corporate Report Requirements: the secretary of state may send a form to be returned within 30 days not more often than once every four years, containing the following information:

1. Corporate name and jurisdiction of incorporation
2. Name and address of registered agent
3. Directors' and officers' names and addresses

STATE CORPORATE TAX EXEMPTION

Corporate Income or Franchise Tax: yes

Name and address of state agency to contact:

Comptroller of Public Accounts
Exempt Organizations Section
111 W. 6th St.
Austin, TX 78774-0100
(512) 463-4600, (800) 252-1381

State Tax Exemption Requirements:

Separate state notification required but determination follows federal

A federally exempt 501(c)(3) organization must send a copy of its federal determination letter to the Comptroller to receive state income tax exemption. Texas also has a $150 annual corporate franchise tax, but new nonprofit organizations are not required to pay for their first 15 months of operation, or until they receive their federal exemption. A corporation that fails to receive an exemption will be liable for the postponed payment, but there is no additional penalty

UTAH

SECRETARY OF STATE INFORMATION

Department of Commerce

Division of Corporations and Commercial Code

160 East 300 South

Box 146705

Salt Lake City, UT 84114-6705

http://www.commerce.state.ut.us/web/commerce/corporat/corpcoc.htm

Phone number of corporate filing section: (801) 530-4849; Fax: (801) 530-6650

Provides Articles of Incorporation: no; provides guideline for creating Articles

Provides statutes: Utah Corporation Laws (nonprofit sections 16-6-18—112), $3, from above address

CORPORATE NAME REQUIREMENTS

Corporate Designator: not required

Corporate name may not contain language that implies the corporation is organized for purposes other than those stated in its Articles; the name may not be deceptively similar to the name of a domestic or authorized foreign profit or nonprofit corporation, or a reserved or registered name, or any registered trademark or service mark, unless submitted with a court judgment authorizing use of the name; may not contain "Olympic" or a form of the word without authorization from the U.S. Olympic Committee

ARTICLES OF INCORPORATION

Articles Statute: Utah Code Annotated, Corporation Laws, Sec. 16-6-46

Registered Agent Requirements:

A statement signed by the registered agent acknowledging acceptance of the designation must be included in the Articles or on a separate page attached to the Articles

Director (Trustee) Qualifications:

Number: 3 or more

Residency: no

Age: no

Incorporator Qualifications:

Residency: no

Age: no

Special Requirements:

BYLAWS

Directors' (Trustees') Quorum: majority of the directors in office or else as specified in Articles or Bylaws

Members' Quorum: as specified in the Articles or Bylaws; if not specified, then the number actually present in person or represented by proxy

Executive Committee: majority of the board may designate two or more trustees to exercise the authority of the full board, except to change Articles or Bylaws; appoint or remove trustees, officers or committee members; adopt a plan of merger or consolidation of the corporation; plan for distribution of corporate assets or authorize any transaction involving most of corporate property and assets; or change a board resolution. The full board remains responsible for the actions of the committee

Directors' (Trustees') Term of Office: as specified in Bylaws; if not specified, one year

Required Officers: as specified in Articles or Bylaws. No statutory restriction on how many offices a single person may hold

Special Officer Requirements: no age or residency requirements

Corporate Report Requirements: must be filed during the month of the anniversary date of incorporation, on a form provided by the Division. It contains the following information:

1. Corporate name and jurisdiction of incorporation
2. Name and address of registered agent
3. Officers' and trustees' names and addresses

STATE CORPORATE TAX EXEMPTION

Corporate Income or Franchise Tax: yes

Name and address of state agency to contact:

Utah State Tax Commission

160 E. 300 S.

P.O. Box 4000

Salt Lake City, UT 84134

(801) 530-4848

State Tax Exemption Requirements:

Separate state notification required but determination follows federal

To apply for corporation franchise tax exemption send a copy of federal determination letter with a written request for exemption in Utah to the State Tax Commission. Exempt organizations file Form TC-20 to report unrelated business income taxes

VERMONT

SECRETARY OF STATE INFORMATION

Secretary of State
Corporations Division
Pavilion Office Bldg.
109 State Street
Montpelier, VT 05609-1104
http://www.sec.state.vt.us

Phone number of Corporations Division: (802) 828-2386; Fax: (802) 828-2496

Provides Articles of Incorporation: yes, and model Bylaws

Provides statutes: no; Vermont Nonprofit Corporation Act (Title 11B, VSA, Chapter 19) is available in public libraries; secretary of state does provide short guide to VT nonprofit corporation law, no charge, from above address

CORPORATE NAME REQUIREMENTS

Corporate Designator: name must include "corporation," "incorporated," "company," "limited," or an abbreviation; may not contain "cooperative

Corporate name may not contain language that implies the corporation is organized for purposes other than those stated in its Articles; may not be the same or deceptively similar to a name granted, reserved or registered by the state, except with written consent of name holder and the consenting company agrees to change its name slightly, or with a court judgment authorizing use of name; if the name is not in English it must be transliterated into letters of the English alphabet

ARTICLES OF INCORPORATION

Articles Statute: VSA, Nonprofit Corporations, Title 11B, Section 2402

Registered Agent Requirements:

Director Qualifications:
    Number: 3 or more
    Residency: no
    Age: no

Incorporator Qualifications:
    Residency: no
    Age: 18 or older

Special Requirements:

Articles must specify whether the corporation being formed is a public benefit or mutual benefit corporation

BYLAWS

Directors' Quorum: majority of the number of directors specified in Bylaws, or a greater number in the Articles or Bylaws

Members' Quorum: as specified in Bylaws or else 10% of the voting membership

Executive Committee: majority of directors may designate two or more directors to exercise the authority of the full board, except to change the Articles or Bylaws; appoint or remove directors, officers or committee members; or recommend or authorize any transaction involving all or most of the property and assets. The full board remains responsible for the actions of the committee

Directors' Term of Office: as specified in Bylaws, but not to exceed 6 years; if not specified, then one year

Required Officers: president, vice president, secretary and treasurer. One person may hold two or more offices, except the offices of president and secretary

Special Officer Requirements: no age or residency requirements

Corporate (Status) Report Requirements: must be filed every two years regardless of the year of incorporation, by April 1, on a form provided by the secretary of state. It must contain the following information:

1. Corporate name and address and jurisdiction of incorporation
2. Name and address of registered agent
3. Brief statement of character of affairs
4. Directors' and officers' names and addresses

STATE CORPORATE TAX EXEMPTION

Corporate Income or Franchise Tax: yes

Name and address of state agency to contact:

Commissioner/Dept. of Taxes
Agency of Administration
Pavilion Office Bldg.
Montpelier, VT 05602
(802) 828-2551

State Tax Exemption Requirements:

Separate state notification required but determination follows federal

For exemption (and to receive an exempt organization number), send copies of federal income tax exemption application, federal determination letter, Articles and Bylaws. Vermont Business Account Number Application applies to all state taxes (income, sales and use, withholding, meals and rooms). To report unrelated business income, exempt organizations file Form 104

VIRGINIA

SECRETARY OF STATE INFORMATION

Clerk's Office
State Corporation Commission
P.O. Box 1197
Richmond, VA 23218-1197
http://www.state.va.us/scc/index.html

Phone number of corporate filing section: (804) 371-9733; Fax (804) 371-9744

Provides Articles of Incorporation: no; provides form (Form SCC819) to be used as a guideline for creating Articles

Provides statutes: no; Nonstock Corporation Act (Ch. 13) can be found in law libraries; commission does provide an detailed "Business Registration Guide," no charge, from the above address

CORPORATE NAME REQUIREMENTS

Corporate Designator: not required

Corporate name may not contain language that implies the corporation is organized for purposes other than those stated in its Articles; must be distinguishable from the name of a nonstock or stock, domestic or authorized foreign corporation, and from any reserved or registered name, except with written consent of name holder and the consenting company agrees to change its name slightly

ARTICLES OF INCORPORATION

Articles Statute: VA Code, Nonstock Corporation Act, Section 13.1-819

Registered Agent Requirements:

Registered agent must be an individual who is a resident of VA and either an initial director of the corporation or a member of the VA State Bar Association, a professional corporation, or a limited liability company

Director Qualifications:
   Number: one or more
   Residency: no
   Age: no

Incorporator Qualifications:
   Residency: no
   Age: no

Special Requirements:

BYLAWS

Directors' Quorum: majority of the directors in office, unless a percentage is specified in the Articles or Bylaws, which may not be less than 1/3 of the number in office

Members' Quorum: as specified in the Bylaws or else 10% of the voting membership represented in person or by proxy

Executive Committee: majority of the board may designate two or more directors to exercise the authority of the full board, except to approve or recommend action required to be approved by the members; fill vacancies on the board; alter Articles or Bylaws; approve merger plan

Directors' Term of Office: as specified in Articles; if not specified, then one year

Required Officers: as specified in Articles or Bylaws. One person may hold any two or more offices simultaneously, without restrictions

Special Officer Requirements: no age or residency requirements

Corporate Report Requirements: must be filed between January 1 and April 1, on forms provided by the Corporation Commission. It must contain the following information:

1. Corporate name, address and jurisdiction of incorporation
2. Name and address of registered agent
3. Directors' and officers' names and addresses

STATE CORPORATE TAX EXEMPTION

Corporate Income or Franchise Tax: yes

Name and address of state agency to contact:

Dept. of Taxation
P.O. Box 1115
Richmond, VA 23208-1115
Fax (804) 367-2062

State Tax Exemption Requirements:

Automatic with federal 501(c)(3) exemption

Exempt organizations must report any unrelated business income on Form 500 but no other income tax filings are necessary after the federal exemption is received

"Business Registration Guide," available from the secretary of state, has useful tax information

WASHINGTON

SECRETARY OF STATE INFORMATION

Secretary of State
Corporations Division
2nd Fl., Republic Bldg.
505 E. Union
P.O. Box 40234
Olympia, WA 98504
http://www.wa.gov/sec

Phone number for general corporate information: (360) 753-7115

Provides Articles of Incorporation: yes

Provides statutes: no, Nonprofit Corporation Act, Sections 24.03.010—925, can be found at libraries

CORPORATE NAME REQUIREMENTS

Corporate Designator : name cannot include or end with "incorporated," "company," "limited" or abbreviation thereof, but may have designation such as "association," "group," "club," "league," "services," "committee," "fund," "foundation," etc.

Corporate name may not include language that implies the corporation is organized for purposes other than those stated in its Articles; may not be the same or deceptively similar to the name of a corporation, limited partnership or limited liability company authorized to do business in the state, except with written consent of the name holder you add or delete one word to the corporate name; must be written in English or transliterated into letters of the English alphabet

ARTICLES OF INCORPORATION

Articles Statute: RCW Title 24, Corporations and Associations, Ch. 24.03.025

Registered Agent Requirements:

Consent to Appointment as Registered Agent is a separate part of the official Articles form and must be signed by the designated agent

Director Qualifications:
  Number: one or more
  Residency:
  Age: initial directors must be 18 or older

Incorporator Qualifications:
  Residency: no
  Age: 18 or older

Special Requirements:

An application for Status as a Public Benefit Nonprofit Corporation must be filed with the Charities Division if your corporation plans on soliciting charitable contributions

BYLAWS

Directors' Quorum: majority of the directors in office, or else the percentage stated in the Articles or Bylaws, which may not be less than 1/3 of the number in office

Members' Quorum: as specified in Bylaws or else 10% of voting membership represented in person or by proxy

Executive Committee: majority of directors may designate two or more directors to exercise the authority of the full board, except to alter Articles or Bylaws; appoint or remove directors, officers or committee members; adopt a plan of merger or consolidation; conduct any transaction involving all or most of the corporate property and assets; authorize voluntary dissolution or revoke resolution to dissolve; adopt a plan for distribution of assets; or change a board resolution. The full board remains responsible for the actions of the committee

Directors' Term of Office: as specified in the Articles or Bylaws

Required Officers: president, vice president, secretary and treasurer. One person may hold any two or more offices simultaneously, except for the offices of president and secretary

Special Officer Requirements: no age or residency requirements; unless the Articles or Bylaws provide otherwise, an officer's term is limited to one year

Corporate Report Requirements: must be filed each year by anniversary date of incorporation on form provided by the secretary of state. It contains the following information:

1. Corporate name, address, and jurisdiction of incorporation
2. Name and address of registered agent
3. Brief statement of character of affairs
4. Directors' and officers' names and addresses
5. Corporation's Unified Business Identifier Number

STATE CORPORATE TAX EXEMPTION

Corporate Income or Franchise Tax: no

Name and address of state agency to contact for other tax information:

Washington State Dept. of Revenue
General Administration Bldg.
AX-02
Olympia, WA 98504-0090
(206) 753-5540

State Tax Exemption Requirements: no corporate income tax

WEST VIRGINIA

SECRETARY OF STATE INFORMATION

Secretary of State
Corporations Division
Capitol Bldg., W-139
Charleston, WV 25305

http://www.state.wv.us

Phone number of corporate filing section: (304) 558-6000; Fax (304) 558-0900

Provides Articles of Incorporation: yes

Provides statutes: provides, on request, a photocopy of WVa Code, Business and Nonprofit Corporations, Sec. 31 et seq., for $16.10

CORPORATE NAME REQUIREMENTS

Corporate Designator: "corporation," "limited," "incorporated," "company" or abbreviation required in corporate name, or you may use "foundation"

Corporate name may not contain language that implies the corporation is organized for purposes other than those stated in its Articles; may not be the same or deceptively similar to the name of a domestic profit or nonprofit or authorized foreign corporation, or to any registered or reserved name except with written consent and you add or delete one word to name to make it distinguishable, plus a certified copy of final court order validating the applicant's prior right to use the name; name must be written in English or transliterated into English alphabet

ARTICLES OF INCORPORATION

Articles Statute: WVa Code, Business and Nonprofit Corporations, Sec. 31-1-27

Registered Agent Requirements:

Director Qualifications:
  Number: one or more
  Residency: no
  Age: no

Incorporator Qualifications:
  Residency: no
  Age: no

Special Requirements:

Incorporators must file a copy of the Articles with the clerk of the county where the corporation's principal office is located

BYLAWS

Directors' Quorum: majority of the directors in office, or else a greater percentage, if stated in the Articles or Bylaws

Members' Quorum: as specified in Bylaws or else 10% of voting membership represented in person or by proxy

Executive Committee: majority of the board may designate two or more directors to exercise the authority of the full board, except to alter the Articles or Bylaws; appoint or remove officers, directors or committee members; adopt a plan of merger or consolidation; authorize a transaction involving all or most of the property and assets; authorize voluntary dissolution or revocation of dissolution; adopt a plan to distribute all corporate assets; alter a board resolution. The board remains responsible for the actions of the committee

Directors' Term of Office: one year between annual meetings to elect directors

Required Officers: president, vice president, secretary and treasurer. One person may hold any two or more offices simultaneously, except for offices of president and secretary

Special Officer Requirements: no age or residency requirements; an officer's term may not exceed three years

Corporate Report Requirements: must be filed by July 1 of each year, on a form provided by the Tax Department. It includes the following information:

1. Corporate name and jurisdiction of incorporation
2. Address of principal office and name and address of registered agent
3. Brief statement of character of affairs
4. Directors' and officers' names and addresses

STATE CORPORATE TAX EXEMPTION

Corporate Income or Franchise Tax: yes

Name and address of state agency to contact:

West Virginia Tax Department
Taxpayer Services Division
P.O. Box 3784
Charleston, WV 25337-3784
(800) 642-9016 (in WV)
(304)558-8609
Fax (304) 558-2501

State Tax Exemption Requirements:

Automatic with federal 501(c)(3) exemption

Federally exempt nonprofit corporations are exempt from paying the state business registration fee, but must still file the business registration form. Exempt organizations are also exempt from the business franchise tax. File unrelated business income tax on Form WV-CNT 112 with a copy of federal Form 990-T

WISCONSIN

SECRETARY OF STATE INFORMATION

Department of Financial Institutions
Division of Corporate and Consumer Services
P.O. Box 7846
Madison, WI 53707-7846

http://badger.state.wi.us/agencies/dfi/corp/corp.htm

Phone number of corporate filing section: (608) 266-3590; Fax (608) 267-6813

Provides Articles of Incorporation: yes

Provides statutes: no; Wisconsin Nonstock Corporation Laws, Sections 181.01—79, available in libraries

CORPORATE NAME REQUIREMENTS

Corporate Designator: name must contain "corporation," "incorporated," "limited" or abbreviation

Corporate name may not contain language that implies the corporation is organized for purposes other than those for which a nonstock corporation may be organized under Wisconsin statutes; may not be the same or deceptively similar to the name of a domestic or foreign corporation or limited partnership or to a reserved or registered name, except with written consent of the name holder and you add or delete one word from the name, or by court judgment authorizing use of the name

ARTICLES OF INCORPORATION

Articles Statute: WSA, Sec. 181.31

Registered Agent Requirements:

A separate form for Designation of Registered Agent must be filed with Articles

Director Qualifications:
  Number: 3 or more
  Residency: no
  Age: no

Incorporator Qualifications:
  Residency: no
  Age: 18 or older

Special Requirements:

Duplicate originals of the Articles must be signed by all incorporators, notarized and filed

The secretary of state will forward duplicate originals of the Articles to the clerk of the county where the corporation's principal office is located. You must submit a check for $16 to the Register of Deeds with your Articles

Name of the person or agency that drafted the Articles must be typed, stamped or written legibly on the Articles or they will not be filed

BYLAWS

Directors' Quorum: majority of the directors in office or else as specified in the Articles or Bylaws

Members' Quorum: unless specified otherwise in the Articles or Bylaws, 10% of the voting membership present or represented by proxy

Executive Committee: majority of the board may designate three or more directors to exercise the authority of the full board to the extent of the resolution creating the committee, except to elect officers or fill vacancies on the board or on committees. The full board remains responsible for the actions of the committee

Directors' Term of Office: as specified in the Bylaws; if not specified, then one year

Required Officers: president, vice president, secretary and treasurer. One person may hold any two or more offices simultaneously except for offices of president and secretary, and president and vice president

Special Officer Requirements: no age or residency requirements; officers' term may not exceed three years

Corporate Report Requirements: must be filed during calendar quarter of the anniversary of incorporation, on forms provided by the secretary of state. Contains the following information:

1. Corporate name and address
2. Directors' and officers' names and addresses
3. Name and address of registered agent
4. Statement of general nature of activities in the 12 months preceding report

STATE CORPORATE TAX EXEMPTION

Corporate Income or Franchise Tax: yes

Name and address of state agency to contact:

Dept. of Revenue
P.O. Box 8906
Madison, WI 53708
(608) 266-2776

State Tax Exemption Requirements:

Automatic with federal 501(c)(3) exemption

Exempt organizations report unrelated business income (or franchise) taxes on Form 4T (to which federal Form 990-T must be attached). Organizations that make payments of rents, royalties or annuities must file the short informational return, Form 9b

WYOMING

SECRETARY OF STATE INFORMATION

Secretary of State
Corporations Division
Capitol Building
Cheyenne, WY 82002-0020

http://soswy.state.wy.us

Phone number of Corporations Division: (307) 777-7311

Provides Articles of Incorporation: yes

Provides statutes: no; WS Nonprofit Corporations, sections 17-19-101 et seq. can be found in libraries or on the Internet, at http://legiswebstat.wy.us/titles/97titles/title17.htm

CORPORATE NAME REQUIREMENTS

Corporate Designator: not required

Corporate name may not contain language that implies the corporation was organized for purposes other than those stated in its Articles; may not be the same or similar to the name of a nonprofit or for-profit, domestic or authorized foreign corporation, trade name, trademark, limited liability company or limited partnership

ARTICLES OF INCORPORATION

Articles Statute: WS, Nonprofit Corporations, Sec. 17-19-202

Registered Agent Requirements:

Director Qualifications:
  Number: 3 or more
  Residency: no
  Age: no

Incorporator Qualifications:
  Residency: no
  Age: no

Special Requirements:

Articles must specify whether the corporation being formed is a public benefit or mutual benefit corporation

BYLAWS

Directors' Quorum: majority of the directors in office, or else the percentage stated in the Articles or Bylaws, which may not be less than 1/3 of the number in office

Members' Quorum: unless specified otherwise in the Articles or Bylaws, 10% of the voting membership present or represented by proxy

Executive Committee: a majority of directors may designate two or more directors to exercise the authority of the full board, except to recommend to members dissolution, merger, sale or transfer of all or most of the assets, appoint or remove directors or committee members, fill vacancies on the board or on a committee, or amend the Bylaws or Articles

Directors' Term of Office: as specified in the Articles or Bylaws, but not to exceed 5 years; if not specified, then one year

Required Officers: president, secretary and treasurer. One person may hold any two or more offices

Special Officer Requirements: no age or residency requirements

Corporate Report Requirements: must be filed by the first day of the registration anniversary month (date of incorporation); the secretary of state will send out forms two months prior to that date. The following information is included:

1. Corporate name and address
2. Directors' and officers' names and addresses
3. Any compensation, profit or pecuniary advantage given to any director or officer

STATE CORPORATE TAX EXEMPTION

Corporate Income or Franchise Tax: no

Name and address of state agency to contact for other tax information

Secretary of State—see above address

State Tax Exemption Requirements: no corporate income tax

Dept. of Revenue
Herschler Bldg.
122 W. 25th St.
Cheyenne, WY 82002
(307) 777-5235

Index

NONPROFIT CORPORATE KITS

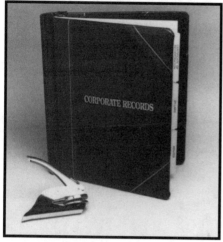

Ex Libris® and Centennial® are registered trademarks of Julius Blumberg, Inc.

Nolo Press, in cooperation with Julius Blumberg, Inc. offers two superior corporate kits. The kits are fully described in Chapter 9, Step 8.

The Ex Libris® and Centennial® kits include:

- A corporate records book with minute paper and index dividers for Articles of Incorporation, Bylaws, Minutes and Corporate Certificates. We are partial to the Centennial book which features a handcrafted, red and black simulated leather binder with your corporate name embossed in gold on the spine.

- A metal corporate seal designed to emboss your corporate name and year of incorporation on important corporate documents.

- 20 lithographed Director Certificates printed with your corporate name. An option is provided for you to add 20 Sponsor Certificates.

- An option is included to order membership materials consisting of a membership index and roll sheets, plus 40 lithographed membership certificates.

ORDER COUPON   *How to Form a Nonprofit Corporation Handbook (NNP)*

Name of Corporation (print exactly as on Articles of Incorporation). Put one character per space (including punctuation and spaces). BE SURE CAPITAL AND LOWER CASE LETTERS ARE CLEAR AND SPELLING IS ACCURATE. CORPORATE KITS ARE NONREFUNDABLE.

45

Year of Incorporation: _____   State of Incorporation: _____

☐ Ex Libris Kit $74.95 (100 DRNL)   ☐ Centennial Kit $84.95 (930 DRNL) .... $ _____
Each kit includes 20 Director Certificates

☐ Ex Libris Kit $84.95 (100 DRSP)   ☐ Centennial Kit $94.95 (930 DRSP) .... $ _____
Each kit includes 20 Director Certificates plus 20 Sponsor Certificates

☐ Membership Materials including 40 Membership Certificates—add $40.00 (9MEMNL) .... $ _____

Long corporate names (over 45 characters) cost an additional $25.00 .... $ _____

California Residents Only: Add your local Sales Tax .... $ _____

Shipping Charges   ☐ $10.00 *or* ☐ $25.00 .... $ _____
Regular delivery by ground costs $10.00 and is within 10-12 business days;
Air delivery is within 4 business days and costs $25.00*

TOTAL ENCLOSED .... $ _____

METHOD OF PAYMENT   ☐ Check enclosed   ☐ VISA   ☐ Mastercard   ☐ Discover Card   ☐ American Express

NAME

STREET ADDRESS (NO PO BOXES)

CITY   STATE   ZIP   PHONE

SIGNATURE   ACCOUNT #   EXP. DATE

EXTRA STOCK CERTIFICATES: $39.00 for 20 extra stock certificates, plus 50¢ for each additional certificate above this amount, plus half the corporate kit
(with Kit purchase)   shipping price. Please indicate the numbers to be printed on the extra stock certificates.

CORPORATE SEAL ONLY: $30.00 each plus half the corporate kit shipping price.

*All delivery dates are calculated from the day after we receive your order. Prices are subject to change without notice.

SORRY, WE DO NOT ACCEPT TELEPHONE ORDERS FOR CORPORATE KITS.

Send: NOLO PRESS/FOLK LAW, INC. 950 PARKER STREET, BERKELEY CA 94710   Fax: 1-510-548-5902

CORPORATE KIT ORDERS ARE NONREFUNDABLE

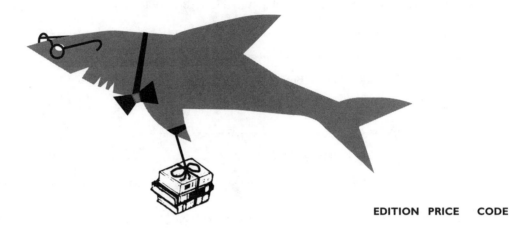

CATALOG

...more from Nolo Press

▣ Book with disk
● Book with CD-ROM

	EDITION	PRICE	CODE
How to Write a Business Plan	4th	$21.95	SBS
The Independent Paralegal's Handbook	4th	$29.95	PARA
Legal Guide for Starting & Running a Small Business, Vol. 1	3rd	$24.95	RUNS
Marketing Without Advertising	2nd	$19.00	MWAD
▣ The Partnership Book: How to Write a Partnership Agreement, (Book w/Disk—PC)	5th	$34.95	PART
Sexual Harassment on the Job	2nd	$18.95	HARS
Starting and Running a Successful Newsletter or Magazine	1st	$24.95	MAG
▣ Taking Care of Your Corporation, Vol. 1, (Book w/Disk—PC)	1st	$29.95	CORK
▣ Taking Care of Your Corporation, Vol. 2, (Book w/Disk—PC)	1st	$39.95	CORK2
Tax Savvy for Small Business	2nd	$26.95	SAVVY
Trademark: How to Name Your Business & Product	2nd	$29.95	TRD
Your Rights in the Workplace	3rd	$19.95	YRW

CONSUMER

	EDITION	PRICE	CODE
Fed Up With the Legal System: What's Wrong & How to Fix It	2nd	$9.95	LEG
How to Win Your Personal Injury Claim	2nd	$24.95	PICL
Nolo's Everyday Law Book	1st	$21.95	EVL
Nolo's Pocket Guide to California Law	5th	$11.95	CLAW
Trouble-Free Travel...And What to Do When Things Go Wrong	1st	$14.95	TRAV

ESTATE PLANNING & PROBATE

	EDITION	PRICE	CODE
8 Ways to Avoid Probate (Quick & Legal Series)	1st	$15.95	PRO8
How to Probate an Estate (California Edition)	9th	$34.95	PAE
Make Your Own Living Trust	2nd	$21.95	LITR
▣ Nolo's Will Book, (Book w/Disk—PC)	3rd	$29.95	SWIL
Plan Your Estate	3rd	$24.95	NEST
The Quick and Legal Will Book	1st	$15.95	QUIC
Nolo's Law Form Kit: Wills	1st	$14.95	KWL

▣ Book with disk
● Book with CD-ROM

▣ Book with disk
● Book with CD-ROM

▣ Book with disk
⬤ Book with CD-ROM

Book with disk
Book with CD-ROM

SOFTWARE

Call for special direct discounts on Software

	EDITION	PRICE	CODE
California Incorporator 2.0—DOS	2.0	$79.95	INCI
Living Trust Maker 2.0—Macintosh	2.0	$79.95	LTM2
Living Trust Maker 2.0—Windows	2.0	$79.95	LTWI2
Small Business Legal Pro Deluxe CD—Windows/Macintosh CD-ROM	2.0	$79.95	SBCD
Nolo's Partnership Maker 1.0—DOS	1.0	$79.95	PAGI1
Personal RecordKeeper 4.0—Macintosh	4.0	$49.95	RKM4
Personal RecordKeeper 4.0—Windows	4.0	$49.95	RKP4
Patent It Yourself 1.0—Windows	1.0	$229.95	PYP12
WillMaker 6.0—Macintosh	6.0	$49.95	WM6B
WillMaker 6.0—Windows	6.0	$49.95	WIW6B

Special Upgrade Offer

Get 25% off the latest edition of your Nolo book

It's important to have the most current legal information. Because laws and legal procedures change often, we update our books regularly. To help keep you up-to-date we are extending this special upgrade offer. Cut out and mail the title portion of the cover of your old Nolo book and we'll give you 25% off the retail price of the NEW EDITION of that book when you purchase directly from us. For more information call us at 1-800-992-6656. This offer is to individuals only.

⌑ Book with disk
● Book with CD-ROM

ORDER FORM

Code	Quantity	Title	Unit price	Total
		Subtotal		
		California residents add Sales Tax		
	Basic Shipping ($6.00 for 1 item; $7.00 for 2 or more)			
	UPS RUSH delivery $7.50–any size order*			
		TOTAL		

Name

Address

(UPS to street address, Priority Mail to P.O. boxes)　　　* Delivered in 3 business days from receipt of order.
S.F. Bay Area use regular shipping.

FOR FASTER SERVICE, USE YOUR CREDIT CARD AND OUR TOLL-FREE NUMBERS

Order 24 hours a day	1-800-992-6656
Fax your order	1-800-645-0895
e-mail	cs@nolo.com
General Information	1-510-549-1976
Customer Service	1-800-728-3555, Mon.-Fri. 9am-5pm, PST

METHOD OF PAYMENT

☐ Check enclosed
☐ VISA　☐ MasterCard　☐ Discover Card　☐ American Express

Account #　　　　　　　　　　　　　　Expiration Date

Authorizing Signature

Daytime Phone

PRICES SUBJECT TO CHANGE.

VISIT OUR OUTLET STORES!　　　　　　　VISIT US ONLINE!

You'll find our complete line of books and software, all at a discount.

BERKELEY　　　　　　**SAN JOSE**
950 Parker Street　　　　111 N. Market Street, #115
Berkeley, CA 94710　　　San Jose, CA 95113
1-510-704-2248　　　　　1-408-271-7240

on the Internet
www.nolo.com

NOLO PRESS 950 PARKER ST., BERKELEY, CA 94710

Take 1 minute &
Get a 1-year Nolo *News*
subscription free!*

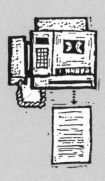

Catalog inside, see p.32
NOLO COMES TO SAN JOSE
See Back Cover

With our quarterly magazine, the **NOLO** *News*, you'll

- **Learn** about important legal changes that affect you
- **Find out first** about new Nolo products
- **Keep current** with practical articles on everyday law
- **Get answers** to your legal questions in *Ask Auntie Nolo's* advice column

- **Save money** with special Subscriber Only discounts
- **Tickle your funny bone** with our famous *Lawyer Joke* column.

It only takes 1 minute to reserve your free 1-year subscription or to extend your **NOLO** *News* subscription.

CALL
1-800-992-6656

FAX
1-800-645-0895

E-MAIL
NOLOSUB@NOLOPRESS.com

OR MAIL US THIS POSTAGE-PAID REGISTRATION CARD

*U.S. ADDRESSES ONLY.
ONE YEAR INTERNATIONAL SUBSCRIPTIONS:
CANADA & MEXICO $10.00;
ALL OTHER FOREIGN ADDRESSES $20.00.

REGISTRATION CARD

NAME _____ DATE _____

ADDRESS _____

_____ PHONE NUMBER _____

CITY _____ STATE _____ ZIP _____

WHERE DID YOU HEAR ABOUT THIS BOOK?

WHERE DID YOU PURCHASE THIS PRODUCT?

DID YOU CONSULT A LAWYER? (PLEASE CIRCLE ONE)   YES   NO   NOT APPLICABLE

DID YOU FIND THIS BOOK HELPFUL?   (VERY)   5   4   3   2   1   (NOT AT ALL)

SUGGESTIONS FOR IMPROVING THIS PRODUCT

WAS IT EASY TO USE?   (VERY EASY)   5   4   3   2   1   (VERY DIFFICULT)

DO YOU OWN A COMPUTER? IF SO, WHICH FORMAT? (PLEASE CIRCLE ONE)   WINDOWS   DOS   MAC

We occasionally make our mailing list available to carefully selected companies whose products may be of interest to you. If you do not wish to receive mailings from these companies, please check this box ❏

NNP 4.0

"Nolo helps lay people perform legal tasks without the aid—or fees—of lawyers."

—USA TODAY

Nolo books are ..."written in plain language, free of legal mumbo jumbo, and spiced with witty personal observations."

—ASSOCIATED PRESS

"...Nolo publications...guide people simply through the how, when, where and why of law."

—WASHINGTON POST

"Increasingly, people who are not lawyers are performing tasks usually regarded as legal work... And consumers, using books like Nolo's, do routine legal work themselves."

—NEW YORK TIMES

"...All of [Nolo's] books are easy-to-understand, are updated regularly, provide pull-out forms...and are often quite moving in their sense of compassion for the struggles of the lay reader."

—SAN FRANCISCO CHRONICLE